Nobody's Girl

Nobody's Girl

A MEMOIR OF SURVIVING ABUSE AND FIGHTING FOR JUSTICE

Virginia Roberts Giuffre

doubleday

TRANSWORLD PUBLISHERS

UK | USA | Canada | Ireland | Australia
India | New Zealand | South Africa

Transworld is part of the Penguin Random House group of companies
whose addresses can be found at global.penguinrandomhouse.com.

Penguin Random House UK,
One Embassy Gardens, 8 Viaduct Gardens, London SW11 7BW

penguin.co.uk

First published in Great Britain in 2025 by Doubleday
an imprint of Transworld Publishers

009

Copyright © 2025 by The Estate of Virginia Roberts Giuffre

The moral right of the author has been asserted.

Jacket photograph from the personal collection of the author.

Every effort has been made to obtain the necessary permissions with
reference to copyright material, both illustrative and quoted. We apologize
for any omissions in this respect and will be pleased to make the
appropriate acknowledgements in any future edition.

Penguin Random House values and supports copyright. Copyright fuels creativity, encourages diverse voices, promotes freedom of expression and supports a vibrant culture. Thank you for purchasing an authorized edition of this book and for respecting intellectual property laws by not reproducing, scanning or distributing any part of it by any means without permission. You are supporting authors and enabling Penguin Random House to continue to publish books for everyone. No part of this book may be used or reproduced in any manner for the purpose of training artificial intelligence technologies or systems. In accordance with Article 4(3) of the DSM Directive 2019/790, Penguin Random House expressly reserves this work from the text and data mining exception.

Printed and bound in Great Britain by Clays Ltd, Elcograf S.p.A.

The authorized representative in the EEA is Penguin Random House Ireland,
Morrison Chambers, 32 Nassau Street, Dublin D02 YH68.

A CIP catalogue record for this book is available from the British Library.

ISBNs:
9781529985245 hb
9781529985252 tpb

Penguin Random House is committed to a sustainable future
for our business, our readers and our planet. This book is made
from Forest Stewardship Council® certified paper.

*Dedicated to my Survivor Sisters
and to anyone who has suffered sexual abuse*

Some names have been changed
to protect the privacy of the people involved.

CONTENTS

A Note from Virginia Roberts Giuffre's Collaborator   *xi*

Introduction   *xix*

Part I. **Daughter**   *1*

ONE. "BABY"   *3*

TWO. GROWING TOGETHER   *10*

THREE. VIRGINIA LEE   *18*

FOUR. LESS THAN NOTHING   *28*

FIVE. VINCEREMOS   *38*

SIX. IF WISHES WERE HORSES   *43*

SEVEN. A GHOST COME BACK   *55*

Part II. **Prisoner**   *65*

EIGHT. THE PINK HOUSE   *67*

NINE. TAPPING A CROOKED VEIN   *76*

TEN. A VERY IMPORTANT MAN   *84*

CONTENTS

ELEVEN. THE BOTTOM OF THE PYRAMID 97

TWELVE. "JUST LIKE YOU DO FOR ME" 103

THIRTEEN. LIFE WITH "OTHER-MAN" 115

FOURTEEN. PUPPETS ON A STRING 126

FIFTEEN. A BRIDGE TOO FAR 137

Part III. Survivor 147

SIXTEEN. THE LAND OF SMILES 149

SEVENTEEN. BULLY BASHER 155

EIGHTEEN. HONEYMOONERS 164

NINETEEN. DOWN UNDER 175

TWENTY. WELCOME TO THE WORLD 186

TWENTY-ONE. A PERSON OF INTEREST 196

TWENTY-TWO. "HE'S A TYLER!" 203

TWENTY-THREE. MY VERY OWN PRINCESS 214

TWENTY-FOUR. A SMALL DENT 228

TWENTY-FIVE. BACK IN THE SUNSHINE STATE 234

TWENTY-SIX. ROCKY MOUNTAIN HIGH 247

Part IV. Warrior 257

TWENTY-SEVEN. THE POINT OF NO RETURN 259

TWENTY-EIGHT. ALWAYS MY DAUGHTER 266

TWENTY-NINE. I SOLEMNLY SWEAR 273

THIRTY. A RECKONING BEGINS 286

THIRTY-ONE. A TASTE OF JUSTICE 296

THIRTY-TWO. SURVIVOR SISTERS UNITE 303

CONTENTS

THIRTY-THREE. UNBROKEN *311*

THIRTY-FOUR. FROM BAD TO WORSE *321*

THIRTY-FIVE. BACKLASH *329*

THIRTY-SIX. MAXWELL ON TRIAL *336*

THIRTY-SEVEN. SETTLING UP AND SETTLING DOWN *343*

THIRTY-EIGHT. NOBODY'S GIRL *355*

Where to Turn for Help *369*

A Note from Virginia Roberts Giuffre's Collaborator

Writing a book with someone is always an intimate exercise. During every project I've worked on, at some point I must ask the author some extremely personal questions. Next, I bolster their memories, no matter how vivid, by working to corroborate them—reviewing all preexisting documentation and talking to others in their lives who may have witnessed or known about the events being described. In that sense, the process I followed while working with Virginia to get her story right was nothing new for me.

Two things, however, made Virginia's memoir different. First, the stories she needed to share were devastating beyond measure for her to tell; second, several of the characters in these stories were among the wealthiest and most powerful in the world. Some of those people had already threatened Virginia to try to keep her quiet. From the beginning, Virginia and I understood that this would have to be a meticulously written book—to ensure accuracy, of course, but also to protect her from those who would have preferred she stayed silent.

A NOTE FROM VIRGINIA ROBERTS GIUFFRE'S COLLABORATOR

I want to say explicitly why Virginia opted *not* to stay silent, which certainly would have been easier for her. From the beginning, she told me she believed that her story would help other people—not just survivors of Epstein's cruelty, but any person, male or female, who'd ever been coerced into sex against his or her will. Over and over, during the hundreds of conversations and text and email exchanges Virginia and I had over four years, she insisted that she wanted to be portrayed authentically, with all her flaws. She wanted the world to know who she really was so that survivors of abuse who might read her words would feel less alone. She hoped that if she painted a real portrait of her suffering, it would inspire more people to fight to make the changes she believed were so desperately needed—prime among them, legislation to eliminate statute of limitations provisions for sexual abusers of children.

Virginia was one of the most sweethearted and generous people I've ever met. She was devoted to her three children, whom she shared with her husband, Robbie Giuffre (from whom she was later estranged). She was also fierce and determined. And that fierceness is what enabled me, at her direction, to tell her whole story, and—just as importantly—to interrogate it, to confirm it, and ultimately to help create the inspiring but also heartbreaking account you are holding in your hands.

When it came to corroborating the abuse Virginia had suffered as a child, I tracked down a childhood friend who was incredibly forthcoming about the abuse this friend endured by her stepfather, the same man who sexually abused Virginia as a child and who later was convicted for abusing yet another minor. Her input and kindness were a huge source of comfort to Virginia. In consultation with a professional factchecker, I spoke at length to Virginia's mother. Her perspective differed from her daughter's in a few key places. She was clear in her denials that she had not had any knowledge at

A NOTE FROM VIRGINIA ROBERTS GIUFFRE'S COLLABORATOR

the time of the abuse Virginia suffered at the hands of her father and his friend, which Lynn explained in part because she was often absent from the family home due to her caring responsibilities for her ailing mother and the demands of her work. She told me she believed her daughter spoke the truth about the abuse she suffered, but could not confirm a few details of Virginia's account. In particular, her recollection of events surrounding the allegation that Virginia's father received hush money from Epstein made her unable to confirm that payment had occurred. I also spoke at length to Virginia's husband, her former boyfriend, and her two brothers to whom Virginia had recounted the abuse by both her father and his friend. I reached out to Virginia's father multiple times seeking his response to his daughter's allegations. He responded by strenuously denying them.*

Virginia's firsthand account of her time in Epstein and Maxwell's orbit was supported by thousands of pages of public court documents, including sworn depositions and Epstein's flight logs. These documents contained the full names of many of the men who Virginia alleged she had been trafficked to. Their contents are supported by numerous other sources, including interviews that Virginia gave to the press (all of which I reviewed) and published books on the subject by authors such as the *Miami Herald*'s Julie K. Brown, Virginia's former attorney Brad Edwards, and former US attorney for the Southern District of New York Geoffrey Berman. I also spoke to many of Virginia's

---

* His response reads, in full: "Just to straighten this out, I never abused my daughter and didn't know that Forrest ——— did that either, if I had known about that, I would have been very angry and taken care of the situation. I gave my daughter every single thing she ever wanted and never ever touched her sexually, I never even knew what was going on with Epstein until I read about it online and getting calls from news agencies. There is so much they are getting wrong, even her middle name, it is Virginia Lee Roberts and not Virginia Louise. I am a moral person and believe that men who take advantage of young children should be prosecuted and then castrated. It really pisses me off that someone would write that I would ever abuse my children, as a father, I only tried to give my children a good life."

A NOTE FROM VIRGINIA ROBERTS GIUFFRE'S COLLABORATOR

attorneys, including Edwards, Sigrid McCawley, and Brittany Henderson. (In the book, Virginia recounts how her lawyers at Boies Schiller obtained a settlement on her behalf from Prince Andrew. That settlement was made without any admission of liability on his part and he continues to deny Virginia's allegations that he had sex with her, that she had been trafficked to him by Epstein or indeed that he had even met her.)

Writing the book involved several stops and starts, in part due to struggles Virginia had with her health. But all along, she insisted that she wanted the book published. She wanted all her suffering to have accomplished something, and if she could help even one survivor of abuse, she said, it would be worth all the effort. In October 2024, she felt ready to resume. We met to finalize the manuscript. I returned to Australia, where I'd already visited her in 2022, to go over it in detail with her, side by side, one more time. We read the manuscript again, with me taking short breaks to revise certain sections, then returning to read them to her again. By the end of that visit, she'd approved all the book's contents, save for this note by me added after her passing. She was deeply grateful to the people from all corners of her life who had supported her efforts to tell her story.

Then, on the night of January 9 (the morning of January 10 in Australia), Virginia called me in a state of extreme distress. She said that the previous evening, she and Robbie had had an argument and that he had assaulted her. We talked for a long time. She sent me photographs of her face, which appeared discolored and swollen. I made sure she was in a safe place and offered to reach out to her mother and her older brother, both of whom I contacted.

Virginia reported the incident to police in Western Australia, but they did not charge Robbie with any crime. Robbie made allegations of his own, which resulted in a restraining order against Virginia that

A NOTE FROM VIRGINIA ROBERTS GIUFFRE'S COLLABORATOR

prohibited contact with her children. This profoundly hurt Virginia—she couldn't stand being out of touch with her kids.

The alleged January incident was not without precedent. At one point, Virginia had told me about a time in 2015, in Colorado, when Robbie was arrested after assaulting her. I tracked down a sheriff's deputy who'd worked the case; he spoke to me at length about the incident and said that a restraining order had been put in place that prohibited Robbie from returning home. But according to the sheriff's department, documentation of that incident was no longer available to the public. Virginia presented this episode as an isolated incident and said that for the sake of her kids, she didn't want it to appear in the book. That was a terrible chapter that had occurred during a very tense time in their lives, she told me, and she and Robbie had worked hard to put it behind them. (Robbie, too, said as much when—in person—he referred to the incident obliquely.) I knew that there were all kinds of reasons that a woman who had been domestically abused might choose to stay silent. I also knew that people who are victims of child abuse are considerably more likely—fifteen times more likely, according to one widely cited study—to be victims of abuse later in life. I abided by her wishes.

Things took a turn for the worse in March 2025, when Virginia was injured in a car accident. Virginia and I spoke for the last time on March 31, 2025. She'd been in the hospital, she said, but had left because she didn't agree with her doctors. I begged her to go back to the hospital, and she said she would. But first, she wanted to talk about her kids, desperate to know how they were. Before we hung up, she said, "If it's in God's hands, I'm not scared. If it's my time to go, it's my time to go, but I want the book published." I begged her, one more time, to let her doctors do their jobs. "I want you around for the rest of my life," I said. She told me she loved me. I told her I loved her, too.

A NOTE FROM VIRGINIA ROBERTS GIUFFRE'S COLLABORATOR

The next day, on April 1, Virginia sent me and Dini von Mueffling, her longtime publicist, an email stating clearly her desire to publish the book. It read, in part:

> I am reaching out to discuss an important matter regarding my book, "Nobody's Girl." It is my heartfelt wish that this work be published, regardless of my circumstances at the time.
>
> The content of this book is crucial, as it aims to shed light on the systemic failures that allow the trafficking of vulnerable individuals across borders. It is imperative that the truth is understood and that the issues surrounding this topic are addressed, both for the sake of justice and awareness.
>
> In the event of my passing, I would like to ensure that "Nobody's Girl" is still released. I believe it has the potential to impact many lives and foster necessary discussions about these grave injustices. I kindly ask for your assistance in making this wish a reality. Thank you for your support, patience and most importantly love ❤ ❤ ❤.

On April 5, Virginia released a statement to *People* magazine, stating publicly for the first time that her husband had abused her and specifically citing the alleged assault on January 9. The statement read, in part: "I was able to fight back against Ghislaine Maxwell and Jeffrey Epstein who, [sic] abused and trafficked me. But I was unable to escape the domestic violence in my marriage until recently. After my husband's latest physical assault, I can no longer stay silent." (Robbie's attorney declined to comment on Virginia's allegations, citing ongoing court proceedings.)

Less than three weeks later, Virginia was dead, having committed suicide at her remote farm.

A NOTE FROM VIRGINIA ROBERTS GIUFFRE'S COLLABORATOR

Before this book went to press, Virginia's two brothers and their wives came forward with their concerns that the book she wrote underplayed the domestic abuse that she had allegedly experienced. They publicly offered their account of what they believed was long-standing abuse that their sister had suffered during her marriage, and they stressed the importance of publishing her memoir with further context to avoid undermining her credibility. At the same time, they expressed their support for the publication of Virginia's memoir and affirmed its importance in holding abusers to account.

As I've reflected on Virginia's life since her passing—all she accomplished, and all the suffering she experienced—I haven't stopped thinking about those last three hearts she sent us. They will stick with me forever. Because despite the unspeakable cruelties she'd endured throughout her life, Virginia opted to keep her heart open and, whenever possible, to lead with love. The world could learn something from Virginia. It was truly an honor to spend four years by her side, helping her tell her story and ensuring that her legacy lives on.

Amy Wallace
August 2025

Introduction

"Life is not a private affair.
A story and its lessons are only made useful if shared."

DAN MILLMAN, *Way of the Peaceful Warrior*

Just a few hours ago, a visit to the Louvre seemed like a brilliant way to cheer myself up. But now the sadness overtakes me. I am so far from home.

It is June 2021, and I am on the second floor of the world's largest art museum, surrounded by strangers and yet very much alone. It is a weird time to be in Paris, which has just reopened after the COVID-19 pandemic swept the globe, and the streets are largely empty of tourists, who have only now been allowed to fly into France. I look like a tourist—another blond American mom in blue jeans and ballet flats. But I did not come to Paris to sightsee. I am here to do a job that never gets any easier. I'm here to stand up to those who have hurt me. I am here to reclaim my life.

Leaving my hotel this morning, I felt strong. The sun sparkled and the air was warm, as if to make fun of all the sweaters I'd packed. I thought of my husband, Robbie, back in Australia, where we live. I knew he was hosting a sleepover for our three kids and three of their

INTRODUCTION

friends, and I could imagine him, frazzled as he telephoned our favorite pizza place and ordered way too many pies. "You are my little warrior," my husband likes to tell me, and he said it again before I boarded the plane from Perth to Paris. I can't always see myself as Robbie does, but today as I set off on foot and headed toward the Seine, I felt connected to his fierce ideal of me.

From my hotel on Rue Scribe, I easily found my way to the Avenue de l'Opéra and headed south toward the Louvre. It had been twenty years since I'd walked these streets, but it seemed as if I knew the route. Visiting the museum was a gift I'd decided to give myself: a few hours away from my lawyers and their questions. For days they had been grilling me, and I understood why. In order to maximize the impact of the testimony I was here to give, I had to be focused—ready for anything. But I badly needed a break. When a morning off presented itself, I knew exactly where I wanted to go. Now I made a beeline for the Louvre's iconic metal and glass pyramid, scanned my ticket, and rode the escalator down. My plan was to relax and wander the galleries, escaping my ugliest memories by immersing myself in pure beauty.

For a while, everything went as I'd imagined. I lost myself in the larger-than-life bronze and marble sculptures, texting my husband photos of *The Four Captives*, a quartet of soldiers in shackles, and of Hercules fighting an oversized snake. I was in no rush. I figured I'd get to the *Mona Lisa* eventually. But then, unsure exactly where I was going, I climbed a flight of stairs, turned a corner, and froze. *I know this room*, screamed a voice inside my head. I'd been in this precise spot before—two decades ago, when I was just seventeen.

THE ROOM I am in is painted bloodred and is dominated by a huge tapestry: a depiction of Louis XIV's garish bed chamber. In 2001, when Jeffrey Epstein and Ghislaine Maxwell took the teenage me into

INTRODUCTION

this room for the first time, they had been sexually abusing and trafficking me for months. Now I am a thirty-seven-year-old wife and mother—a full-fledged adult—and it's been two years since Epstein died in jail. Still, I can practically see him standing next to me, admiring the tapestry, whose dark palette he was determined to mimic in the decor of his opulent Manhattan townhouse. In my mind's eye, I imagine Maxwell beside him, as always. A molester with posh manners and an aristocratic pedigree, "G-Max," as she called herself, played den mother to Epstein's dysfunctional family of underage girls. I was one of those girls, and I spent more than twenty-five months in their house of shame. Even decades later, I can still remember how much I feared them both.

My ears are ringing. As I stand here, my rational mind knows that they cannot hurt me anymore: a year after Epstein's lifeless body was found in his cell, Maxwell was arrested, and at this moment, in 2021, she remains in jail awaiting trial on various charges, including sex trafficking a minor. Yet still I feel haunted by their hungry ghosts. Fighting dizziness, I focus my eyes on the elaborate wall-hanging in front of me. It depicts a young man kneeling before the king, begging forgiveness as a crowd looks on. I glance at my feet, rooted to the parquet floor. My breath catches, and the familiar thrum of a panic attack rolls over me.

Even as a child, I never liked to cause a scene. I would rather envelop my pain, holding the turmoil in my chest, instead of risking more danger by screaming and letting it out. So I stay quiet, trying to soothe myself. I look down at my pretty fingernails—freshly manicured and painted a glossy ivory. I read the bracelet on my left wrist, a gift from a dear friend, that spells out "B-A-D-A-S-S" in lettered beads. I take one careful step and then another. My stomach churns, but I keep going. *"Please,"* I beg without speaking. "Please don't let me faint in this exquisite place." I find a bench and sit, looking around

INTRODUCTION

for exit signs. "I can make it," I tell myself—a mantra I've relied on so many times before. I know from experience that I should not yet try to run.

Trauma is such a cunning enemy. Those of us who've survived its terrors often marvel at how quickly it can recede, at least at first. Once you get to safety, your visible wounds—your cuts, your bruises—heal and fade. Your psyche, too, revives, like a drowning man who, pulled from the depths, somehow spits up dark water and opens his eyes. But recovering victims like me know too well how trauma lurks in the shadows, always there. No matter how many years go by, or how many therapists you see, it can rise, unbidden, seemingly out of nowhere. A song on the radio may summon it. Or the scent of a stranger's cologne. For you, the trigger probably won't be a wall-size tapestry in the Louvre, but you never know.

I have come to France to stand up to one of Epstein's coconspirators, the modeling agent Jean-Luc Brunel. During his years in the modeling business, Brunel became a scout of some renown—he boasted of launching the careers of Jerry Hall, Milla Jovovich, Rebecca Romijn, Sharon Stone, and Christy Turlington. But he was also known to solicit sex from young women whose careers he managed. Now, Brunel is in custody and is awaiting trial on charges of rape, sexual harassment, and human trafficking of minors for sexual exploitation. But lately he's been asking if he can be free in the months before his court date. That's why I've traveled here from Australia: to help keep Brunel, who procured so many young girls for Epstein, behind bars.

In the sworn testimony I'm here to give, I will assert, as I've asserted before, that Brunel repeatedly raped and abused me. While in Paris, I will also connect French prosecutors with other victims of Brunel who have sought me out after seeing me on TV and on social media, and I will turn over my handwritten notes about what he and Epstein and Maxwell put me and others through. French prosecutors

INTRODUCTION

tell me I am a critical witness because, unlike many Epstein victims who were abused in a single location, I spent more than two years traveling the world with him and Maxwell. I knew their cruel habits, and those of the men, like Brunel, to whom they trafficked me. I saw these men—endured them—up close.

Can it be any wonder that I struggle with post-traumatic stress disorder (PTSD)? But speaking out as I'm doing now costs me more than an anxiety attack or an interrupted outing to an art museum. Coming to Paris to reveal the past means missing out on my life in the present. My fifth grader, Ellie, has her first school dance this weekend and has dyed her gorgeous dark hair purple to protest my absence. (Robbie texted me a photo, and I have to admit it looks pretty good.) Just now, Ellie texted me that she wants to complete her "grunge" outfit with a pair of fishnet stockings, and despite the six-hour time difference, we have scheduled a FaceTime call so I can weigh in, yes or no. When I was a teen, I, too, was a grunge fan, but still: I think fifth grade is a little early for fishnets. While I'm glad that Ellie and I have plans to discuss it, I feel sad our debate will have to be over the phone. If I were home in Perth, I'd commemorate Ellie's first dance by taking a million photos. Instead, I'll be fighting loneliness and jet lag in a tiny hotel room nine thousand miles away.

I have to believe, however, that my trip to Paris benefits my kids. Years ago, after a teacher asked one of our children what their mother did for a living, Robbie and I put our heads together and decided that the truth was too complicated, so they should simply answer: "My mom fights bad guys." Since then, more than one teacher has wrongly assumed I am a cop. I'm not a cop, and I've never claimed to be an angel either. But I hope I have done some good. Seeking to silence me, my powerful enemies have threatened to bankrupt me and even to have me killed. I haven't stopped talking. When I was a sex slave, I had no say. I have promised myself that I will never have "no say" again.

INTRODUCTION

So, did my demons cause me to flee a world-class museum today before I could see my favorite paintings? Yes, they did. Did I retreat afterward to my hotel room to engage in one of my favorite calming rituals: binge-watching that most satisfying of TV's police procedurals, *Law & Order*? Yes, that happened too. But I won't let demons win. Three days from now, I will return to the Louvre, to sit across from that spooky tapestry and take back possession of that red-walled room. I will ground myself in my hard-won strength. Then afterward I'll finally track down the *Mona Lisa* to say a quick hello.

A few days later, I will face off with Brunel in an eight-hour, closed-door hearing, answering the most dehumanizing questions you can imagine about what he—then a man in his midfifties—did to me when I was seventeen, eighteen, and nineteen years old.

In an interview with NBC News later that same day, I will explain that I gave testimony against Brunel because I wanted him "to know that he no longer has the power over me, that I am a grown woman now, and I've decided to hold him accountable for what he did to me and so many others." Then I will deliver a call to arms that will soon be broadcast around the world. "I'm urging more witnesses—even if it is outside of the statute of limitations—to come forward," I'll say, explaining that even something as simple as confirming Brunel's whereabouts on a particular day can help those who are seeking to convict him of his crimes.

"The judge is listening," I will say. "The authorities are listening. I'm listening. We want to help put this monster away where he belongs. We can't do that unless we all work together."

I KNOW ABOUT monsters. As a child, I suffered nearly every kind of abuse: incest, parental neglect, severe corporal punishment, molestation, rape. As a teen, I had been sexually trafficked by another pedo-

INTRODUCTION

phile even before I met Jeffrey Epstein and Ghislaine Maxwell. But these two doubled down on my suffering. In my years with them, they lent me out to scores of wealthy, powerful people. I was habitually used and humiliated—and in some instances, choked, beaten, and bloodied. I believed that I might die a sex slave. Then, just after my nineteenth birthday, I met someone who seemed to give a damn about me. I took a chance, and in 2002 I escaped.

As I write this, I have enjoyed twenty-two years of freedom. That period has not always been easy, but I am beyond grateful for it. My life since 2002 has been marked by several turning points, none more important than when, unexpectedly, I became a parent. Doctors had told me that was highly unlikely, but they were wrong. My son Alex came first, then Tyler. I loved being the mom of two boys. But when Robbie and I had our third child, a daughter we named Ellie, I felt something shift inside me. Given what I've been through, I know that sexual predators don't stop until they're made to stop. For years, however, I'd hung back, hoping someone else would take the lead in holding abusers accountable. Ellie ended that period of passivity. Looking into my daughter's eyes, I knew I had to act to keep other girls from suffering the way I had. Not long after that, I began to fight.

One of the first things I did was try to answer some hard questions: Was the abuse I suffered merely the result of bad luck? Had my family's shameful secrets marked me for tragedy? Or is there something going on in our culture that contributed to my bad situation? There has always been evil in the world. But human trafficking—the use of force, fraud, or coercion to obtain some type of labor or commercial sex act—is particularly venal, especially when the victims are minors. Underreported and understudied, child sex trafficking is not just a problem that exists in Third World countries, as many people mistakenly assume. In America, incidents have been reported in all fifty states. And in recent decades, the internet and social media have

INTRODUCTION

made it easier for traffickers to make contact with their victims. According to the National Center for Missing and Exploited Children, during the COVID-19 pandemic, predators took advantage of children being even more online, which resulted in a 106 percent increase in cyber-tip-line reports of suspected child sexual exploitation in just one year.

My point: while Jeffrey Epstein is dead and gone, there are many others around the world who are still committing the same kinds of crimes that he did. There are countless victims of sex trafficking who have not yet escaped their exploitative situations, as I was fortunate enough to do. Those girls and boys, women and men, will likely attempt to flee between three and seven times before they succeed, according to recent research. Many of them will not be offered help by a single caring stranger. In America, where only 4 percent of law-enforcement agencies have personnel dedicated to exposing human trafficking, most victims must rely on their own wits, and on luck, to survive.

I want to change that. I want not just to hold abusers accountable but also to challenge the ways that all too often our legal system protects those abusers. It is estimated that most victims of childhood sexual abuse don't come forward and share their experiences until they are in their forties or later. In my view, survivors of sex trafficking and abuse should be able to seek justice whenever they are ready to do so, but many states have statutes of limitations that make that impossible. These are systemic problems that no single person can solve, which is why it's so important for survivors to unite. As I said in that NBC interview in Paris in 2021, no matter how weak survivors of sexual abuse are made to feel, we will always be stronger when we work together.

In recent years, bits and pieces of my story have been told and retold by others in countless books, podcasts, interviews, articles, movies, miniseries, and televised specials. But until now, I have never

INTRODUCTION

told my whole story. Doing so allows me to fill in gaps, to provide context where it has been sorely lacking, and in key places to set the record straight. Young girls (and boys, too) don't end up being sexually trafficked in a vacuum. Serial sexual abuse doesn't happen to them—to us—out of the blue. In many cases, we are first abandoned by those who claim to love us. By describing my history, I hope to help others prevent it from being repeated.

Nobody experiences extreme trauma and emerges unscathed. I certainly haven't. Even before I met Epstein, I'd experienced awful things that made some observers label me his "perfect victim." But I was also resilient, or I wouldn't be here now. I still have night terrors and panic attacks. I still have moments of feeling worthless. Perhaps I always will. But on many days—especially when I've been able to help another survivor—I thrive. My hope is that this book can aim some light at the darkness and force it to crawl back into its cave.

Once I was silent, but now I have found my voice. This book is a result of that metamorphosis. Because my husband is right about me: I *am* a warrior. A warrior with a story to tell.

Part I

DAUGHTER

"Do you know why this world is as bad as it is? . . . It is because people think only about their own business, and won't trouble themselves to stand up for the oppressed, nor bring the wrong-doers to light. . . . My doctrine is this, that if we see cruelty or wrong that we have the power to stop, and do nothing, we make ourselves sharers in the guilt."

—Anna Sewell, *Black Beauty*

ONE

"Baby"

Picture a girl sitting alone on a curb, her face stained with tears. She is fifteen, but so skinny that she appears even younger. She could be pretty, with her blue eyes and long blond hair, but her freckled face is swollen, her throat is bruised, and in her mouth is a taste she will never forget: gunmetal. Bleeding from places she didn't know she could bleed, this girl has been hurt before, but not like this. A gust of wind makes the palm trees above her shudder. She wipes her bloody lip. What would it be like, she wonders, to matter?

Then she sees the stretch limousine. As it glides toward her, black and shiny, the girl catches a glimpse of the driver behind the wheel. Her mind flashes on the limo in Disney's *101 Dalmatians,* the one that Cruella de Vil drives around London, looking for puppies to skin. How many times has she watched that movie? But this isn't a scene from a cartoon. That's kids' stuff, and the girl hasn't felt like a kid in years. This is real life in Miami, Florida. And the girl is me.

Busting out of the juvenile detention facility in Palm Beach County forty-eight hours earlier, I'd been so full of hope. I knew from experience that I needed to ditch my juvie uniform—a navy polo and khakis—or the cops would pick me up right away. So my first stop had been a Marshalls discount store, where I quickly changed into a new T-shirt and jeans and made a show of returning my prison-issue garb, neatly hung on a hanger, to a rack. Then I exited the store without paying and headed straight for Delray Beach.

I've always been good at talking to strangers. On the sand, I met a stoner dude—way older than me, but with a mellow energy. He was smoking a joint, which he offered to share as we looked out at the Atlantic. When I told him I planned to sleep outside that night, he said I could crash on his couch. I worried that he wanted sex, but I was wrong. When we got to his place, we just smoked some more pot and then he found me a clean towel so I could take a shower. "Please be gone by the morning," he said before he went to bed. "I go to work early. And please don't fuck up my house. Do the right thing."

Not all men are monsters.

The next morning before dawn, I did the right thing, pulling the front door shut with a quiet click. Then I headed for the train station, where I took most of the money I had—a twenty-dollar bill I'd panhandled from a gas-station attendant—out of my ponytail scrunchie, where I'd hidden it, and bought a one-way ticket to Miami. An hour and a half later, I arrived at the Miami-Dade station, fifty miles south of Palm Beach. I'd run away dozens of times before, but I'd never made it this far.

From the station, I headed east on foot, figuring I was about an hour's walk from the ocean. Right away, I saw the pink and orange glow of a Dunkin' Donuts up ahead. Back home in Loxahatchee, I'd often begged for change outside the local Dunkin', so the sight of its logo—a cheerful steaming coffee cup—felt like a good omen. I went inside and bought two of my favorite chocolate-topped donuts. With

"BABY"

food in my stomach for the first time in days, I walked out feeling confident. I had no place to go, but I'd figure it out, somehow.

I must have been walking for about twenty minutes when a white van pulled over just ahead of me. "Need a lift?" the driver asked, sounding friendly. "I'm going your way." Maybe it was the sugar high, but my guard was down. Besides, it was hot and humid, and the dark-haired driver looked like a skinny shrimp—bigger than me, but not by much. I got in and buckled up. The driver glanced at me, then back at the road. He was probably in his late thirties and dressed as if he worked construction. "I need to make one quick stop," he said. He owed someone money, he said, and needed to pay them back. That's cool, I replied, in a voice I hoped sounded tough. The van turned west, away from the water, then parked in front of a seedy-looking motel. "Come upstairs with me," the construction worker said. "It'll only take a sec." I followed him up, then through a door into a dingy, worn-out room.

He was on me immediately, and I knew right away I had underestimated his strength. He overpowered me and held me down on the bed, one hand around my neck. Then he pulled a gun and put its muzzle into my mouth. He raped me from the front first, then from the back. The only lubrication was the saliva he spit into his palm. He choked me until I lost consciousness, then let me breathe, then choked me again. I imagined myself dead, dumped in a ditch. And then a miracle: the man's cell phone rang, and he released me so he could answer it. "Stay here," my attacker told me. "Try to leave, and I'll find you and kill you." Then he turned back to his phone and stepped outside. I suspected he was going to kill me either way. So I waited until I couldn't hear his voice anymore. Then I ran.

That's how I became this tearstained girl sitting on a curb in an empty beach parking lot. It is dusk when I see the limousine slow to a stop in front of me. The tinted rear passenger window hums as it opens, revealing the pasty face of a stranger in his sixties. He is heavy-set, balding. I watch his eyes as they roam over my swollen, bruised face and battered body. "Oh, you poor baby," the old man says. His concern sounds genuine. Peering into the car, I see a pretty girl in a short red dress sitting next to him. She smiles at me. The old man wears black slacks and a collared shirt. The men in my family tend toward blue jeans or coveralls. I hope this stranger is different from them in other ways too.

"Come in here so we can take care of you," the old man says, as the girl nods encouragement. I think of my attacker driving around in his white van, his gun in his lap, searching for the girl who got away. I stand up, wobbly. The limo door opens, and the old man slides over to make room for me.

The old man tells the limo driver where to go, then introduces himself. His name is Ron Eppinger, and he runs a modeling agency called Perfect 10, he says. He gestures toward Yana, the girl next to him, who is from the Czech Republic. Would I like to become a model like her? He asks me how old I am, and at first I say sixteen because it sounds better to me, less vulnerable. Eppinger shakes his head; he isn't buying it. So I tell him the truth, that I'm fifteen, which seems to please him. "As long as you never lie to me again, I will take you in," he says. "What does that mean?" I think, but don't ask out loud. Then Eppinger's fleshy face turns sad. He had a daughter once, he says. Susan Marie. She died when she was fifteen, when the driver of a truck she was riding in fell asleep and crashed into a utility pole in Pompano Beach. Eppinger has never gotten over it, he tells me, and for a moment, I feel sorry for him.

That's when he reaches for me and strokes my hair. "If you want," Eppinger says, "I can be your new daddy."

How quickly he does that, twisting the father-daughter bond into something sickening. But I already know that trick, and I want to believe it doesn't work on me anymore. I don't trust parents—especially fathers. I don't need a daddy, old or new. I just want a break from fending for myself. When you grow up female, danger is everywhere. I've known that for as long as I can remember. Just hours ago, the construction worker in the white van showed me a darker shade of evil. I know I can't go home again. There's no safety there. My whole body aches, inside and out. I have no good options.

The old man, the model, and I order takeout from an oceanfront stand. As we eat—I scarf mine down like an animal—we listen to the waves. Then Eppinger says he wants to take me shopping. We go to a nearby GapKids, and he steers me toward short shorts that don't cover my backside and tops that are way too small. From the look on the saleswoman's face, it's easy to tell what she's thinking: This isn't what most grandfathers buy their granddaughters. Next, we go to a lingerie store where Eppinger seems to be a regular. He picks out G-strings and other lacy things that I've only seen grown women wear in the movies. He holds them up to my newly developed body, leering. Finally, he tells the chauffeur to take us home.

Inside his huge apartment in Key Biscayne, with its sweeping views of Miami across the Rickenbacker Causeway, Eppinger introduces me with a wave of his hand to five other girls, most of them wearing underwear or nothing at all. Only a few speak English. Then, he takes me to a back room—his room. There is a circular bed and a mirrored ceiling. I ask where I can sleep. "With me," he says.

Part of me feels a familiar dread. Is it too late to get away? But another, bigger part remembers how life was in rehab and in foster care and, worst of all, on the run. Maybe this is the way all men behave? I am tired. I want to feel nothing. The old man calls me "Baby." I am the youngest girl there, so the nickname sort of fits. I want to become someone new so badly that I accept it. "Baby" is now who I am.

IT'S BREAKFAST TIME, and my kids—ages eleven, fourteen, and fifteen—are tearing around the house, almost late for school. At the sunny end of our kitchen island, I sip a perfect cup of coffee, cherishing the chaos. My husband, Robbie, hands out the lunches he's packed: three healthy snacks and one oversized sandwich. (Robbie's family is from Sicily, and his Italian subs are hard to beat.) My job is to confirm that everyone has their homework, their permission slips, their *gi* uniforms for their after-school martial-arts classes. As Robbie herds them toward the car, I hug my daughter and two sons tight, ignoring how they wriggle to get free. "Hurry up!" Robbie yells. "That bell is about to ring!" Then, impulsively, I decide I want to come too. Though still in my pajamas, I jump in the front passenger seat as Robbie opens our electric security gate, and I marvel that this is my life.

Later, I'll take a Pilates class and make coq au vin for dinner, giving Robbie (our family's primary chef) a well-deserved night off. But first I must return to the job of examining what came before. It's no fun, this task I've assigned myself, but it is necessary. Would it be easier to spend my waking hours walking on the beach with Juno, my French bulldog, or taking my daughter, Ellie, shopping for earrings, or getting ready to overdecorate our house for Christmas? (My husband complains every year, but I can't help but go overboard on Christmas.) Yes, it would be easier. And I do all those things too.

But it's finally time, I've decided, to put all the puzzle pieces of my life together. I couldn't do that as a child, which is part of the story. Children don't have the luxury of that kind of reflection. Especially if they are in bad situations as I was, they must focus all their energies on simply trying to survive. In the present, my life is organized around two things: my devotion to my husband and children and my determination to hold my abusers accountable. Part of me would prefer to

"BABY"

start in the here and now, describing the gratitude I feel as I arrange Santa Claus figurines, say, or shiny strands of tinsel. But my past demands an audience. It has been hidden for too long.

So how did I end up in Miami, penniless, battered, and alone, at the age of fifteen? There are so many answers to that question, but if you'd asked me in 1998, unpacking them all would have hurt too much. Instead, I would have offered the shortest explanation. "I ran away," I would have said. "I ran away from Growing Together."

TWO

Growing Together

Growing Together marketed itself as a tough-love treatment center, but the truth was that it left the love out of it. By the time I took a seat in Eppinger's limo, I'd been trying to escape for nearly a year. I hadn't volunteered to become a Growing Together "client." My mother, Lynn, tricked me, saying we were going to the eye doctor. Instead, when we entered the tall blue intake building about twenty miles from my family's one-and-a-quarter-acre farm in Loxahatchee, Florida, I found myself surrounded by uniformed men holding clipboards and a few muscled guards. Mom ducked out—I can still recall what she looked like, walking away. Even from the back, I'd know her fiery red hair anywhere.

My mother had recently declared me "out of control," which was basically true. Once an enthusiastic reader and hardworking student, I had become an angry truant, defiant and prone to emotional meltdowns. Whenever I could, I hung out with older kids, drinking and partying, and there was hardly a drug I hadn't taken. So yes, Mom, you were right that as a young teen, I was a rebellious mess. I just wish you'd asked me why.

Growing Together's banana-yellow building sat just south of West Palm Beach, in a town called Lake Worth. That was funny to me, since it seemed that the facility was determined to make the thirty or so teenagers enrolled there feel worthless. In the name of healing, Growing Together's staff forced kids between the ages of thirteen and seventeen to stand in front of the mirror and berate themselves at the top of their lungs. "I am a whore, a slut, a druggie," we girls would yell, staring into our own eyes. We had no choice but to comply. The place was like a fortress, with security gates and barred windows, as well as a special cell—the White Room—where staff sent us when we fought back. Eventually, I would spend a lot of time in the White Room, which had no toilet, no mattress, only a cold concrete floor coated in the filth previous occupants had left behind. My longest stretch in solitary confinement was three weeks. But that came later.

At the beginning of my time there, I tried to give Growing Together a chance. During the day, in group-therapy sessions, I opened up a bit to the counselors. I told them about how when my mom was drinking, it was as if she became another person. One moment she'd be laughing, the next she'd be yelling. She threw things—coffee cups, cold macaroni and cheese—at me and my little brother, Skydy, who was five years younger and whom I adored. But Skydy was just caught in the crossfire. I was the one Mom always seemed furious at. She'd get this look in her blue eyes—Skydy and I called it "The Evil Eye"—that felt as if it could pierce skin. When she was really angry, she'd send me out to the yard to cut a thorny branch from one of her prized rosebushes. "Pick a switch," she'd say. Then, she'd make me pull down my pants, in front of the neighbors and anyone else who was around, so she could whip me with it.

At Growing Together, I began to talk about these painful things, removing a few bricks from the psychic wall I'd built around myself. I told staff about a time just months before when two boys, one seventeen and the other eighteen, assaulted me in the back of a car while I was unconscious. We'd been drinking and smoking pot before I passed out, but I awoke to find them taking turns on top of me. I would never forget their giddy voices or how hot and sour each boy's breath felt on my face. In all, I said, the ordeal had lasted five to seven hours. Talking about all this with the counselors at Growing Together was difficult, but it gave me something I hadn't expected: the first stirrings of relief.

That reprieve wouldn't last, though. Not for nothing would Growing Together eventually be dubbed "Suffering Together" in an exposé in *New Times,* an alternative weekly newspaper that was a sister publication of *The Village Voice.* In December 2004, seven years after I entered Growing Together, this article would report that for years, kids there had endured "beatings, restraint, imprisonment, and systematic humiliation." The piece identified families that had sued Growing Together for hurting, not helping, their children. It described a girl whose arm had been broken by a counselor, a boy who'd attempted suicide but was never referred to a psychologist. One mother called the program "a concentration camp for clients and parents." The article also noted that the nonprofit facility raked in roughly $1 million a year from donations and fees—typically $14,000 a year per "client"—paid by parents of drug-addicted kids, some of whom were ordered by judges to attend. (I'm not sure who paid to put me there, since my parents had no money.) Eighteen months after the *New Times* piece ran, the place closed for good. But for two decades, it was a miserable hellhole for kids like me.

Growing Together's treatment model was a JV version of Alcoholics Anonymous, with six steps instead of twelve. But unlike AA, this protocol depended on pitting kids against one another as we attempted to move between steps, or "levels." When kids first arrived, they were called "newcomers," and the goal was to graduate to become an "oldcomer." If you succeeded, your reward was to be put in charge of other children. Newcomers were not allowed to move around the facility without an oldcomer holding them by the belt, or "belt looping" them. This meant no privacy—not in the toilet, not in the shower, nowhere. Belt looping didn't just make kid-on-kid violence possible, it actively encouraged it.

Having kids supervise and restrain other kids was illegal, yet it must have been efficient, financially speaking (you don't need as many paid staff when you've assigned your wards to police each other). The result was a *Lord of the Flies*–like atmosphere, with terrible hazing rituals and near-constant physical and sexual abuse. Though boys and girls were not supposed to speak to one another, I befriended a slight, pale boy named Chris. When older, bigger boys arrived in the program, they singled him out from across the room: Rape Kid. After they did their worst to Chris, I'd hold his hand and tell him I was sorry. Looking in his flat, gray eyes, I worried that a part of him was already dead and that the rest was not far behind. The girls treated each other just as savagely. A gang of the meanest ones accosted a girl I knew, holding her down and molesting her with some sort of object. That wouldn't happen to me, I vowed. I'd been hypervigilant since long before Growing Together. I saw no reason to change.

Peril was everywhere. Staff members were either ineffectual or cruel. There was one guard, a white guy with curly, blondish hair and a burnt-orange tan, who we called The Enforcer. He loved to put his hands on kids and throw them to the floor or against the walls. Roslyn, meanwhile, was a Hispanic chick with a power complex. She did to our psyches what The Enforcer did to our bodies. She seemed to enjoy humiliating us.

The food was disgusting, and the dinner menus never changed: Mondays, tacos; Tuesdays, Salisbury steak. On Wednesdays, we were served a nasty mushroom soup. I hated mushrooms, but I forced myself to eat because I knew that kids who didn't clean their plates were made to sit at the table until they obeyed, chewed, and swallowed. One Wednesday, though, I just couldn't do it. The smell of the watery, gray liquid made me gag. *"Eat!"* Roslyn yelled, so I tried. But after a few spoonfuls, it wouldn't stay down, and I vomited into my bowl. Roslyn's face broke into a sadistic smile. "No problem," she said. "Now eat until that bowl is empty."

"What goes on here, stays here," staff would often say. The longer I spent at Growing Together, the more I understood why. Rules were rigid. Boys had to keep their heads shaved nearly bald. Girls, though, weren't allowed to shave their legs or underarms. It was as if the staff wanted to mark us, to make us look as abnormal on the outside as they told us we were on the inside. Strip searches and pepper spray were the methods they used to keep us "in line." The squalid building, meanwhile, was overrun with cockroaches and rats.

Nonetheless, every Friday, parents gathered in a large, well-lit room that hid all that. Friday was open-house night, and I remember well the dog-and-pony show the administrators put on. Imagine fifty adults at one end of a banquet room, their "problem kids" herded together at the other end, all dressed in those matching navy-and-khaki uniforms. Before open house began, parents and children were separated by an accordion-like room divider. But when the meeting was called to order, the partition was pulled back, music burst from a loudspeaker, and we kids were made to sing. We knew that if we refused, we'd be sent to the White Room.

"I am a promise, I am a possibility," we chirped, sounding more like nursery schoolers than troubled and abused teens. "I am a promise with a capital *P*. I am a great big bundle of potentiality. And I am learning to hear God's voice. And I am trying to make the right choice. I am a promise to be anything that God wants me to be."

Staff would then hand a microphone to one of the moms or dads and ask them to describe their child's misdeeds. Chosen parents would recite their lists—drug abuse, petty theft, fistfights, violent outbursts, whatever—without a nod to whatever role they might have played in their kids' acting out. It was like watching prosecutors during a trial, except that when the microphone was finally handed to the accused, he or she was not allowed to mount a defense. Instead, we were expected to use our time to confess. Only by confessing could we move up in the hierarchy that divided the punishers from the punished.

That's a snapshot of what happened inside the facility during the day. Other abuses occurred each night, when we were shipped off to sleep at private foster homes endorsed by Growing Together administrators. Typically these were houses owned by parents of children enrolled in the program, and most accommodated five kids at a time. All these homes—mine included, because my parents sometimes took in kids—had been renovated to meet Growing Together's specifications. Pictures and mirrors were removed from walls, so there'd be no glass to break. Kitchen knives were hidden. Bathrooms were stripped, leaving only the sink, toilet, and bathtub. Usually, the windows and doors of the bedrooms where we slept were rigged with alarm systems. Bedtime was 10:00 p.m., and we couldn't exit our rooms until the next morning. That meant no bathroom visits. We had to hold it or pee in buckets.

There was one ritual at Growing Together that I embraced: before bed, we were expected to write in our journals. Staff called these entries "moral inventories." They told us to catalog bad things we'd done, painful things we'd endured, and how we'd been affected by both. The more you confessed, the higher up the hierarchy you were allowed to move, which meant more freedoms—the right to go to the toilet unsupervised, say, or to attend school outside the facility. Inventories that included sexual abuse or underage sex were particularly encouraged. Given these incentives, lots of kids made stuff up. I, however, didn't need to lie. I had plenty of awful experiences to draw on. In the beginning, I hoped that after reading my accounts of past abuses, the staff would take steps to punish those who'd hurt me. Maybe the boys who raped me in the back of that car could be held to account? But I soon realized that wasn't the purpose of our journals. The purpose was to gather information that the staff could use to keep us inmates in check.

I've kept a journal, off and on, ever since. At times I've felt as if the act of recording what's happened and how I feel about it is the only thing keeping me sane. But back then, in that horrible place, the journaling—not the cockroaches or the mushroom soup—is what ultimately broke me. To have chronicled, in blue ink on white paper, even a few of the atrocities I'd suffered and to have nothing done about them? Counselors told me they'd alerted the police about my rape allegation, but apparently the boys said I had consented to the threesome, so no charges were filed. That's what made me see the truth. At Growing Together, my pain was nothing more than a sick form of currency, valuable only if used to climb the program's supposed ladder of "achievement." Once I figured that out, I reinforced my psychic brick wall. "See? There's no point," I scolded myself. "Nobody cares. Fuck the world."

I responded by running away. Over and over. Sometimes I fled from the cars that delivered us from Growing Together to our overnight lodgings. The moment the door locks popped open, I'd make a break for it. That was by far the easiest way to escape. Other times I waited until I got inside those fortified foster homes, with their deadbolts and their alarms. Then I'd find any sharp object and hold it to my throat, threatening to kill myself. More often than not, the parent host would crumble. Who needs the hassle of a dead teenager in their kitchen? So they'd throw open their doors and let me run into the night. I would then be free, sort of, until I was caught and returned to Growing Together. Though I usually disguised my identity when I was on the run, introducing myself as Rachel (my "runaway name") to anyone who asked, I wasn't hard to track. The facility's staff had figured out where I liked to loiter and beg for change—the local Dunkin' Donuts was my spot. Eventually they'd find me and take me back to the White Room. But the next chance I got, I ran again.

This is just some of what I'd been through before I met Eppinger. Perhaps it helps explain why I so readily got into a limousine with an old man I didn't know. It wasn't just that I'd been brutally raped a few hours before, barely fleeing with my life. No, I had felt worthless for years. Sometimes I worried that what the counselors at Growing Together made me say was true: that I was a whore, a slut, a druggie.

But even if I were all those things, I hadn't always been. Once, I'd been a daughter, a sister, a beloved little girl. I hated to think about that. But thinking about it was crucial, I see now. Remembering a better time, a time when I had value, may have been the only thing that kept me from giving up.

THREE

Virginia Lee

In my earliest memory, my uncle Speed scoops me into his arms and sits me on the bare back of his favorite horse. I am three years old, and it seems as if I am a mile off the ground. I grab a fistful of the horse's mane, steadying myself. I love how it feels up here, but I don't get to stay very long. My mother is worried that I'll fall, and she scolds my father's eldest brother for putting me in danger. My first horseback ride is brief, but it changes me. From then on, I'll be obsessed with animals, particularly horses.

To hear my relatives talk, ours is a proud family of athletes, cowboys, and war heroes. Dad always liked to tell the story of how he and his brothers got their names. Their father, Fred, was a radio operator in World War II, but mostly he loved to be up in the clouds, airborne. While serving in the Eighth Air Force in England, Fred was a gunner on a B-17, and in 1945, when he was twenty-six, he was awarded a medal for meritorious achievement. For my grandpa Fred, that sealed it. When he came home to California, and he and my grandma Daisy started a family, he insisted their sons' names reflect his passions:

Speed came first; then Sky, my father; and finally, Jet. (My grandparents had daughters, too, but they had normal names: Sandi and Carol.)

My dad and his siblings grew up in the 1960s and 1970s in Sacramento, which couldn't have been more different from San Francisco, though it's only a hundred miles away. While the hippies in Haight-Ashbury dressed in tie-dye and embraced antiwar activism and free love, my dad's neighbors wore Wrangler jeans, held conservative values, and believed in hard work. My uncle Jet, for example, became a square-dance caller at the age of eight, and that's still what he does for a living. For his part, my dad liked to fix things with his hands. Lanky, with an easy smile, my dad rarely went anywhere without his Stetson hat.

My mom, Lynn, was more of a free spirit. She was born in 1960 to my grandmother Shelley and her second husband, a guy I never met. That marriage ended after Mom's younger sister came along three years later, at which point Shelley sent both her daughters to live with their maternal grandmother, Deedee, in Richmond, Virginia. A Vassar tennis-team alum, my mom's mom was one of the first female tennis pros in the country, and she had no intention of retiring. In the late 1960s, Shelley stayed close to her daughters, serving as head tennis pro at clubs in Virginia Beach and Richmond. But in 1970, Shelley moved eight hundred miles west to Chicago, where she'd grown up, to manage the Mid-Town Tennis Club. I'm not sure my mom ever got over being left behind.

Even from afar, Shelley imposed a lot of rules on her daughters. Both my mom and her sister (also named Virginia) were required to keep their hair bobbed short, which my mom hated. Their grandma Deedee came from money, meanwhile, and appearances mattered to her. She was hell-bent on turning her two granddaughters into well-mannered Southern belles.

Then Shelley married husband number three, a ranking tennis player named Bucky Walters Jr., and moved to Florida to join the

Tennis Club of Palm Beach. At that point, she sent for her daughters, but after they arrived, my mom made clear she wasn't interested in having a stepfather, let alone an older stepbrother (Bucky had a son from an earlier marriage). Mom and Shelley argued constantly. My mom had always been headstrong, and she resented this new family, especially since her mom hadn't seemed to care much about family until now. So my mom ran away, hitchhiking all the way to San Francisco. I don't know much about what that trip was like, but I do know that she started calling herself a hippie, and let her red hair grow long and wild. By the age of sixteen, she'd gotten married to an army man named Craig, and they soon had a son, Danny. By seventeen, Mom was divorced and sharing an apartment with another single mom. She had her hands full, but somehow she finished high school.

Then one afternoon, while buying Danny a soft-serve cone at Dairy Freeze, Mom met Sky Roberts, a cute auburn-haired boy in a big hat. They were both smitten, or so I've always been told. Sky loved Lynn's shiny mane of hair, her freckled skin, and her big toothy smile. Lynn liked how Sky swaggered when he walked—and how he wasn't put off by her already having a kid. Later, my dad would grow a beer belly and develop what I've come to think of as the Roberts nose, wide at the base and bulbous at the tip. But back then, he was long and lean, with a close-cropped beard and mustache. Mom couldn't stay away.

From the start, Dad treated Danny as his own. He said he also wanted more children, which tugged at my mom's heart. Maybe, she thought, they could make a family that was better than the fractured one she'd come from. So in December 1982, my parents married at St. Peter's Lutheran Church in Elk Grove, just south of Sacramento. Eight months later, they had me: Virginia Lee Roberts. Everyone called me Jenna. Family legend has it that my arrival made my grandma Shelley want to reconcile with my mom, her estranged eldest daughter. In a series of long-distance phone calls, she and my mother patched things up, and soon my dad, my mom, Danny, and I were speeding east in a used Winnebago we'd picked up for cheap.

THE FIRST THING that struck me about Florida was the ocean—I'd never seen one. I loved its salty smell. We stayed with grandma Shelley in West Palm Beach at first, not far from the beach, and I soon discovered a lot about her. She wouldn't let us call her Grandma, for starters; I guess because it signaled her age. We kids were to call her Gamma. What's more, she seemed to wake up with a Bloody Mary in one hand and a cigarette in the other. Gamma always spent peak tanning hours poolside at her tennis club, bronzing her already brown and leathery skin and playing backgammon with friends. She kept a bottle of baby oil in her purse. She had other quirks, too. A clean freak, Gamma was the kind of woman who kept her furniture covered in plastic and who made me stand in the driveway when I brushed my hair. She didn't have a nurturing bone in her body. But I admired how she lived life on her own terms.

Given Gamma's control issues, Mom never intended for us to stay long under her roof. Soon my parents found a small three-bedroom ranch house on a dirt road in Loxahatchee, about thirty minutes away from West Palm Beach. Loxahatchee is prime horse country now, but back then it was known for its renegade residents, loose land restrictions, and exotic animals. Partly surrounded by citrus groves, Loxahatchee edged up against the last remaining section of the northern Everglades. Living next to something so wild, our new neighbors felt free to keep not only broken-down school buses in their yards, but also iguanas, peacocks, alpacas, and emus. Years later, one neighbor would stash the body of an endangered panther in his garage freezer. That was Loxahatchee in the 1980s: untamed and off the grid.

Our new house wasn't much, but my parents worked hard to fix it up. Mom planted sunflowers and daisies in the front yard. Dad seeded a lawn, built a shed, raised a barn. And me? In the daytime I explored the woods that bordered our land. There were two kinds of cypress trees in our part of Florida—the pond cypress and the bald cypress—neither one of which resembled the tall Italian cypresses I remembered from Sacramento. These trees grew in areas saturated by water. I remember a neighbor explained that the bald cypress, a wispy breed, got its name because it lost its leaves in winter. But I was more fascinated by how when it flooded, these trees created specialized root structures—everyone called them "knees"—that grew out of the submerged ground, through the water and up into the air, bringing oxygen to the canopy above. These cypresses were survivors—some had been alive for six hundred years—and I admired that. I also loved what I could see from the uppermost branches of our tallest slash pine trees, which are the kind that grow on swampy ground. I would ascend and hang upside down like a possum, laughing at the world flipped on its head. I got so good at climbing that my parents began calling me Peter Pan. I couldn't fly, of course, but I had the fearlessness and confidence of someone who could.

A month after I turned five, Mom put me in kindergarten at Haverhill Baptist Day School. Classes were only a few hours a day and were mostly intended to get kids used to attending school. But I still have the report card, which features a drawing of two smiling children, a boy and a girl, sitting together on the floor, both holding books open in their laps. I remember the delight I felt as I learned to read that fall, and how amazed I was to learn there was a place called a library where anyone could go to borrow books, free of charge.

Five months after I'd enrolled at Haverhill, in February 1989, my little brother, Sky Rocket Roberts, was born. I called him Skydy Bump, or just Skydy. When he came home from the hospital, my parents put his crib in my room, so I felt almost as if he were my baby. When he cried at night, I was the one who got up and comforted him. I adored Skydy, and as he grew up—white-blond, brown-eyed, and handsome—good things began to happen. My mom worked briefly as a bank teller after Skydy was born, but she quit after being robbed at gunpoint. I understand now that the robbery must have been terrifying for her, but at the time, it seemed a boon to us kids: we were glad to have her around more. For his part, Dad began to find work doing maintenance and construction. My half brother, Danny, was a scrappy kid. Even after getting one of his front teeth knocked out being rambunctious, he always seemed to lean into trouble. But he was my big brother, and he looked out for me. More and more, it seemed Mom and Dad walked around with beer cans in their hands. Still, I was happy, and I thought my family was too.

In those days, I was buoyed by the knowledge that my mom loved having a daughter. I still have the baby book she made for me, which is so jammed with photos I can barely close it. There's me, perched on a chair next to a favorite tabby cat; me barefoot at the beach, shoveling sand into a bucket; me dressed up as Snow White on Halloween. There's a lock of my hair tied with a pink ribbon, and Mom wrote monthly entries, each one addressed to me. "My Special Girl!" she wrote. When my freckles popped out, just like Mom's, she called them "angel kisses" and insisted they made me prettier. And Mom trusted me completely with Skydy. One day, while playing in the sandpit under the treehouse Dad had built for us, Skydy tugged on my T-shirt. "Sissie," he said, and when I turned around, he pointed at a snake slithering toward us. I wasn't particularly afraid of reptiles—at one point, I'd kept a lizard in a shoebox under my bed, filling a bottle cap each night so he had water—but something told me this viper was trouble. I grabbed Skydy and ran for the house, screaming. Mom came out just in time to see the deadly water moccasin slipping into the grass. Later, she said I'd saved Skydy's life.

I loved our neighborhood. We lived in the second house on the left on Rackley Road, just down the street from the Rackley family. You might think that since our dirt road was named after them, they'd be sitting pretty on the nicest plot of land. Instead, it seemed they'd sold off the best parcels around them, keeping the mangiest, muddiest piece for themselves. By the time we moved in, the Rackley clan were what people called hillbillies—rough as guts, with a lot of barking dogs but no front lawn.

Our land had its own small pond with a tiny island in the middle of it, and after my father built a narrow bridge linking it to the nearest stretch of shore, the island was my spot. I spent hours there reading, drawing, and daydreaming about how my life might turn out. One day, while I was lolling about, I spotted an alligator snapping turtle, as big as a truck tire, stick his head out of the water. I'd never seen a turtle that large, so of course I wanted to catch it. Mom said I should ask the Rackleys. "They'll know what to do," she said. And they did. One of their boys—there were several, including one set of twins—put a hunk of meat on a hook tied to a string with a bell on it. Two days later, when the bell started ringing, I watched in awe as the Rackleys pulled the bloody turtle out of the pond, its jaws snapping. Later that night, there was a knock at our door—yet another Rackley boy. He said his mom had made turtle soup if anyone wanted to taste it. I thanked him, but declined. I'd already decided I wanted to be a veterinarian—ever since I'd heard that taking care of animals was a job some people got paid to do. So I didn't want to eat the turtle. I was excited just to see the turtle's sharp beak and scaly shell up close.

We kids never lacked for adventure. We'd build makeshift bike ramps out of boards and cinderblocks that sent us flying, but we somehow managed not to get too hurt. We prided ourselves on being able to handle whatever Loxahatchee dished out. One time, after Dad installed an electric fence on the property, we took turns seeing who could grab it and hold on the longest. Another time Danny fell through a rotten roof that we were not supposed to be climbing on and broke his arm. If you'd asked, we'd have told you we lived in heaven. Whenever Mom took us to visit her sister's kids in their North Palm Beach housing development, we couldn't believe our cousins had to live in such a boring place. "What do you guys do for fun?" I'd ask, trying not to reveal how sorry I felt for them.

My tomboy ways were about to be interrupted, though, by the realities of starting elementary school. Maybe it was a holdover from her own upbringing, but Mom had very clear ideas about how she wanted her only daughter to appear to the outside world. Suddenly I was forced to trade my jeans for frilly dresses that I hated almost as much as the brightly colored ribbons Mom insisted on tying into my hair each morning.

Still, I loved first grade. My favorite teacher was Mrs. McGirt, who recommended I check out *Charlotte's Web*, about a girl named Fern who, like me, lived on a farm. Like Fern, I was an early riser, always eager to get a jump on the day. Like Fern, my family had dogs and goats and chickens—though no pigs like the adorable Wilbur. I loved that book. On the nights Mom tucked me in, I had her read it to me. On the nights when my parents were drunk and I put myself and Skydy to bed, I practiced reading it aloud, especially the end, when Charlotte tells Wilbur about the wonderful life he will lead—"this lovely world, these precious days." I adored the idea that Wilbur was so dear to Farmer Zuckerman that the little pig would never, ever be harmed.

Around this time, Mom made clear that being a girl meant more than dresses and hair ribbons. I had never balked at my chores with the animals—feeding them, cleaning their stalls, putting them in their pens at night. I'd spent hours teaching our goat, Cordelius, how to walk on his hind legs. But suddenly my mother said I had to help her take care of the people in our family too. My new jobs included setting and clearing the table every evening, then helping with the dishes, and vacuuming every room in the house once a week. Neither of my brothers had to take a turn, but when I asked Mom why, she said girls needed to learn things that boys didn't. "You'll have a husband someday," she said, "and you'll need to do this for him." It's funny to think about now, because it's not as if my mother was a very good housekeeper. The inside of our house often looked as if a tornado had just torn through. But the message was clear: we were both female, and I was going to shoulder some of her load.

My family had its rituals. Every night we'd assemble around our coffee table for dinner: fish sticks, chicken tenders, anything that was on "special" at the local Pantry Pride. The TV was always on—usually *M*A*S*H*, which I hated, or *The Simpsons*, which I loved. Every morning I packed my lunch (and, eventually, Skydy's) before school, even though no one showed me how. I'd just smear some grape jelly on white bread and put it in a brown paper bag, no baggie. By lunchtime my backpack gave off a musty smell, as if something were fermenting inside. I envied the kids who brought lunch money for a hot meal. But without even asking, I knew that wasn't an option for me. In our house, what little money there was seemed always to get spent on my dad's whims: his latest pickup truck or construction project. Either that or beer.

When my dad decided he wanted something, though, he went out and got it. When I was about six years old, I stepped off the school bus one day and encountered Dad standing in the road. "I've got something to show you," he said, and the grin on his face said it was something good. He turned toward our house, with me right behind him, and when we got within sight of the barn, I spotted her: a beautiful black-and-white paint. "Her name is Alice," Dad said, nodding to the horse who hadn't been there that morning. "She's all yours."

I was stunned. I approached her as Dad told me to: slowly, with my hand extended so she could nuzzle it. Looking in her big brown eyes, I saw intelligence. I couldn't believe I had my very own horse.

From that point on, Alice and I were inseparable. I could have changed her name, I guess, but I didn't because it reminded me of *Alice in Wonderland*, a book I'd adored. My Alice was gentle, patient, and easy to get a saddle on, though usually I rode her bareback. Skydy was jealous: I had to reassure him that Alice would never take his place in my heart. But the truth was that my little brother—then barely a toddler—couldn't expand my world like Alice did.

Every day when the final school bell rang, I'd hurry to the bus, counting the minutes until it dropped me off. I had a longer walk home now; the school bus had been rerouted after a pig farmer drowned in the collecting canal at the end of our dirt road—the fourth person in a year whose car had rolled into the canal's swampy water. The county school board didn't want to risk a bus full of kids meeting the same fate. So now, instead of delivering me right to the end of Rackley Road, the bus dropped me an eighth of a mile away. I didn't care. I would run all the way home, sling a halter around Alice's neck, and off we'd go.

Alice wasn't fast, and she wasn't slow. She was perfect because she was mine. I delighted in the way she smelled, especially after a ride, and the way she'd wrap her head around me to hold me close as I brushed her mane. I couldn't wait to do the jobs that kept her happy: mucking her stall, putting fly spray on her. When I taught her to swim in our pond, we'd float and paddle together, just a girl and her horse, enjoying the same cool water. When we headed for the woods, she never startled or bucked. She was sensitive as well as smart. On her back, I felt taller. Stronger. I knew that she understood me, and I her, without words. Alice was my ally, my protector—like Charlotte-the-spider was for Wilbur-the-pig. With her I felt completely safe. I didn't yet know there were reasons to be afraid.

FOUR

Less Than Nothing

In her novel *Black Beauty*, which I read and reread as a child, Anna Sewell describes horses like this: "We call them dumb animals, and so they are, for they cannot tell us how they feel, but they do not suffer less because they have no words." I've thought a lot about that idea: that you can be in pain even if you can't articulate it. When I was small, I loved that *Black Beauty* was written from the horse's point of view. It took me inside the horse's mind, describing his memories of his mother ("a wise old horse") and what she wished for him: a life built on kindness and freedom. Reading that book, I vowed never to cause suffering when I could help it. Just like the story's main character, I wanted to grow up gentle and good, never learning bad ways.

What many people don't know about horses is that despite their size and power, they are vulnerable prey animals. They depend on flight—their ability to outrun predators—as their primary means of survival. That requires that they use their well-honed intuitions to sense danger in their surroundings. I've described how, from the moment I met my horse, Alice, I felt in sync with her. Little did I know that she and I would soon share even more in common: a reliance on wariness and, eventually, a need to escape.

The first signs of trouble came with a few subtle changes to our family routine. First, Skydy started sleeping in my parents' room, leaving me alone each night in the room the two of us had shared. Then, my mom—who up to that point had usually run my bath, washed my hair, and gotten me in my pj's each night—stepped back for some reason, and Dad began doing that. Now, once I was ready for bed, Mom would say a quick goodnight, but it was Dad who tucked me in, read me a story, and cuddled me. At first, all that felt normal and good. I loved my dad. He'd taught me to ride Alice. When I competed in horse shows, which I was learning how to do, he was always my biggest fan. I saw Dad as capable and even invincible. I trusted him.

Then, during bath time one night, Dad abruptly told me to stand up. "We've got to make sure you're extra clean," he said. The command felt weird to me. I stayed submerged, the soapsuds hiding my nakedness. I wasn't sure why I felt embarrassed, but I did. "Can Mom come in?" I asked.

"No, Mom's busy," Dad said, impatient. He had a washcloth in his hand. I stood up, and he began to soap me all over, spending extra time between my legs.

That night in my room, Dad touched me in ways nobody had before. He told me I was his special girl, his favorite, and that this was his way of giving me "extra love." He used his fingers at first. Then, days later, his mouth. He called my private parts my "tee-tee" and his penis his "pee-pee." It wasn't long before he asked if I wanted to touch his genitals. I didn't want to, but he wanted me to. He was my father, so I did.

I tried to stop these things from happening. "I don't want bedtime stories anymore," I announced one day. "I don't want cuddles anymore. I can do bath time by myself. I'm a big girl now." And so the bedtime rituals ended, but the abuse didn't. At night in the dark, I'd wait. Dad didn't always come in, but every night I feared he would. The door would open a crack, revealing a stripe of light from the hall, and the hinges would creak slightly—I'll always remember that soft squeaking sound. Then Dad would close the door behind him and slip into my twin bed, fondling me, forcing himself on me. For a while, I tried hiding in the tight space under my box spring, but that didn't work. "Get out from under there," he'd say, "or I'll take Alice away." I couldn't imagine that. So out I'd crawl.

At this point, Mom—once so warm and loving—became cold and remote, at least when it came to me. I was already a pleaser; up early, I'd make my bed, trying to help her manage the mayhem of getting three kids ready for school. Now, I tried even harder to make her love me, offering to go grocery shopping with her—anything to not be left alone with Dad. But Mom seemed unreachable. The whippings with the thorny rose branches started around this time. And it seemed to me she was drinking more beer. Once I had been her beautiful, angel-kissed girl. But now she told me a story I'd never heard before: she'd always wondered if I was really her daughter. In the hospital right after my birth, she told me, one of the nurses had briefly given her a different baby girl to breastfeed, but the woman soon rushed back in and took that infant away. Maybe I'd been switched with another child, she said. Maybe I was just a big mistake.

I was confused. Why was Mom mad at me? Did she know what Dad was doing to me? I have a distinct memory of my bedroom door opening slightly one night as Dad molested me—I heard that squeaking sound again. Was that Mom, or did I just desperately want it to be her? I didn't see her face. Could she have seen Dad under the covers with me? The door slowly closed again.

I began to get painful urinary tract infections. Mom took me to the doctor again and again. The nurses were mystified. After one examination, a doctor told my mother that my hymen had been broken. My mother didn't hesitate. "Oh, she rides horses bareback," she explained. That was the end of that. I didn't even know what a hymen was.

My infections were so severe at times that I couldn't hold my urine. Mortified, I started tying a sweater around my waist at school so that when I sat down, the sweater would absorb what leaked out. The other kids recognized the smell and where it was coming from, though, and nicknamed me "Pee Girl." At home, Mom flew into a rage whenever she found my wet underwear, beating my bottom until it stung. So I tried to hide the soiled clothes—and, God forbid, the sheets when I wet the bed. They stank, so she'd always find them. But I figured getting a single beating for a pile of dirty underwear was better than getting beat one pair at a time.

Around this time, Danny was sent away to a Baptist reform school in Washington State. Dad then changed up his tactics, doing what he wanted to me more obviously, not just in the middle of the night. If Mom was out, he'd molest me in the afternoon, promising me that afterward, we'd put on a movie—he loved scary films best—make some popcorn, and stay up late together. By mixing his sick behavior with cozy bonding, he normalized it, at least partly. I still hated what Dad did to me, but I began to bargain with myself: just get the icky part over with so the good parts of life can go on.

Then something happened that made sure life had no more good parts. Forrest was a friend of my father's. He was tall and muscular, with a military bearing, and he had a tattoo on his chest. I knew this because he liked to show off his physique at the pool-and-beer parties our two families began having together. Suddenly, Forrest—who had his own landscaping business—was around our house a lot. My dad encouraged Skydy and me to call him "Uncle Forrest" and told me to befriend his stepdaughter, Sheila, which I was happy to do. She was sixteen—nine years older than me—so I thought she was the epitome of cool. But she could seem distant sometimes too. I later found out why.

One night Mom, Dad, and I were out on our porch with Forrest, Sheila, and Sheila's mom. I've corresponded with Sheila about this recently, and she remembers this too. We think our little brothers were playing somewhere inside the house when our parents—who were drinking beer, as usual—began joking around about how "naughty" Sheila and I were. Either my dad or Forrest then suggested that they "trade" us for a night. I recall Forrest glancing at my father and saying something about "a backwards sleepover. Jenna can come sleep at our house, and Sheila can sleep here."

I didn't know it then, but by this point, Forrest had been sexually abusing Sheila for two years. Since Sheila and I have reconnected, she's told me she was never "traded" to my dad for him to abuse. I wasn't so fortunate. I'll never know the exact date I was first left with Forrest. I do remember that it was with my father's permission. I recall being in a bathtub—I've always thought it was in Forrest and his wife's home, but Sheila wonders if it may have been in one of the empty vacation homes whose lawns Forrest was paid to tend. Forrest walked into the bathroom. I told him I wanted to bathe myself, but he wouldn't leave. He sat on the toilet next to me and acted as if this were the most natural thing in the world—a grown man scrubbing the naked body of someone else's young daughter. "We've got to wash you good. You're a dirty girl," he said.

That time, Forrest did things to me that my father had done and other things my father had not. When he put his fingers inside me, like my dad did, Forrest narrated his actions out loud. "I think you can take another finger," he said, implying that was a good thing. His chest was shaved, and he wanted me to admire its smoothness. "Touch my muscles," he commanded. "Tell me how big they are." Forrest lay on top of me, crushing me. He tried to kiss me, but I turned my face away. When he put his mouth down there, I remember he held my wrists tightly. He was very strong. I couldn't escape.

TO THIS DAY, I rely on music to make the world make sense. I'll be in the front passenger seat on one of those early morning drives to school, my children buckled in behind me. With Robbie at the wheel, my hands are free to plug my iPhone into the sound system and push shuffle. Chances are good that as it clicks through my two thousand or so songs, it'll land on one from the period during which I began to process how much my dad and Forrest had hurt me. I have a lot of songs from the 1990s and early 2000s among my favorites, I guess because that's when I leaned on music the hardest. Tracy Chapman will start singing "Give Me One Reason" ("I don't want no one to squeeze me / They might take away my life"). Or Matchbox Twenty will launch into "Bright Lights" ("I got a hole in me now / I got a scar I can talk about"). Or the thunderclap will sound at the beginning of Garth Brooks's "The Thunder Rolls." When that happens, all three kids start screaming. They are born-and-bred Australians, and while they love a lot of American music, they think my taste is terrible. "Oh, Mom," they'll moan, rolling their eyes. "You've *got* to update your tunes!" Nonetheless, we all enjoy this ritual—my ancient hit parade, their merciless teasing—so I just laugh and turn up the volume. Then I lose myself a bit, remembering how, as a young girl, I wielded my Walkman like a talisman, to ward off evil.

As I have become a "public person"—by which I mean a woman whose story of survival has been told and retold by the media—I have kept much about my childhood private. When I began working with a collaborator on this book, I had never said publicly that my father molested me and then gave me to another man to molest. When asked, I had always been vague, saying only that I was abused by a family friend. Well, that was true, as far as it went. But there was so much more awfulness left unsaid.

Forrest was the first man to penetrate me with his penis. Not long afterward, my father did the same. Sometimes what they each did to me was so similar that I suspected they were comparing notes. Other times they liked to spend time with me together. They once insisted on taking me to see the movie *Arachnophobia*, about a species of South American spiders that is smuggled into the United States inside a coffin. I remember they thought it was funny to take me, a small child, to a horror film about eight-legged insects that breed and kill. I've been terrified of spiders ever since.

Sheila, meanwhile, stopped coming to our house altogether. Only while writing this book have I discovered that in 1990 she filed a formal complaint with the Florida Department of Children and Families, alleging that Forrest had sexually abused her. Her mother didn't believe her then, but the state did. In September of that year, she got a restraining order against Forrest and went to live with another relative. From what Sheila and I have pieced together, it seems that at this point, Forrest turned his attentions to me.

Recently, Sheila told me that we were not the only girls Forrest molested. In 2000, he was convicted of abusing another girl in North Carolina in 1996. He served fourteen months in prison and was a registered sex offender for ten years, from 2001 to 2011. Sheila says more girls came forward over the years to accuse him of abuse, but her mom disbelieved them. Sheila's mom stood by Forrest until 2010, when she found pornography on his computer and threw him out for good.

I feel so grateful that Sheila and I have found each other again, and I wanted to make sure I didn't drag her into the spotlight. Many survivors have made that decision, to remain anonymous, and I respect that choice. But Sheila wanted me to use her real first name here. "I have had to be silent for so long," she wrote in an email. "This is me and I'm not afraid to be me. I didn't do anything wrong to be ashamed of. I don't want to hide from the truth."

I love Sheila's self-confidence, and today I am inspired by it. But as a child, I had no such inspiration. "It's hard to believe that there's nobody out there / It's hard to believe that I'm all alone," the Red Hot Chili Peppers sang from the cheap transistor radio I'd begun keeping next to my bed. Their lyrics seemed meant for me. I turned to Alice for help. I was trying to hang onto the feeling that I was part of a family and that I belonged—if not to my parents, or entirely to myself, then maybe to my horse, to our groves of slash pines, to the island in the middle of our pond. But day by day, that feeling of belonging was fading away.

Some nights Alice and I would stay out long after sunset, missing dinner and whatever came after it. I got in trouble with Mom, but I didn't care. I felt she was willfully ignoring what was in front of her face. Her outgoing tomboy had become withdrawn. Her straight-A student had begun cutting class. Her Peter Pan wasn't so confident anymore. That's what happens when a girl is preyed upon. Mom had to know that *something* was up, but she didn't ask me what, and she didn't intervene. More than once, she even implied I was trying to steal her husband from her. One night I was hiding under the kitchen table to avoid bath time with Dad. Mom got the broom and jabbed me with it until I came out. "Look what you're making me do!" she yelled, as if what was happening were something I'd set in motion. My response: defiance. I didn't want her husband or his nasty friend Forrest! So what if I missed dinner every night? Throwing food away was nothing compared to throwing a daughter away. And that's what I believed she was doing.

Not surprisingly, I guess, during this period I clung to even the tiniest expressions of affection, even disturbing ones. While sexually abusing me, for example, my father would often ask me questions about what his actions were causing me to feel. He was fascinated by my body's reactions, and sometimes what he did felt good, sort of, though any pleasure I felt was mixed with disgust. I didn't know what an orgasm was, but I knew I didn't want to encourage him. Still, sometimes my body betrayed me, shivering under his touch. That's when my father would say he was proud of me. "This is why we do this," he'd say. "This is why I give you all this extra love." A part of me relished feeling special—especially since my mother had labeled me good-for-nothing. But when Dad would compare me to Mom, saying, "You're my star. I don't even do this with your mother," I felt sick to my stomach.

I guess some instinct for self-preservation made me try to claim my body as my own, because I started to experiment with boys. My best friend, Kyle, lived on the same side of Rackley Road as us with his dad, J.D.—who I'm pretty sure was using Kyle as his punching bag—and his mom, who everyone called Chicken. One day when we were maybe eight or nine years old, Kyle showed me a *Playboy* magazine he'd found in his dad's closet, and we took off our clothes, then shyly started to kiss and gently touch each other. When I think back on this behavior, I'm struck by the pure innocence of it. We were children; my chest at that point was as flat as Kyle's (which is why we were both equally wowed by the breasts we saw in that pilfered *Playboy*). Guided more by curiosity than anything approximating lust, we weren't sure what we were doing, but we knew that it felt good. At first I was the leader, mimicking things Dad and Forrest did to me, and Kyle was bewildered. But my friend was inquisitive, too, and soon, we were playing this game every day. Then, my mother caught us. She went nuts, banishing Kyle from our house and telling me I was a bad, dirty girl.

LESS THAN NOTHING

Kyle and I weren't allowed to see each other for a long time. We were even forbidden from talking across the fence that separated our properties. That's when I got angry. Before this, I'd questioned the ways my life was changing, but I was confused about who to blame. Now, I chose to blame my mother. "How can she say what I'm doing with Kyle is bad, when Dad and Forrest do things to me that are so much worse?" I asked myself.

In *Charlotte's Web*, a lamb tells Wilbur that pigs mean "less than nothing" to her. Wilbur is outraged and argues there is no such thing. "Nothing is absolutely the limit of nothingness," he protests. "It's the lowest you can go . . . If there were something that was less than nothing, then nothing would not be nothing, it would be something—even though it's just a very little bit of something." Every night, as I lay in my bed, dreading the now-familiar creak of the door, I tried to remember a time when I'd been more than nothing. I longed to be worth something again.

FIVE

Vinceremos

There were moments when I could glimpse the Mom I used to know. I remember one weekend—I was probably nine or ten years old—I'd been invited to a sleepover party by a girl I didn't know very well. At this point, I didn't have any close friends—I had walled myself off from kids my age because I no longer felt I was like them. But a sleepover meant one less night at home, so I went. Immediately, I regretted it. The girls were cliquish; I didn't fit in. So when I got the chance, I stepped outside of our host's house and headed for the barn. It was getting dark, but I figured I could sleep out there. Inside the barn, I found myself face-to-face with a horse that was locked in its stall. A bonus, I thought—I wasn't alone. But as my eyes adjusted to the dim light, I saw that the horse was having trouble moving. Peering into the stall, I saw the animal was standing in several feet of its own excrement: a captive, left to drown in its own shit.

I may not have been able to save myself, but there was no way I was leaving this horse behind. I marched straight into the kitchen and called my mom. "Mom, you need to bring the trailer," I told her when she picked up. "You need to do it right now." And you know what? She believed me. It wasn't long before Mom pulled our horse trailer into the driveway. I'll never forget how she squared off with my sleepover hostess's parents, telling them we were taking their horse and that if they put up a fight, she'd call the authorities. We packed up the poor animal, whom we'd soon rename Baloo after the bear in *The Jungle Book* (I just called her Blue-y because she had one brown eye and one blue eye), and drove her home. In that moment, I felt proud of myself and of my mom. We'd banded together and done something good! But as the days went by, that feeling turned in on itself. Why was Mom willing to fight for an abused animal, but not for me? Why did she hear my cry for help when I called about a horse but didn't see my own suffering when it was right under her nose?

There was one woman in my life, though, who didn't make me feel like an afterthought. I'd met Ruth Menor in 1989, when she and her husband and kids became our back-gate neighbors. Even though her son and daughter were a few years younger than me, we three (and later Skydy, too) had played together off and on almost as long as we'd been in Loxahatchee. Soon I found out that Ruth ran Vinceremos Therapeutic Riding Center, which she'd founded a year before I was born. As a young woman, Ruth had had a dream of using horses to help change the lives of handicapped and disabled kids. She was determined to create a place that used horses to heal. Nothing like that existed in the area, so she opened her own center and chose a name inspired by the Spanish word for "we will overcome." She started off with one client and one horse and began growing Vinceremos on a leased plot of land.

A few years later, Ruth's nonprofit needed a permanent home, and she managed to scrape together the money to buy a fifteen-acre parcel half a mile from my family's land. The place was pretty broken-down when she bought it, but I didn't care. Ruth introduced me to Spring, her quarter horse, and to Malarkey, an Arabian who she often let us ride all the way home to Rackley Road. Ruth called Malarkey her "heart horse" because of their strong connection. Sometimes, when Malarkey was visiting Ruth's yard, Ruth would open a sliding glass door and Malarkey would walk over and stick her head in the house. Ruth joked that Malarkey was watching cartoons with us kids, and I believed her.

But it was a rescue horse named Millie that captured my heart. Millie was just three years old, but she'd already been terribly abused. When Ruth adopted her, she had cuts on her legs that went all the way down to the bone. Usually the horses Ruth used for therapy were at least eight years old. Ruth said they needed that maturity to work with disabled kids. But Millie started working at Vinceremos right away. Ruth said Millie seemed to know she had been rescued because she acted grateful. When I was around Ruth, I knew just how Millie felt.

As the abuse I was suffering continued, I came to see the riding center—and Ruth herself—as a safe haven. Ruth had thick reddish-brown hair and warm, sparkling brown eyes, and I admired how capable and self-assured she was. It seemed there was nothing in the barn she didn't know how to do. I told Ruth I'd work any job if she'd just let me hang around. I didn't dare tell her what was happening to me—my dad had said if I ever told a soul, he would kill my little brother and bury his body in the woods, where no one would find him. Still, Ruth seemed to sense that I needed help, because she kindly put me to work. First, she helped me sign up for 4-H, a year-round club whose members worked together on a farm or in a stable. The idea was if you give kids responsibilities and impress upon them how their actions make a difference in the lives of the animals they are tending, they will become more capable, confident, and self-aware.

Back then, I'm not sure I could have told you what the four *H*'s stood for (heads, hearts, hands, and health). All I knew was that Ruth recommended 4-H and that joining would let me spend more time with her. I had already learned from Alice how intuitive horses were, but Ruth expanded my knowledge. "A horse can feel a fly land on its back," she'd say. "Imagine all it can feel from you. If you think it, the horse feels it." I already knew how to feed a horse, but now I learned about the different styles of riding and how to groom Alice properly. In the meantime, I must have mucked a thousand stalls at Vinceremos, shoveling soiled wood shavings and hay into my wheelbarrow with a pitchfork. It felt good to scrub something clean.

At the same time, I began helping where I could with Ruth's disabled clients. Every few months, Vinceremos hosted camping trips for its members. Eager to get out of our house, I begged Mom to let me go along to DuPuis State Reserve, a twenty-two-thousand-acre park interspersed with ponds, wet prairies, and remnants of Everglades marsh. Officially, I went to help stake tents and tend animals. But I found I also connected with the kids, who were blind or had cerebral palsy or other ailments. One girl, Maddie, was hearing impaired. Sitting around the campfire one night, I could tell she felt out of place, so I sat down next to her. We couldn't communicate, really, but I made her smile by goofing around and toasting her marshmallows. Maddie didn't want to sleep in a tent, but her parents had a minivan, so we slept together there, rolling out our sleeping bags on the long, narrow back seats. Over a weekend, Maddie and I became wordless best buddies—kind of like me and Alice. Ruth praised me for sensing that Maddie needed a little extra TLC. But later I wondered if Maddie sensed the same about me. Though not disabled, I was definitely wounded, with no end to my abuse in sight.

It was Ruth who first taught me that horses reflect the emotions of their riders. When working with her most-vulnerable clients—children with autism, say, who had trouble identifying and communicating their feelings out loud—Ruth would often urge them to appraise the horse on whose back they were sitting. "Is your horse anxious?" she'd ask.

"Do you think he feels like you feel?" Later, she'd tell me that mirroring is just one superpower that horses have. Here's another one: As alert as they are to potential danger, horses don't carry fear with them all the time. Once a mountain lion leaves their pasture, for example, horses will return immediately to grazing peacefully. Even in the wake of trauma, most horses are able to quickly embrace calm.

I wish I could say the same about myself. At ten years old, I saw my preadolescent body as an enemy. I couldn't control how it drew the attention of the men who caused me pain, so I began to starve it. "You don't deserve to eat," said a voice in my head. About the only thing I allowed myself to devour in those days was a videotape of Disney's *Cinderella*. Though I knew I was too old for it, I still found the animated classic comforting. I watched it so many times on our beat-up VCR that Skydy, who usually liked to be plastered to my side, got bored and wandered off. "Cinderella, you're as lovely as your name," a chorus sang, as the opening credits rolled. And then Cinderella herself would appear, waking up in her bed, combing her fingers through her long blond hair. "A dream is a wish your heart makes when you're fast asleep," she'd sing to the birds and mice who gathered around her—and also to me. I related to the story of an unloved daughter doing chores while her family mistreated her. And I enjoyed the fantasy of being swept off my feet by a handsome prince. No matter how sad I was, Cinderella sang, if I kept on believing, my hopes for a better life would come true. Still, I couldn't help but wonder: Was it really that simple?

SIX

If Wishes Were Horses

When I was eleven, I got my period. For years, as adults had forced me to do things no child should know about, I'd been praised sometimes for acting "grown up." But no one had bothered to tell me what happened when a girl *actually* grew up. I had no idea what was coming. I remember being outside at one of my parents' boozy bonfire parties, running around with some other kids, when I looked down at my jeans and saw a creeping red stain. Was I bleeding to death? I wondered. Pale and terrified, I sought out Mom, who glared at me as she appraised my bloody pants. Then, without putting down her beer, she headed into the house, scrounged around in the cupboard under the bathroom sink, and handed me a sanitary pad. "Figure it out," she said, turning on her heel and leaving me alone. Locking the door behind her, I sat down on the toilet and cried.

Around this time, Sheila's mom called my mom, and what she said set off an explosion in our house. My memory is that Mom got the impression that Forrest had impregnated Sheila. (He hadn't, as it turned out. Sheila has recently told me that after a Florida court emancipated her, she moved to North Carolina with a boyfriend and got pregnant with him. She married that boyfriend when she was eighteen, and they had a daughter. But my mom didn't know that.) My parents fought for hours that night as Skydy and I huddled together, covering our ears. For a while, Dad moved out—but not before I was exiled to the home of one of my dad's sisters. Aunt Carol lived in California, three thousand miles west. Maybe my mother was trying to protect me when she sent me into this other galaxy, but it didn't feel that way to me. In my mind, my mother had once again chosen my father over me.

"Alone, listless / Breakfast table in an otherwise empty room," Eddie Vedder of Pearl Jam would sing into my earphones. When he'd belt out the chorus, in which a young girl demands again and again, "Don't call me daughter," I'd chime in at the top of my lungs.

When I arrived in Salinas, a dusty farming town just inland from Monterey, I was a skinny wreck, and I couldn't have been less interested in starting at a new school. I wasn't a racist like my father, who'd told us that black people were born with tails that doctors cut off when they were young. I knew that was bullshit, and that I was no better than anyone else, no matter their skin color. But it was still hard to be one of only three white kids, and the only white girl, in a school that was ruled by Latino gangs. I may have been seething inside, but on the outside, I wasn't very scary looking, with my emaciated frame and my sunken blue eyes. When a classmate told me I had two choices—"You can either be beat into a gang, or fucked into a gang"—I had an idea. That afternoon, I convinced Aunt Carol to take me to get a haircut by threatening her with the truth: "If you don't take me, I'll call Mom and tell her you're spending all the money she sends you on things that are not for me." The minute I got into the salon chair, though, I told the beautician to shave my head. The poor woman was reluctant—my hair was almost to my waist—but I insisted. When I emerged with my buzzcut, my aunt was horrified. But my plan worked. The next day at school, I looked so crazy that even the gangs steered clear.

Though not raised religious, Aunt Carol had become a devout Mormon, and I had no use for her proselytizing. With all that had happened, how could I believe that the Spirit of the Lord was trying to inspire me? I doubted my aunt knew what her brother had been doing to me. If she had known, she wouldn't have kept pleading with me to use the Book of Mormon to bear my testimony. Still, her faith sounded like mumbo jumbo to me, and it wasn't long before I'd had enough of her. Remembering how Mom had run away to San Francisco as a teenager, I hatched a plan. If San Fran was good enough for Mom, I figured, maybe it'd be good enough for me.

The night before Easter, I crawled out a window and hitchhiked more than a hundred miles north. Almost instantly, I regretted it. Not knowing how cold San Francisco could be, I hadn't brought any warm clothes. A few days later, the cops nabbed me for panhandling. Aunt Carol called my father and said she was done with me. That was that: my dad flew out and took me home to Florida.

When we got back to Rackley Road, the first thing I did was run to Alice's empty stall. "Where is she?" I demanded. My parents said that when they'd shipped me off to California, they'd sold Alice. I cried for weeks, begging them to tell me where she was. Could I at least visit her? But neither Mom nor Dad would tell me Alice's whereabouts, saying only that she'd been sent to "a good home."

"Well, that makes one of us," I thought to myself.

AT THIS POINT, for reasons I will never know, the sexual abuse stopped. Forrest was gone, and Dad was steering clear of me. I was relieved, of course, but I can't say that life became entirely easy, either. What was left of my relationship with my parents was a river of anger that flowed in both directions. All this came to a head when Mom, Dad, Skydy, and I drove our camper van cross-country to a reunion of my dad's family near Sacramento. For the whole trip west, I stayed in the way back of the van, huddled under a blanket, headphones over my ears. At this point I'd discovered Enya, whose New Age, ethereal style felt foreign in a good way. "I walk the maze of moments / But everywhere I turn to / Begins a new beginning / But never finds a finish," Enya sang in her lilting Irish accent. I knew how she felt and sang along when she told me, "Sail away. Sail away. Sail away. Sail away."

When we arrived at the campsite where the family reunion was being held, I couldn't help but cheer up a bit. The massive redwoods were different from Florida's trees, and as we sat around the campfire each evening, I liked staring up at the stars. Then one night toward the end of the four-day gathering, there was a dance that was open to all campers, not just our family group. I went, grateful to be around kids my own age, but also to be in a place where no one knew a thing about me. For a few hours, I pretended I was a carefree camper from a wonderful, loving home, and after the DJ played the night's final song, a shy boy whom I'd danced with once or twice offered to walk me back to our campsite. Gratefully, I accepted. My mom always said that my sense of direction was so poor that I could get lost in a circle, and on this night, I knew I needed help finding my way. But minutes later, as the boy and I walked down the middle of a moonlit asphalt road, Dad's van suddenly appeared and screeched to a halt. "What the fuck are you doing?" my father screamed from the driver's seat, and I could tell from the high keen of his voice that he was drunk.

My gracious escort looked as if he might swallow his tongue. "I'm sorry, sir," he stammered. "I didn't do anything. I'm just walking Jenna home." But my dad wasn't listening. "Get the fuck out of here," Dad ordered, stepping toward the boy. Then he turned on me. "You're a fucking slut," he said, as he threw me into the van.

Back at our campsite, Dad kept up with his yelling, calling me a dirty whore, an ungrateful piece of shit, and worse. I'd heard it all before, but that night I snapped. "What, you think you're the only one who's allowed to touch me?" I asked, my voice loud. My mom was inside the camper, out of earshot. But if I was going to finally call Dad out, I wanted to make sure at least my uncles and aunts could hear. "This guy has been fucking me for years, since I was a little kid," I yelled in their direction, "and no one's done shit about it." I wish I could say that they all stood up then to form a protective barrier around me. But they didn't move. So after a startled silence, Dad grabbed me by my neck with one hand and punched me in the face with the other. Then he shoved me into the borrowed camper where we'd all been sleeping and continued beating me until my lips were split open and one of my eyes was swollen shut. Skydy tried to come in to help me, but he was too little to do much. Finally, I got Dad off me by kicking him in the groin, and the beating stopped. He'd worn himself out raging at me.

The next morning, I woke up thinking that since I'd finally revealed my father's abuse out loud, something would have to change. Maybe, at the very least, someone would acknowledge what I'd been through. Instead, before we left to drive back to Florida, the entire extended family acted as if nothing had happened. "You want some bacon and eggs?" Aunt Peggy (not actually my aunt, but a family friend; we'd been told to call her that) asked me when I emerged, black and blue, from wherever I'd passed out. She offered me some Percocet. Then my family piled in our van, and I sought out my blanket in the back.

I didn't speak to my father again until we got to Loxahatchee.

WEEKS LATER, I started at Crestwood Middle School. I was thirteen. Maybe this will be hard to understand, but for a while I stopped fighting. It was as if my anger were a balloon, but all the air had leaked out. I'd lived on the streets of San Francisco, surviving pangs of hunger that even I—a girl who'd become expert in denying myself nourishment—found excruciating. I guess part of me was just glad to be living under a familiar roof again.

It was around this time that I came home and found Forrest sitting with Dad on our back porch.

"Uncle Forrest has something he wants to say to you," Dad said, as a bump of adrenaline hit me. I wanted to run, but my feet wouldn't move. "He is a man of God now, born again," Dad continued, "and it's important that you respect your elders and hear him out." I don't know what I expected to hear from Forrest's ugly mouth. Maybe: "I'm sorry I raped you and fucked up your life"? Besides, my legs weren't working. So I just stood there, trying to breathe.

What happened next would be funny if it weren't so appalling. Forrest stood up and grabbed me by my shoulders, then pushed me to my knees, where he'd forced me to be so many times before. This time, though, he was clothed. "You need to ask God for forgiveness," he said, sort of bellowing, "for what you did with your dad and me." I couldn't believe what I was hearing. As horrible as I felt about myself, some part of me knew that what had happened with Dad and his friend wasn't *all* my fault. But standing over me now, Forrest just kept on, half-yelling, half-preaching. Suddenly, I knew what hate tasted like. It was bile in my mouth, bitter, and I had an appetite for it. I hated Forrest. I hated my parents. I hated every living being in Loxahatchee.

AFTER THAT, MY rage stayed at a full boil. I ran away so often my parents put alarms on my windows to try to keep me in, but I'd watched *MacGyver* and I always got out. Though I went to school each day, I skipped more classes than I attended, whiling away the hours under the bleachers, smoking pot. English class was the exception. I never cut English because I loved reading and escaping into other people's stories. But one compelling class wasn't enough to tether me to school. Though I was on the basketball team, I stopped going to practice. For years my parents, who attended every one of Skydy's games and tournaments, had always skipped mine. I was done trying to win them over.

My middle school shared a campus with the high school, so now I sought out older kids—the "bad" kids, the "rats," who did drugs and got into trouble. There was one boy, Ian, whom I'd meet in the woods to smoke pot and fool around with. I think he was a senior in high school, while I wasn't yet a freshman, but I told myself this was proof I was just more grown-up than my peers. Up to that point, all sexual encounters had been against my will, so there was something freeing about choosing sex for myself. That said, Ian wasn't anything close to a boyfriend or a first love. At the time, I thought that I was taking back control of my life by lying down in the woods with him, but I see something else now. Pathetically, I was trading on the only part of me that anyone seemed to care about—my body—while my soul remained on the sidelines, ignored.

I KNOW THIS is a lot to take in. The violence. The neglect. The bad decisions. The self-harm. Imagine if a trauma reel like this played in your head all the time, as it does in mine, and not just on the pages of a book you can put down if you need to, just for a moment, to steady your nerves. But *please* don't stop reading. I know exactly how to help you get through these tough parts, just as I help myself: by focusing on the present.

It's dinnertime in the Giuffre household, and Robbie has made his famous shepherd's pie. "AlexTylerEllie!" he yells from the kitchen, making their names into one word. Suddenly the kids are running full steam toward the table. "Shotgun!" Tyler says. Because he's first to claim it, he gets the coveted chair to the right of Robbie, who sits at the head of the table. The shotgun seat is the only one with a direct line of sight to the living-room TV, catty-corner from our dining area. The TV isn't usually on when we're eating, but a family tradition has been cemented nonetheless: the best seat at the dinner table is that one, and every night, the kids compete for it.

For a few minutes, everyone chews. Everyone except Alex, who's half asleep. "Eat your dinner, Alex," Robbie commands. "I'm trying," our eldest protests. "Your hands are in the pockets of your hoodie," Robbie observes. "That's not the definition of trying." Robbie worries that Alex is too skinny. "You look like a stick figure," he says. But I remember how thin I was as a teenager, and I've seen photos of Robbie as a beanstalk at that age too. I reach over and put my hand on Robbie's knee to signal: let him be.

"Hey, Dad, what is the most intelligent species on this planet?" Ellie asks.

"You're looking at him!" Robbie boasts, as Ellie rolls her eyes.

But here's what occurs to me all the time: Robbie may not be highly educated, but he has taught me and the kids so much. Our children are polite. They take out the trash bins when asked. They are kind to one another—when Ellie was cold at the beach the other day, Tyler offered her his sweatshirt without anyone asking. While I'd love to take credit, I know Robbie is a big part of the reason why. Our kids know something I never knew as a child: that their father would do anything to keep them safe. And that allows them to thrive. "How you doing, beastie?" he'll ask Ellie, when she looks out of sorts. My husband is difficult to ignore. He gets her talking. And when any of us is truly in a funk, it is Robbie who suggests that we "drop anchor."

"Envision yourself on a boat," he'll say. "Now throw that weight overboard. What are you really feeling? Let's stop, get centered, see what's going on." When we lash out or act angry, it is Robbie—no stranger to anger himself—who pushes us to look for what he knows is there: the underlying hurt. (I've got plenty of that.)

Full disclosure, though: when dropping anchor doesn't work, Robbie's been known to drop his pants and moon us. Anything to get through—to get us out of our own heads. That's my husband: part guru, part goofball. He helps me more than I can say.

AT THIRTEEN, I would walk a mile for a fistfight. I particularly liked confronting bullies, which is probably part of the reason I befriended a boy named José. He didn't call himself gay, because that wasn't a word we used then. But he liked boys "that way," and he refused to hide it, so he was always getting picked on. I was José's only friend—we used to do each other's makeup—and the fact that he made no sexual demands on me was a relief. Wearing brightly colored outfits and heavy eyeliner to school, José seemed intent on forcing our school's bigots to accept him for who he was. I wanted his plan to work. When it didn't, though, one insulting word aimed in José's direction was enough for me to throw the first punch. When he took me home and his mom heard how I was defending him, she told me I was welcome there anytime. Soon I was regularly sleeping on their couch. But then my mother called the cops looking for me, and two officers knocked on José's front door. I hid, but after they left, José's mom told me I needed to sleep elsewhere. I was on the move again.

Then I met a fellow middle schooler, a boy named Tony Figueroa, who would play a big part in my life off and on for years to come. Tony's mom was from Honduras and his dad was from Chile, and he had the most beautiful long black hair. A self-proclaimed goth, with combat boots and all-black clothing, Tony could spend hours listening to Led Zeppelin and Metallica. I thought he was rad. Tony had black lights in his bedroom that made his neon-colored posters glow in the dark. He also had a lock on his door, so when his mom would knock, I had time to slip under the bed before he opened it. On nights when I didn't want to go home—that was most nights—Tony would bring me scraps from his family's dinner table, like in the movie *E.T. the Extra-Terrestrial*, when the little boy sneaks food to the alien hiding in his closet. I was truly fond of Tony, but this relationship—like so many others—was colored by my desperation. At first we were just friends, but I felt I owed Tony for letting me stay with him, and at this point, I saw sex as the primary way to pay my debts. One night we were in his room, and rain was pouring down outside. Tony put The Doors' "Riders on the Storm" on his stereo, and we ended up having sex. I was probably fourteen. I'd find out later that it had been his first time.

I WAS BARELY sleeping at my parents' house, but I guess they wanted me gone for good, because this was when Mom tricked me into entering Growing Together. I've already described the terrors I endured at that teen rehab facility. I've told of my escape to Miami when I was fifteen, and what the armed stranger in the white van did to me when I accepted a ride from him. I've tried to explain how that rape made me easy prey for the old fat man in the black limousine: Ron Eppinger, who was then sixty-three. What I didn't know when Eppinger picked me up in his limo in December 1998 was that Perfect 10, the "modeling agency" he told me he was running, was in fact a $1,000-a-night escort service. Federal prosecutors would eventually prove that between 1997 and 1999, Eppinger and two Czech accomplices procured young women abroad, then sent them to South Florida to work as call girls.

So when Eppinger discovered me sitting on that curb and took me home, he made an exception: I was the only American girl in his stable.

Eppinger wanted me to look as young as possible, so the first night I was there, before he demanded sex from me, he shaved my pubic area and told me to keep it that way. He said I should be grateful, when he forced me to have intercourse with him, because he was teaching me a valuable skill: how to please men. Later, he required that I watch porn so I'd understand "what sex is about." He had a certain all-American look he wanted me to emulate. He insisted I have my blond hair dyed a lighter platinum, like a teen Barbie doll's, and sent me to a tanning salon to bronze my skin. He also liked to show me off in public, driving me around in his convertible. During these drives, he usually required that I be topless.

Early on, Eppinger was relatively gentle with me. But as time went by, he revealed a violent streak. He was aggressive with me during sex and seemed to enjoy making me feel afraid. On one particularly awful night, he grabbed me by the back of my neck and forced my face into his crotch. I closed my eyes and began to count—one, two, three—hoping the numbers would keep my brain from focusing on what was happening. I had to count to over a hundred before he ejaculated in my mouth. Raped again and again, I began to take the drugs Eppinger and his girls offered me: Xanax, oxycodone, anything to numb the pain. Determined to change my fate one way or another, I began fantasizing about killing myself. "It would be so much easier if you just died," said the voice in my head.

In some published accounts about this period in my life, I've been inaccurately described as an eager participant in Eppinger's world. In her book *Perversion of Justice: The Jeffrey Epstein Story*, the *Miami Herald's* Julie K. Brown writes that after I heard from Eppinger's other girls about the expensive clothes and jewelry that their clients gave them, I "began to think that this lifestyle wasn't only exciting; it was an acceptable way to earn a living." That's bunk. I wasn't excited. I was a defeated, hopeless child. I knew what was happening wasn't right. Soon, after Eppinger began trafficking me to his friends, I knew how it felt to be a puppy picked from a litter, just hoping its new owner wasn't the whipping kind. I was merely trying to survive.

The only bright spot in this dark chapter came when Eppinger, sensing that law enforcement was onto him, sent me away to a horse ranch in Ocala, in northern Florida. While there, I was made to sexually service the owner of the ranch, who was repulsive. But being near horses again helped me stay in touch with myself. While I didn't get to groom or ride them, I could watch them from afar, standing together, tossing their tails and grazing happily. I imagined these animals were my guardian angels.

Have you ever heard that nursery rhyme, "If wishes were horses, beggars would ride"? It means that success in life depends not just on how much you desire it but on what actions you take to achieve it. I like that idea: that a person has the power to push her own life forward. But when I was held prisoner by Eppinger, I didn't have any power. I felt if I took action to save myself, I'd be caught and physically punished—or worse. In the years since, I've come to believe that in Ocala, my wishes really were horses. The horses outside my window embodied the freedom I lacked—the freedom I wished for. Watching them lazily munching sweetgrass, even as they trained their ears to perceive any threats, was the only time I dared imagine that my life might someday get better.

SEVEN

A Ghost Come Back

Eppinger held me captive for nearly six months before he gave me away to a friend of his. Yes, you read that right: he gave me away, as if I were a used bicycle or an unloved toy. The man Eppinger gifted me to was in his fifties and had connections to Fort Lauderdale's seedy nightclub scene. Every night at a place called Hot Chocolates, which the man said he owned, he introduced me to everyone as his girlfriend. Maybe someone there noticed how young I looked and reported it, because on a bright June morning in 1999, the Federal Bureau of Investigation and the local police broke down the door of the man's apartment, where I was sleeping naked next to him. "This is a raid!" one black-clad officer yelled as they forced their way in. "Hands on your head!" When they dragged my abuser from the room, I could hear him yelling at me: "If you say anything, you-know-who will find you!" He meant Eppinger. The FBI agents wrapped me in a sheet and let me go to the bathroom to get dressed. I wished I'd had jeans and a T-shirt, but the only clothes I owned had been chosen by my captors, so I put on a metallic blue miniskirt and a tiny shirt that barely covered my breasts. The officers took me back to the Wilton Manors Police Station in Broward County, and for the next few hours, they grilled me about who had done what to me. When they were finally finished, they called my dad.

Even today, I remember Dad's face when he walked into the police station. At that moment, I was holding tight to the arms of a borrowed swivel chair and spinning in circles. By then, I'd seen things no child should ever see, things that made me feel so much older than my fifteen years. From a distance, I may have looked like a kid enjoying the dizzy thrill of a makeshift Tilt-a-Whirl. But there was no joy in me. When Dad walked in, he flinched at the sight of me, his listless, abused little girl. "Goddamned slut," he spat. "Fucking whore." Then, though, he did something I'd never seen him do. He started to cry.

Some of this is a blur for me. I know the outline of what happened, and I can summon many of the feelings I felt, but my mind protects me by not bringing the scene into too sharp a focus. I remember Dad with his head in his hands, telling me Mom didn't want me to come home, so he was sending me back to Growing Together. I pleaded with him, but he said he needed a week to find me somewhere else to stay. "One week," he promised, "and I'll come get you out." A police officer handcuffed me then and put me in the back of a squad car to return me to juvie. Everyone believed I would try to run. But I was too tired to run. I would give Dad the week he asked for. I hoped that maybe, just this once, he'd keep his word.

Walking back into Growing Together, I recognized only a few of the kids. One girl told me I looked like "a ghost come back" from the other side. That felt about right. I bided my time, but with every passing day, I had less faith in my father. Finally, when Growing Together sent me out with a chaperone to get my blood and urine tested, I made a break for it. Finding a pay phone in a mini-mall parking lot, I called my parents' house. Dad answered, full of excuses. "I'm trying to convince your mother to sign the papers to get you out of there," he said.

"Well, you can quit that, because I'm already out," I said. "Now come pick me up so I can come talk to Mom." Dad wasn't happy, but he did what I asked.

When we got back to Rackley Road, Mom was nowhere to be found. I looked in the kitchen and stuck my head into my old room, which they'd made into an office. Finally, I went out back, where I found her sitting in an old rusty lawn chair, smoking a cigarette, a beer can in her hand. When she saw me, she stood up and walked toward me. I knew better than to hope for a hug. She greeted me with a hard slap in the face, but then we both were crying. She didn't want to hear where I'd been, she said. She couldn't bear the thought of it. But I could stay, at least for the night.

When I think about this day, I can't linger on my parents. Thinking of them is too awful. Instead, I think of Skydy, running out the back door, the screen slamming shut as he flung himself into my arms. He held me so tight that the rest didn't matter. Someone loved me, truly. That didn't fix everything, but it would have to be enough.

I stayed in my parents' house only a short while. While they didn't throw me out, exactly, Mom soon made it clear I wasn't welcome on Rackley Road. I moved in with the family of a girl named Lorna, who I'd met at Growing Together. But that ended just a few months later, after Lorna's dad announced that I was a bad influence on her. Lorna was back to partying again and had been caught shoplifting. I protested that I hadn't been with her when she stole anything, but her dad was done with me. I couldn't totally blame him—it's not like I was helping Lorna get clean, and I'm sure he was wondering why my own family didn't want me. But I was resentful and told him so. Are you noticing a pattern? I was unwanted, so I acted like a girl no one would want. A captive for so long, I had no idea how to harness my freedom.

That's when Lorna's stepbrother, Michael, said I could live with him in Fort Lauderdale. Michael was a kind but troubled boy who was two years older than me. We'd met when he visited Lorna's family's house—where he'd once lived—and I could tell he had a crush on me. So when he suggested being roommates, I had an idea of what he was hoping for. But I still said yes. Once again, desperation—not affection—determined my love life. Michael rented us an apartment, which we shared with a friend of his named Mario. Michael was working full time as a manager at Taco Bell and eventually helped me get a job there too. One thing led to another until we started having sex. But I had no romantic feelings for him. I just didn't know how to set boundaries with men who wanted things from me. On Valentine's Day 2000, Michael asked me to marry him, offering me his grandmother's ring. I couldn't say yes—I was just sixteen, two years short of Florida's age requirement without parental consent. But I didn't clearly say no, either, or tell him the truth: that I wasn't in love with him. Years later, he'd say he believed that I'd accepted his proposal. I can understand why. For all the changes I wanted to make, it seemed I was paralyzed. Instead of choosing my own path, I was letting life happen to me. When I had opportunities to take control and advocate for myself, I often found it easier to get fucked up on alcohol or drugs instead.

"I need to hear some sounds that recognize the pain in me," Richard Ashcroft sings in "Bitter Sweet Symphony." I must've listened to that song by the Britpop rock band The Verve a thousand times that year, wanting to believe, as Ashcroft asserts, that "I can change, I can change," but knowing that, like the song says, I was "a million different people from one day to the next." When I heard the Goo Goo Dolls song "Slide," I again felt the sting of recognition. "Your father hit the wall / Your ma disowned you," they sang. "Do you wanna get married? Or run away?" I knew the answer—run!—but I didn't act on it.

Michael and I lived in that Fort Lauderdale apartment until we were evicted for failure to pay rent and for living, in all honesty, like wild beasts—or should I say among them? One of the few things Michael and I had in common was our love of animals, and we had a lot of pets: dogs, cats, even a ferret. We sort of tried to keep the place clean, but when we were thrown out of it, it was a pigsty.

Homeless again, I broke down and asked my parents if Michael and I could live in a travel trailer they'd parked in their back horse paddock. The trailer looked out on the pond, where years before I'd taken refuge on our tiny island and where I'd taught Alice to swim. The trailer had a bed, a bath, a kitchenette, and a small sitting area—plenty of room for us, at least for a while. My parents said yes, and days later, I was back on Rackley Road.

Today, I see this as a moment that could have set me on a better path. Through a stroke of luck, I'd landed the perfect job for a girl who'd dreamed of being a veterinarian. I worked the morning shift at a pet store called The Kookaburra's Nest, where I was learning to run its aviary. The pay was good—more than $8 an hour—and I found I loved breeding, feeding, grooming, and selling exotic birds. I hand-raised Sugar, a yellow-crested cockatoo, from a chick. Sugar used to ride around on my shoulder, and when I gave her a bath, I'd tell her she was my baby, and she'd coo with happiness. Sugar was a beauty—all white but for a yellow comb on her head, and yellow ear patches and flight feathers—and I was determined to make her mine. Every two weeks, I set aside money from my check. But before I'd saved even half of Sugar's $1,200 price tag, someone came in and bought her out from under me.

"The customer always comes first," my boss said, when I pitched a fit. And in truth, the last thing I needed was another mouth (animal or human) to feed. Still, I was inconsolable. Losing Sugar felt like losing Alice all over again. So when another aviary recruited me to work for them, I accepted their offer just to spite the boss who'd sold Sugar. That decision proved a mistake, though, when my new employer abruptly shut down. I was unemployed again.

During this period, Mom and Dad and I forged a fragile peace. You may wonder how this could be. I guess I knew them so well that being around even their most hurtful behavior felt weirdly comfortable to me. More than that, though, who am I kidding? I had no place else to go, no one else to turn to. Setting aside all the indignities I'd suffered at the hands of my parents and others, the consequences of my own choices were becoming evident, even to sixteen-year-old me. I was a high school dropout. I had a boyfriend I lived with but didn't want a future with. I was damaged in more ways than I even knew, and I was a long way from getting the help I needed to repair myself. I had little money and few prospects for making any. "Well, I've been down so long / Oh, it can't be longer still," Jewel sang into my earphones around this time. "I've been down for so long / That the end must be drawing near." I thought I had nowhere to go but up. What happened next, then, seemed like a gift. In the summer of 2000, my father—then a maintenance man at Donald Trump's Mar-a-Lago Club in Palm Beach—got me a job there as a $9-an-hour locker-room attendant.

I CAN STILL remember walking onto the manicured grounds of Mar-a-Lago for the first time. It was early morning—my dad's shift began at 7:00 a.m., and I'd caught a ride to work with him. Already the air was heavy and moist, and the club's twenty acres of carefully landscaped greens and lawns seemed to shimmer. To look at the beachfront site that Mar-a-Lago occupies, you'd never suspect that before the original estate was built in the 1920s, it was just a thicket of undergrowth and swampland. I sure couldn't see that. Instead, as I watched an army of gardeners set out on their daily rounds, the attention being paid to each shrub and palm and blade of grass soothed me. This, I could see, was not a place that rewarded neglect.

My dad was responsible for maintaining the resort's in-room air-conditioning units, not to mention its five championship red-clay tennis courts, so he knew his way around, both indoors and out. I remember he gave me a brief tour before presenting me to the hiring manager who—after I passed both a drug test and a polygraph—agreed to take me on. That first day, I was given a uniform—a white polo shirt, emblazoned with the Mar-a-Lago crest, and a short white skirt—and a name tag that said JENNA in all capital letters. I was also given a sixty-five-page employee handbook. My uniform would be laundered by Mar-a-Lago, free of charge, said the handbook, which went on to specify everything from basic hygiene ("Body odors are offensive.") to how many earrings I could wear in my ears (one per lobe, each no larger than a dime); from telephone etiquette ("All calls are to be answered within three rings.") to general behavior ("Horseplay and practical jokes are prohibited."). I wasn't annoyed by the rules and regulations—far from it. Their formality made me feel good—as if working at a place that took itself so seriously might make the world take me seriously too.

It couldn't have been more than a few days before my dad said he wanted to introduce me to Mr. Trump himself. They weren't friends, exactly. But Dad worked hard, and Trump liked that—I'd seen photos of them posing together, shaking hands. So one day my father took me to Trump's office. "This is my daughter," Dad said, and his voice sounded proud. Trump couldn't have been friendlier, telling me it was fantastic that I was there. "Do you like kids?" he asked. "Do you babysit at all?" He explained that he owned several houses next to the resort that he lent to friends, many of whom had children who needed tending. I said yes, I'd babysat before, omitting the fact that the last time I'd done so, I'd been reprimanded; in an attempt to entertain the kids in my care, I'd ignited a huge cache of fireworks I'd found hidden in the house. Clearly I was right to leave that out, because soon I was making extra money a few nights a week, minding the children of the elite.

But it was my day job that gave me my first real vision of a better future. The spa, like the resort itself, was gilded, with luxe finishes and an immaculate, sparkling decor. It smelled delicious, like sandalwood and lavender. I remember there were giant gold bathtubs, like something a god would soak in. More than that, I marveled at how peaceful everyone seemed to feel within its walls. My duties—making tea, tidying the bathrooms, restocking towels—kept me just outside the inner sanctum of the massage rooms, but still I could see how relaxed clients looked when they emerged. Whenever possible I questioned the massage therapists about what they did and how they'd learned to do it. I seized on the idea that, with the right training, I could eventually make a living by helping others reduce stress. Maybe, I thought, their healing would fuel my own. For the first time in my life, I allowed a flicker of hope to build inside me. After all I had been through, I believed I might finally leave my abusive past behind.

Then one steaming hot day some weeks before my seventeenth birthday, I was walking toward the Mar-a-Lago spa, on my way to work, when a car slowed behind me. I wish I could say that I sensed that something evil was tracking me, but as I headed into the building, I had no inkling of the danger I was in. In the car I didn't see were two people I'd not yet met: a British socialite named Ghislaine Maxwell and her driver, Juan Alessi, whom she insisted on calling "John." Alessi would later testify under oath that on this day, when Maxwell spotted me—my long blond hair, my slim build, and what he called my notably "young" appearance—she commanded him from the back seat, "Stop, John, stop!"

Alessi did as he was told, and Maxwell got out and followed after me. I didn't know it yet, but once again, a predator was closing in. This one, however, would prove different from any I'd met before. Unlike my father or Forrest or Ron Eppinger or the man Eppinger had given me away to, this was an apex predator—as greedy and demanding on the inside as she appeared to be beautiful, poised, and self-assured on the outside. Again, I wish I could say that I saw through Maxwell's polished facade—that, like a horse, I intuited the immense threat she posed to me. Instead, my first impression of Maxwell was the same one I formed when I greeted any well-heeled Mar-a-Lago guest. I'd be lucky, I thought, if I could grow up to be anything like her.

Part II

PRISONER

If you feel like letting go (hold on)
If you think you've had too much
Of this life, well hang on

　　　　　　—"Everybody Hurts," R.E.M.

EIGHT

The Pink House

Picture a girl in a crisp white uniform sitting behind a marble reception desk. She is sixteen and wears a name tag pinned to her chest. The girl is slender, with the freckled face of a child, and her long blond hair is held back with a tie. A new employee at the Mar-a-Lago spa, the girl is usually in the locker room, handing out towels. But on this blisteringly hot afternoon, the spa is mostly empty, so the girl is at the front desk, which is outside, under an awning that provides shade. The girl is reading a book about anatomy that she's borrowed from the library. The girl loves to read, and she hopes that studying this book will give her something she's lacked for too long: purpose. What would it be like, she wonders, to excel at something?

Suddenly, I look up from my book to see a striking woman with short dark hair striding toward me.

"Hello," the woman says warmly. She looks to be in her late thirties, and her British accent reminds me of Mary Poppins. I couldn't tell you which designers she's wearing, but I bet her purse cost more than my dad's truck. The woman extends her manicured hand for me to shake. "Ghislaine Maxwell," she says, pronouncing her first name "Giilen." Her grip is firm. I point to my name tag. "I'm Jenna," I say, smiling like I've been told to smile. Mar-a-Lago employees are required to make guests feel welcome. The woman's eyes alight on my book, which I've jammed with sticky notes. "Are you interested in massage?" she asks. "How wonderful!"

Remembering my duties, I offer this mesmerizing woman a beverage, and she chooses hot tea. I go and fetch it, returning with a steaming cup. I expect that to be the end of it, but the woman keeps on talking. Maxwell says she knows a wealthy man—a longtime Mar-a-Lago member, she says—who is looking for a massage therapist to travel with him. "Do you do massage on the side?" she asks. "Oh, no," I reply, worried I've given her the wrong impression. "I'm not trained, but I hope to learn someday." My lack of experience doesn't concern her a bit. "I'm sure you'd be terrific," she insists, looking me up and down. "Will you come for an interview?"

I glance at my library book, with its illustrations of muscles and tendons. "I don't think I know the body well enough yet," I protest, but Maxwell shakes her head. What's important, she says, is my desire to learn. If I impress her friend, she says, he'll happily pay to get me trained. He's a mathematician—a genius with a knack for making money. "He loves to help people," she says, adding that the rich gentleman's home is right here in Palm Beach, less than two miles from Mar-a-Lago.

"Come meet him," she says, her pretty face glowing. "Come tonight after work."

Even today, more than twenty years later, I remember how excited I felt. Could my dreams of becoming a professional masseuse be on their way to coming true so quickly? Something about how this proper, well-spoken lady focused on me made that seem possible. I told her I had to get permission from my dad first, but that I really wanted to come. So, as she instructed, I wrote down her phone number and her rich friend's address: 358 El Brillo Way. "See you later, I hope," Maxwell said, waving her right hand by twisting it slightly at the wrist. Then she was gone.

The next break I got, I ran to the tennis courts to tell my father I was in the running for a potentially life-changing opportunity. He said he could drive me over after work. I used the phone at the spa's front desk to call Maxwell and let her know we were on. "Great," she said. "See you soon."

A few hours later, Dad gave me a lift up South Ocean Avenue to El Brillo Way, a short hedge-lined spur of a road that dead-ended into the Palm Beach Intracoastal Waterway. The drive took five minutes, and we didn't talk much. No one ever had to explain to my father the importance of making a buck.

When we arrived at the high wall in front of 358, the last house on the left before we hit the water, Dad pushed a buzzer and spoke into the intercom. A security gate rolled open. We eased into a driveway lined with palm trees and found ourselves in front of a sprawling two-story, six-bedroom mansion. In countless TV documentaries, this house has been shown to be painted a tasteful white, as it was years later. But in the summer of 2000, the home we pulled up to was a garish pink, the color of Pepto-Bismol.

Eager to be punctual, I jumped out of the car before my dad could turn off the engine, walked to the big wooden front door, and rang the bell. Maxwell answered and came outside, the door still open behind her. She shook my father's hand. "Thank you so very much for dropping her off," she told Dad, all smiles, but in retrospect, she seemed impatient for him to leave. "We'll get Jenna home safe," she said, practically shooing him back into his truck. Then she turned and ushered me into an elegant foyer with a spiral staircase and a huge star-shaped chandelier.

"Jeffrey has been waiting to meet you," she said, starting up the stairs. "Come."

Walking behind her, I tried not to stare at the walls, which were crowded with photos and paintings of nude women. Maybe this was how wealthy people with sophisticated taste decorated their homes? "Be cool," I thought. "Don't let her see how nervous you are." I fixed my eyes on the stairs, which were covered in pink, plush carpet. When we reached the second-floor landing, Maxwell turned right and led me into a bedroom. We made a U-turn around a king-size bed, then entered an adjoining room with a turquoise-green massage table. A naked man lay face down on top of it, his head resting on his folded arms, but when he heard us enter, he lifted up slightly to look around at me. I remember his bushy eyebrows and the deep lines in his face as he grinned a Cheshire-cat smile.

"Say hello to Mr. Jeffrey Epstein," Maxwell instructed. But before I could do so, the man spoke to me: "You can just call me Jeffrey." I nodded at the gray-haired stranger as he lay back down. He was forty-seven years old—nearly three times older than me.

Faced with Epstein's bare backside, I looked to Maxwell for guidance. I had never gotten a massage before, let alone given one. But still I thought, "Isn't he supposed to be under a sheet?" Maxwell's blasé expression indicated that nudity was normal. "Calm down," I told myself. "Don't blow this chance." I wanted to be a good student. Palm Beach was just sixteen miles from Loxahatchee, but the economic divide made it seem way farther. I needed to learn how rich people did things. Besides, while the man on the table was nude, it's not like I was alone with him. The fact that a woman was with me made me breathe easier. "Fake it 'til you make it," I thought, as I tried to project a can-do energy.

Maxwell took the lead. "First, you must wash your hands," she said. "Hot water." She pointed toward a white, marble-tiled bathroom, complete with sauna and steam shower, where I did as she asked. Then she began the lesson. When giving a massage, she said, I should keep one palm on the client's skin at all times, so as never to startle him. "Continuity and flow are key," she explained. She turned to a dresser littered with bottles, pumped lotion into both our hands, and showed me how to keep an extra blob of the stuff on my forearm, so I could reload without interrupting the rhythm. She then positioned us at Epstein's feet, on either side of the table, and rubbed her hands together swiftly before placing them on the toes of his right foot. She nodded for me to do the same on his left. "Just do what I do," she said.

We started in on his heels and arches, then moved up his body. "Don't pull his leg hair," Maxwell cautioned, explaining that our goal was to circulate the blood by firmly pushing it up his calves. I paid close attention, mimicking her as we moved higher, to Epstein's thighs. When we got to his buttocks, I tried to glide past them, landing on his lower back. But Maxwell put her hands on top of mine and guided them to his rear. "It's important that you don't ignore any part of the body," she said. "If you skip around, the blood won't flow right."

Only later would I see how, step by practiced step, the two of them were breaking down my defenses. Every time I felt a twinge of discomfort, one glance at Maxwell told me I was overreacting. And so it went for about half an hour: a seemingly legitimate massage lesson. As Maxwell encouraged me—"You're getting the hang of it!"—Epstein asked me questions. "Do you have siblings?" Two brothers, I said. "Where do you go to high school?" I told him I'd quit after ninth grade, but I was only sixteen—I hoped to get my GED. "Do you have a boyfriend?" I said I lived with an older boy in a trailer on my parents' land. "Do you take birth control?" Epstein asked. Was that a weird question in a job interview? Epstein indicated this was just his way of getting to know me. After all, I might soon be traveling with him. I told him I was on the pill.

"You're doing great," Maxwell said, as I kept my hands in sync with hers.

"Tell me about your first time," Epstein said then. I hesitated. Who'd ever heard of an employer asking an applicant about losing her virginity? But I wanted this job, so I took a deep breath and described my rough childhood. I'd been abused by a family friend, I said vaguely, and spent time on the street as a runaway. Epstein didn't recoil. Instead, he made light of it, teasing me for being "a naughty girl."

"Not at all," I said defensively. "I'm a good girl. I've just always found myself in the wrong places."

Epstein lifted his head and smirked at me. "It's okay," he said. "I like naughty girls."

Then he rolled over onto his back, and I was startled to see he had an erection. I'd seen men's private parts before, obviously, but I hadn't expected to see his. Without thinking, I raised both my hands, holding them up in the air as if to say, "Stop." But when I looked at Maxwell, she remained unfazed. Ignoring his aroused penis, she put both hands on his right pectoral muscles and began kneading. "Like this," she said, continuing as if nothing were amiss. "You want to push the blood away from the heart." Unsure whether I was right to feel alarmed, I again followed her example, putting my hands on the left side of his chest, which was covered in thick gray hair. Moving my fingers in circles, I could feel Epstein staring at my face, but I refused to meet his gaze, focusing instead on what I thought I was there to do.

"Not in a circle," Maxwell corrected. "Don't be afraid to use pressure."

Epstein winked at her then and moved his right hand down to his crotch. "You don't mind, do you?" he asked as he began stroking himself.

This is the moment that something cracked inside me. How else to explain why my memories of what came next are splintered into jagged shards? Maxwell peeling off her clothes, a mischievous look on her face; Maxwell behind me, unzipping my skirt and pulling my Mar-a-Lago polo shirt over my head; Epstein and Maxwell laughing at my underwear, which were dotted with tiny hearts. "How cute—she still wears little girl's panties," Epstein said. He reached for an electric vibrator, which he forced between my thighs, as Maxwell commanded me to pinch Epstein's nipples as she rubbed her own breasts, and mine.

A familiar emptiness flooded me. Just minutes before, I had arrived at Epstein's mansion hoping that I was turning a corner. Now I knew I was right back where I'd worked so hard not to be. How many times had I put my faith in someone, only to be hurt and humiliated? But this time the disappointment was excruciating. I blamed myself. "Is sex all anyone will ever want from me?" a voice inside me shrieked, as another harsher voice chided: "Yes, you idiot. You knew that already." I tasted the tang of adrenaline in my mouth, and I could feel my brain begin to shut down. My body couldn't escape from this room, but my mind couldn't bear to stay, so it put me on a kind of autopilot: submissive and determined to survive.

"Pinch him harder," Maxwell said, as Epstein moaned. So I did. "Go down on him," she said. I did that too. Eventually, Maxwell ordered me to straddle Epstein so he could penetrate me. Again, I obeyed. Once he finished, I was told to bring two warm washcloths to clean him up. Then Epstein led the way to the steam room, where he told me to rub his feet. As I did so, kneeling before him, he lectured me about the history of sweat lodges and how opening the pores allows toxins to leave the body. It was important to make healthy decisions, he said, adding, "I can teach you so many things." From that first meeting, Epstein wanted me to regard him as a mentor, not a predator.

Next, we entered the shower, where Maxwell instructed me to wash Epstein with soap and a loofah. Again, I obeyed. Epstein told me to shampoo his hair and massage his scalp. I did. "She's a keeper," he told Maxwell, appraising me as if I weren't there. When Maxwell left the bathroom, Epstein had me take a towel from a heated rack and pat him dry. I did so, shivering a little in my own nakedness. Finally, he pulled on a pair of sweatpants, and I put my Mar-a-Lago uniform back on and wiped smudges of mascara from under my eyes. Epstein then led me down a back stairway to the kitchen, where Maxwell waited. I remember the gleaming stainless-steel appliances and the black-and-white checkerboard floor. When she handed Epstein a black leather duffel bag, he pulled out two hundred-dollar bills and pushed them across the counter toward me. "This is probably what you make in a week at that spa," he said. He and Maxwell smiled knowingly at each other, as if this were funny.

"You did great," Maxwell told me, almost cooing. She said I had strong hands, good instincts, and such huge potential. "You're a natural. Who knows where this could lead?" She reached for a pen and paper. "Can you come back tomorrow?" She asked for my cell-phone number, but I didn't have one. I recited my work number. And then the butler, Juan Alessi—the same man who'd been driving Maxwell when she first spotted me at Mar-a-Lago—led me out to the driveway, where I climbed into the front passenger seat of a shiny black Chevy Suburban.

Only after buckling my seat belt did I begin to return to myself. Having escaped from an imminent threat, my brain came back on-line, but all it wanted to do was scream. During the half-hour drive inland to Loxahatchee, Alessi and I didn't speak. If I opened my mouth, I just knew I'd start sobbing, so I clamped my lips shut. I didn't know then what a therapist would tell me a decade later: that when children are abused by people they love, as I had been by my father, they start to believe that love and pain, love and betrayal, love and violation all go together. I didn't know that abuse victims struggle to see red flags because they've become desensitized to inappropriate behavior. I didn't know that a common coping mechanism during sexual abuse is to distance oneself from what is happening in the moment—to "split" into parts: the obedient body and the walled-off mind. All I knew as the black Suburban headed west was that I felt gutted, as if someone had reached down my throat and scraped out my insides with a silver spoon.

When the butler dropped me at Rackley Road, I went into my parents' house, not the trailer Michael and I shared. I'd built the job interview up so much that I knew Mom and Dad would expect to hear how it had gone. Given the state I was in, however, I kept the conversation short. I get flushed when I'm upset, so as I ticked off what I'd learned—push the blood away from the heart; always be consistent with a firm, warm touch—I sensed Mom noticing my reddened face and neck. So before she could ask questions, I pleaded exhaustion and excused myself to take a shower. For what seemed like an hour, I sat on the wet tile floor and let my tears mix with the hot water pounding my skin.

So begins the period of my life that has been dissected and analyzed more than any other. I don't enjoy repeating this story; it hurts to relive what I did and what was done to me. What's more, as I describe the chronology, transgression by transgression, I worry that the awful details distract from a broader truth. Yes, I was sexually abused. My body was used in ways that did enormous damage to me. But the worst things Epstein and Maxwell did to me weren't physical, but psychological. From the start, they manipulated me into participating in behaviors that ate away at me, eroding my ability to comprehend reality and preventing me from defending myself. From the start, I was groomed to be complicit in my own devastation. Of all the terrible wounds they inflicted, that forced complicity was the most destructive.

I was about to spend more than two years in Epstein and Maxwell's orbit. My job: to do whatever they asked whenever they asked it. There were no bars on the windows or locks on the doors. But I was a prisoner trapped in an invisible cage.

NINE

Tapping a Crooked Vein

After dinner in Perth, Australia, I'm biding my time in my favorite local shopping mall, which stays open late on Thursday nights. Our twelve-year-old daughter, Ellie, who is already taller than me and still growing, needs new clothes. "Mama, do you think these will fit me?" she asks, holding up a pair of black cargo pants.

Having weathered the fond taunts of two older brothers her entire life, Ellie often presents as a tomboy: athletic, capable, unafraid. Just a moment ago, she turned our shopping cart into a race car—first sprinting to get momentum, then jumping aboard with both feet on the back axle, grinning as she flew across the mall's main rotunda.

Now we are in a boutique that caters to tweens. When we first walked in, I spotted an orange sundress that I knew would look wonderful on her, but when I said so, she shook her head and scowled like I was out of my mind. I didn't push it. That never works with Ellie. So it makes me happy when I see her circle back, checking out the dress again. She's already picked out two pairs of pants and an oversized Guns N' Roses T-shirt, but I can see her considering whether maybe a pretty sundress wouldn't be so bad after all. Without looking at me, she adds it to her growing pile and moves to the next rack.

After a few more minutes, our cart is full to overflowing. "You ready, Ellie?" I ask, and she nods, blazing our trail to the checkout line. That's when I see the display of oversized orange-and-yellow-striped beach towels. I know I shouldn't, but I can't resist. I grab six of them and head to the cash register, even though I can predict how exasperated my husband will be when we get home.

Since becoming a mom, I've developed a near-addiction to buying crisp new sheets, pillowcases, and towels. I could say what motivates me is the simple desire to feather my family's nest, to make my kids feel cozy and loved. But Robbie believes there's something else at work, too—something so powerful that I'll risk him rolling his eyes and bellowing: "Jenna! No! We have enough towels in this house to keep an army dry!" Whenever he protests like this, I always promise to "do a quick closet cleanse," as Robbie sighs, resigned. I understand his frustration, but it can't be helped. My perpetual need to fill our home with new, fresh things is driven by a feeling I can't shake: Even after all this time, I remember how dirty I once felt. I will do anything to make my world feel clean.

So many young women, myself included, have been criticized for returning to Epstein's lair even after we knew what he wanted from us. How can you complain about being abused, some have asked, when you could so easily have stayed away? If you didn't like feeling dirty, you could simply have never gone back. But that stance wrongly discounts what many of us had been through *before* we encountered Epstein, as well as how good he was at spotting girls whose wounds made them vulnerable to him. Several of us had been molested or raped as children; many of us were poor or even homeless. Before meeting

Epstein, one of his victims had watched her father beat an eight-year-old boy to death; another was present when her boyfriend killed himself. We were girls who no one cared about, and Epstein pretended to care. At times I think he even believed he cared. A master manipulator who excelled at divining the desires of others, he threw what looked like a lifeline to girls who were drowning, girls who had nothing, girls who wished to be and do better. If they wanted to be dancers, he offered dance lessons. If they aspired to be actors, he said he'd help them get roles. If they said the only thing they yearned to do was paint, he bought them canvases and introduced them to key people in the art world. And then, he did his worst to them.

When I met Epstein just before my seventeenth birthday, all I wanted was to learn a skill that would give me the means to live an independent life. At least that's what I told myself. With hindsight, though, the grown-up me can see that the teenage me also wanted something else. What had Epstein said that first night? That I was "a keeper"? By now you know how long I'd hoped to hear words like those—and to believe I was worth keeping. Every time I went to Epstein's mansion in those early days, he or Maxwell would pay me, peeling two or sometimes three hundred-dollar bills off the huge stack in his black duffel bag. But money wasn't the only thing that lured me into their twisted world. For so many years, I had been sexualized against my will and had survived by acquiescing. Even as a girl on the precipice of womanhood, I was a pleaser, even when pleasing others cost me dearly. For ten years, men had cloaked their abuse of me in a fake mantle of "love." Epstein and Maxwell knew just how to tap into that same crooked vein.

The day after my "job interview," I did as Maxwell requested and returned to the pink house behind the high wall. On this, my second visit to El Brillo Way, I again followed Maxwell up the pink stairs, around the king-size bed, and into the room with the green massage table. Again, Epstein was lying there naked. Again, Maxwell walked me through the steps that a professional masseuse might follow. And again, after a few minutes, Epstein—who had a thick gray head of hair and a long face that reminded some people of the fashion designer Ralph Lauren and others of actor Richard Gere—rolled over and the "massage" turned into sex. You may wonder why the two of them kept up the pretense of a massage lesson at all. Why didn't they take me straight to the bedroom? I think the charade was meant to keep me off balance. Hadn't I said I wanted to learn this skill? But also, abusing me in a therapeutic setting jibed with how Epstein thought about sex. He would soon explain that he needed to climax at least three times a day. It was a biological imperative, he said, like breathing or eating. For him sex wasn't connected to intimacy or love. It was a purely physical release. Epstein viewed sex almost as a procedure—one that he preferred to be performed by nubile young girls like me.

My second visit to the pink house differed from the first, however, because this time, Maxwell and Epstein formally appointed themselves my sexual tutors. Much like Ron Eppinger had when I was his captive, they stressed the importance of learning what men liked and said this was the beginning of my "training period." If I performed oral sex on Epstein, for example, he would tell me to slow down. "You want to bring a man to an orgasm, not just give him an orgasm," he corrected. Maxwell cautioned that no man wanted a woman to talk during foreplay. "Asking 'How do you like this?' is okay," she said. "But you should mostly be quiet."

Afterward, Maxwell joined Epstein and me in the steam room. As Epstein talked about himself—he was a successful financial manager who used his talents to benefit only the most select clients, he said—Maxwell ordered me to massage *her* feet and legs. I knelt before her and obeyed. Apparently, Epstein wasn't my only responsibility. I had to meet Maxwell's needs too.

A day later, Maxwell called me at Mar-a-Lago. "We need you to come again tonight," she said, her voice more curt than before. Having successfully recruited me, Maxwell had turned off the charm. I said I'd be there, and a few hours later, Dad dropped me off at the house. The butler took me into the kitchen and offered me a drink and some fruit that was prettily arranged on a small plate. I was starving, so I sat down and was about to take a bite when Maxwell appeared, shooting me a cold look. I jumped up, as if I'd had my hand in the cookie jar.

"I've got plans, so you're on your own tonight," Maxwell said. "Jeffrey is waiting upstairs. Don't disappoint him."

My skin prickled with nervousness as I climbed the spiral stairway by myself for the first time. Maxwell hadn't protected me from Epstein—far from it. But without her there, I'd be alone with him, and that felt scary. My senses were heightened. I could smell the cleaning fluids the housekeepers used. The light in the house was turning golden as the sun set, and I allowed myself to look more closely at the photos displayed on the walls. There were so many of them: topless girls, bottomless girls, girls with shy expressions, girls from the back, their faces obscured.

In the massage room, Epstein was face down, as usual. He turned and gestured toward a schoolgirl outfit—pleated skirt, white starched button-down, knee socks—and told me to put it on. "Leave your underwear off," he said. I did, then had sex with him as he demanded. On this day, he continued to critique my performance. "Stop. Stop!" he told me more than once. "That's not how we taught you to do it. Start over again." He also ordered me to seem more "into it." Men liked it when women appeared to love sex, he said. In that area, I needed to do better. "Relax," he demanded, and I tried to comply. A half hour later, our "session" complete, I again bathed Epstein with two warm washcloths.

From that point on, when Epstein and Maxwell were in Florida, I was a daily presence at El Brillo Way. Some days Epstein and I were alone in the massage room. Other days Maxwell joined us; or another young woman, a brunette named Sarah Kellen, who was introduced to me as Epstein's assistant. Epstein liked to watch women together, so sometimes he ordered me to have sex with Maxwell or Kellen. I had never had a sexual experience with a woman, but I soon found forced sex with women was less threatening than with men. I didn't look forward to it, but it was less intrusive and therefore less terrifying.

Little by little, I was welcomed into the sorority of Epstein's girls. One day, for example, Maxwell led me upstairs as usual, but then turned left, away from the massage room, to a yellow guest room where Emmy Tayler, Maxwell's blond, blue-eyed personal assistant, stayed. Tayler, a Brit whom Maxwell jokingly referred to as her "slave," was already there, smoking a cigarette on the balcony. By then I knew Epstein hated cigarettes. Like drugs and alcohol, which he also shunned, he saw tobacco as a poison and forbade it in his house. But here Tayler stood, puffing away, and Maxwell now joined her, lighting up and taking a long drag. When the women offered me a cigarette, I took it, anxious to fit in. I wasn't much of a smoker, though, so I inhaled too deeply and started coughing.

"I guess you're inexperienced," Maxwell teased as she and Tayler giggled. I don't know what got into me, but when I caught my breath, I teased her right back. "I'd rather be inexperienced," I said, "than be an old lady with a chronic hack." Maxwell wasn't used to being challenged, but she could enjoy it if she had the last word. "Touché," she said, tapping her ash over the railing and onto the patio below. Talking back to Maxwell was risky, but that day I must've threaded the needle perfectly, because for the next few minutes, she, Tayler, and I chatted and laughed like girlfriends playing hooky from school. Then I excused myself to brush my teeth and douse myself in body spray to eliminate all traces of nicotine. Epstein was waiting for me. There was work to do.

As I became a regular at Epstein's house, it was difficult to avoid the demeaning nature of this transactional relationship. Epstein took delight in explaining to me, for example, that he had painted his house pink because "I love pink. Pink is for pussy!" But so many of my connections to men had been humiliating that I think I saw this one as a challenge; maybe for once, I thought, I could make it work for me. This only makes sense, of course, when you consider how little I'd grown up hoping for. As Epstein used me to satisfy his perverse appetites, I rationalized that perhaps he might also help me to better myself. If he and Maxwell made good on their promise to get me trained as a masseuse, perhaps that would set me on a path to freedom and prosperity. I told myself it was worth the gamble.

But then, probably two weeks after I'd met them, Epstein upped the ante.

I was upstairs, cleaning up after another "massage," when Epstein told me to come to his office. "How about you quit your job at Mar-a-Lago," he said, "and work for me full time?" Unsure what to say, I admitted I was worn out from pulling double shifts each day—the first at the spa, the second at El Brillo Way. Epstein nodded. He wanted to make things easier on me, he said. But he had a few conditions. As his employee, I would be at his beck and call, day and night. No exceptions. When he said, "Jump!" my response would have to be, "How high?" And another thing: I could no longer live in my parents' trailer. Seeing me come and go at all hours might make them suspicious, he said, and he didn't want that. He held out a wad of cash—probably $2,500. "Use this," he said, "to rent yourself an apartment."

I was stunned. I'd never held that much money in my hand before. I thanked him, even as a twinge of worry crept into my head. By this point, I had seen dozens of girls coming and going from his house. Many came once and never returned. If he got rid of them so quickly, would Epstein eventually throw me away too? It felt foolish to rely on him for my livelihood. Epstein must've sensed my qualms, though, because he walked around his desk, picked up a grainy photograph, and handed it to me. The image had been taken from some distance, but it was unmistakably my little brother. Skydy was walking away from the camera; I could see his backpack, and the outline of the side of his face. I felt a stab of fear. Why did Epstein have a photo of the person I loved most in the world?

"We know where your brother goes to school," Epstein said. He let that sink in for a moment, then got to the point: "You must never tell a soul what goes on in this house." He was smiling, but his threat was clear: should I ever be tempted to betray him and go to the authorities, he would hurt Skydy. I stared at him. He stared back. "And I own the Palm Beach Police Department," he said, "so they won't do anything about it."

That threat was still rattling around in my head days later, when Epstein casually mentioned that he knew Eppinger—not well, he said, but they'd met once, at a party. The news only confirmed my emerging understanding of how the world worked. My approximately seventeen years on the planet had taught me that some grown men forced children to have sex with them and suffered no repercussions. So the idea of Epstein and Eppinger socializing made perfect sense. It was simply the way of things. I had no choice, I believed, but to accept that and make the best of it—for Skydy's sake, if not my own.

TEN

A Very Important Man

I turned seventeen on August 9, 2000, and used Epstein's money to lease and furnish a third-floor apartment in Royal Palm Beach, about three miles from Rackley Road. Michael moved in with me, even though our connection was now one of mere convenience. We sometimes ate Domino's pizza on the couch together. We took care of our animals—which now included a miniature Chow Chow puppy I'd named Mary-Jane. But we didn't talk much. Notably, Michael never questioned why anyone would pay me to do a job I didn't know how to do.

From the start, Epstein and Maxwell held me to my promise to be available at all times. Some days, the call would come in the morning. I'd show up, perform whatever sex acts Epstein wanted, then hang out beside his vast swimming pool while he got some work done. After a few hours, I'd usually be summoned to have sex with him again. If Maxwell was there, I was often told to attend to her sexually as well. She kept a bin of vibrators and sex toys handy for these sessions. But she never demanded sex from me one-on-one—only when we were with Epstein. Sometimes there were other girls there, too, and I'd end up staying at El Brillo Way all day.

Other times, my phone wouldn't ring until Epstein was preparing to go to bed. "Come over," Maxwell would command when I answered. "He's requesting you." When that happened, I'd tell Michael I had a work emergency and head out the door. Michael didn't bat an eye.

My relationship with my family, meanwhile, was both better and worse. My mother had confronted me early on, asking what this older couple wanted with a teenage girl who had no credentials. I'd laid it on thick, crowing about the doors Epstein had said he'd open for me. I guess I was glad she cared enough to have suspicions, but at the same time, wasn't it a little late for that? I knew she couldn't save me; she'd never saved me before. But also I wanted to believe I didn't need saving. I'd survived my early childhood, hadn't I? In those initial weeks with Epstein and Maxwell, I told myself I could weather this, too, and maybe even come out ahead.

I remember my first break from servicing the two of them came in what was probably late August, when they went on a trip to two of Epstein's far-flung properties. Zorro Ranch was an eight-thousand-acre spread near Santa Fe, New Mexico, where Epstein said he'd custom built a three-level thirty-three-thousand-square-foot "castle" decorated with rococo flourishes: ten-foot-tall marble fireplaces, sculpted moldings, trompe l'oeil frescoes, and iron chandeliers. In addition to manicured grounds and gurgling fountains, a tennis court, and a grass airstrip and hangar, the property had its own miniature town that housed his servants and groundskeepers. The town also had an eight-stall stable and tack room, a firehouse, a large glassed-in kitchen garden, and even a general store. It sounded like Disneyland to me, and I told Epstein so.

"Wait until you see my Manhattan townhouse," he replied, and then proceeded to brag about his Upper East Side mansion. Formerly a K–12 academy for well-to-do children, the seven-story, thirty-room manse at 9 East Seventy-First Street was one of the city's largest private homes. I'd never been to New York and knew very little about fine art, so when he told me his house sat right across from the Frick Collection, it meant nothing to me. But I could still read the message Epstein seemed determined to deliver: he was a Very Important Man.

As for Maxwell, who told us girls to call her G-Max, I was figuring out she was important too. In October 2000, she jetted off to New York to meet up with her old friend Prince Andrew, Queen Elizabeth II's second-born son, who was then fourth in line to ascend the British throne. On Halloween, along with other guests that included Donald and Melania Trump, Maxwell and Prince Andrew attended a party hosted by German supermodel Heidi Klum at The Hudson, a swank hotel. Maxwell boasted that she knew the man who'd just renovated it—hotel impresario Ian Schrager.

Maxwell was proud of her friendships with famous people, especially men. She loved to talk about how easily she could get former president Bill Clinton on the phone; she and Epstein had visited the White House together when Clinton was in office. Maxwell also enjoyed repeating that once, at some random event, she'd taken the actor George Clooney into a bathroom and given him a blow job. Whether that was true or not, we'd never know. She was less forthcoming about her upbringing, but I began to piece that together too. I remember that Epstein once showed me a mural she'd had painted of a happy-looking family sitting on a bench overlooking a pond, as a hunting party chased foxes nearby. In a hushed voice, Epstein said to me, "This is a portrait of Ghislaine's childhood—the part she can be proud of." The youngest of nine children, she'd been born in France but was raised in a fifty-three-room mansion in the south of England, and she held both French and British passports. Her late father, Robert Maxwell, had been a media mogul in England before he was accused of embezzlement and then found dead, perhaps by suicide, after falling off his yacht in the Canary Islands. That was nine years before I met Maxwell, but his death clearly haunted her. In happier days, she had been his favorite child (he'd named the yacht he was sailing when he died the *Lady Ghislaine*). I gathered that she'd met Epstein not long before her father passed, and I suspected that had something to do with their connection.

And what was that connection like? While they usually slept in separate bedrooms, and rarely kissed or held hands, it seemed to me that Maxwell and Epstein lived in complete symbiosis. Epstein, who described Maxwell as his best friend, valued her knack for connecting him to powerful people. Maxwell, in turn, appreciated that Epstein had the resources to fund the lavish life she thought she deserved yet had trouble affording after her father's death. In social settings, Maxwell often appeared vivacious, entertaining, the life of the party. But in Epstein's household, she functioned more as a party planner: scheduling and organizing the endless parade of girls who she and others—particularly Sarah Kellen—recruited to have sex with him. I remember that at one point I asked her why she wasn't bothered by Epstein's desire to have sex with so many others. She said that it was a relief. Epstein's sexual appetite was so relentless, she said, that no one person could satisfy him. Her lack of jealousy seemed odd but genuine. Over time, I would come to see Epstein and Maxwell less as boyfriend and girlfriend, and more as two halves of a wicked whole.

During my first months working for them, I learned more about Epstein as well. He'd studied physics at Cooper Union and math at New York University, then dropped out two years shy of graduation. Still, Epstein saw himself as an intellectual prodigy, and that self-confidence propelled him forward. The story went that as a young man in the 1970s, he'd talked his way into more than one job he lacked the qualifications for—first as a teacher of high school–level math and physics at the esteemed Dalton School in Manhattan (he told me he gave pretty girls there good grades if they agreed to sleep with him), then as a floor trader at Bear Stearns, the global investment bank where he eventually became a limited partner. In the 1980s, he'd run a consulting firm that assisted clients recovering stolen money, then formed a firm to manage the assets of people whose net worth, he claimed, was no less than $1 billion. This was a point of pride for Epstein: that he, raised by a groundskeeper and a homemaker in Coney Island, only did business with the wealthiest people. For all his cultivation of the upper crust, however, he often appeared unsophisticated and even oblivious. His enormous brainpower couldn't hide his working-class Brooklyn accent. And though he wanted people to know he had money, he usually wore a Harvard sweatshirt and jeans or sweatpants, even when attending fancy events.

The incongruities didn't end there. Epstein was strictly disciplined about what he ate, subsisting on tofu, salmon, chickpeas, ginger, and other foods he deemed healthy (and insisting that the girls around him do so too). A germaphobe, he was equally meticulous about what he touched. He mostly refused to shake hands, and he required his sheets be changed every other day. And yet he relentlessly sought sexual contact with young girls who were strangers to him—some who lived rough, terrible lives outside his gated compound—and he never wore a condom. While he required girls like me, who he forced to have intercourse with him regularly, to be tested every three months for sexually transmitted diseases, no one could guarantee the health of all the girls who streamed in and out of El Brillo Way. I guess this lack of caution can be chalked up to arrogance; Epstein believed he didn't have to follow the rules everyone else did.

In the fall of 2000, Epstein and Maxwell announced that it was time for me to accompany them for the first time on a trip. We were celebrating that I'd successfully completed my "massage training," they said, as they unveiled the itinerary. First, we'd take one of Epstein's private planes—he owned a Gulfstream IV, a Boeing 727, and a helicopter—from Palm Beach to New York. Then, after a few days in New York, we'd fly south to the most luxurious of Epstein's properties: a seventy-two-acre island he owned in the US Virgin Islands, right next to Saint Thomas. The private sanctuary was called Little Saint James, but Epstein liked to call it "Little Saint Jeff's." The place sounded exotic, especially to a girl who'd never left the mainland United States, and I told Epstein and Maxwell that I looked forward to seeing it. I remember when Dad dropped me off at El Brillo Way on the day we were to depart, Epstein came out to the driveway and introduced himself. "We'll take care of her," Epstein told my father.

In the decades since, flight logs made public in various lawsuits show that during my time with Epstein, I accompanied him on his private jets, both domestically and internationally, at least thirty-two times (on twenty-three of those trips, Maxwell was there too). But that tally represents just a tiny fraction of my travel with them. For one thing, we often flew together (or I flew solo to meet Epstein) on commercial airlines. Maxwell always booked those flights through the same travel agency—it was called Shoppers Travel—but those records are not public, so I have no access to them. When it comes to our travel on Epstein's jets, meanwhile, only one of Epstein's pilots, David Rodgers, has turned over his records to authorities. This first trip I took with Epstein and Maxwell was on a plane flown by another pilot, Larry Visoski Jr., who'd worked for Epstein since 1991.

Visoski and Epstein were close. In addition to maintaining Epstein's planes, Visoski built Epstein's home theaters in the Caribbean and in Palm Beach and advised Epstein on which boats and cars to purchase (he once said he helped Epstein with "anything that moves"). At one point, Epstein gave a Hummer he owned to Visoski for his personal use, and when the pilot's wife wanted to build a house in New

Mexico, Epstein gifted Visoski forty acres near his ranch's western boundary on which to do so.

So when exactly was my first trip with Epstein? Without Visoski's logs I can't be sure, but I think it was in the latter part of 2000. I'll never forget how, on our first flight, Epstein told Visoski to let me sit in the cockpit during takeoff. I'd been on a plane just twice before: when I flew to and from Salinas for my exile in California. But on those trips I sat in a coach seat in the back. Being up front, with a 180-degree view, was thrilling. I told Visoski it felt like riding a roller coaster, and I loved roller coasters.

The rest of our flight was less exciting. When I returned to the cabin, where Maxwell and Kellen seemed to be napping in their reclined seats, I saw that Epstein was wide awake and had his socks off. He looked at me expectantly. I would spend the next two hours massaging his feet.

After landing at a private airport in Teterboro, New Jersey, we were picked up by a trim Filipino man in a sober black suit: Epstein's New York butler, Jojo Fontanilla. Jojo and his wife, June, took care of Epstein in Manhattan, managing a housekeeping staff that numbered in the dozens. Always dressed in suits and pristine white gloves, these servants waited hand and foot on Epstein and his guests. Who knows what the Fontanillas' real first names were, since Epstein—like Maxwell—insisted upon calling servants by American-sounding names of their own choosing.

Jojo loaded our luggage into an SUV and got behind the wheel, and it wasn't long before we arrived at Epstein's Upper East Side townhouse. Some have said the place looked more like an embassy or a museum than a private home, and I would have to agree. Outside the entrance—a fifteen-foot-tall double door made of solid oak and adorned with a huge brass doorknob shaped like a knotted rope—two polished brass letters were affixed to the stone facade: JE. The sidewalk there was heated, Epstein told me, so no snow could pile up. To enter, we passed under a stone archway topped with a gargoyle's grimacing face, then climbed eight steps to an enormous marble foyer. Inside, caramel-colored tiles—Epstein said they were imported French limestone—covered the first floor, which was lavishly furnished and brightened by arched windows. Everything inside seemed bigger than necessary—the chandeliers could've lit up a train station; the dining-room table, surrounded by chairs upholstered in a loud leopard print, seated twenty. The walls were lined with massive shadowy paintings and tapestries depicting violent scenes. A staircase led up to Epstein's office, which housed a gilded desk, a nine-foot ebony Steinway concert grand piano, and an antique Persian rug so big that, as Epstein liked to say, it must've been made for a mosque. There was also more than one elevator. For a girl from Loxahatchee, such grandeur was almost impossible to process. I felt as if I had stepped inside an architectural monument the likes of which I'd only seen in books: the Vatican, say, or the Taj Mahal.

Announcing that he was tired from the flight, Epstein led me down a hallway lined with art and antiquities. He favored sixteenth- and seventeenth-century religious statuary, including a bronze casting of the half-human, nymph-loving Greek god Pan, whose goatlike horns and haunches, Epstein told me, symbolized fertility. I followed Epstein into a black-marbled alcove with a massage table at its center—a place so gloomy that I would nickname it "The Dungeon." He pointed at a hutch on one wall that housed a collection of massage oils and a CD player, which he told me to load. By this time, I was used to choosing the music before each day's "session." Back in Palm Beach, I had gotten good at reading Epstein's mood to determine which of his favorite albums to play. Sometimes he wanted opera, other times classical. The only popular artists he favored were female vocalists such as Whitney Houston and Celine Dion.

I don't remember what CDs I chose that day. I only remember that when I had satisfied Epstein sexually, I was escorted to an apartment in a building owned by his brother, Mark, on East Sixty-Sixth Street. The one night I slept there I luxuriated in having my own space, but that freedom would be short-lived. The next day, I foolishly went out for a long walk, discovering New York City for the first time. But because I had no cell phone, Epstein and Maxwell couldn't reach me as I walked around for hours, filled with awe. I remember that the skyscrapers ringing Central Park looked like toy soldiers standing at attention. There were so many people on the sidewalks, bundled up to enjoy the chilly afternoon. I had some money in my pocket, and I bought a disposable Instamatic camera—the first of many I'd purchase over the coming months. I didn't know how much longer I would be seeing the world as part of Epstein's entourage, so I wanted photos to remember where I'd been.

When I returned to Epstein's townhouse, however, both he and Maxwell were pacing in the entryway, frantic. "Where have you been?" Epstein demanded angrily as Maxwell glared at me. That was the last time I saw the Sixty-Sixth Street apartment. From that day forward, whenever we were in New York I would occupy a fifth-floor bedroom in Epstein's house: an enormous loftlike space, its carved moldings coated in gold paint, that was dominated by a menacing wall-hanging that gave me the creeps—it showed wild boars feeding on the carcasses of other animals as a few screaming children looked on. There was also an intercom that Epstein used to summon me. I quickly learned not to keep him waiting.

Today when I recall the sumptuous trappings of Epstein's homes, I feel conflicted. In too many media accounts, descriptions of Epstein's over-the-top lifestyle have fueled the perception that the girls Epstein victimized were lucky to find themselves in such surroundings. I don't want to add to that degrading narrative. To be sure, traveling with

Epstein meant being introduced to a level of luxury I would never have experienced otherwise. And I will not dispute that it feels nicer to sleep under sheets made of premium Egyptian cotton, not low-rent polyester. But the comforts of Epstein's glamorous life—while I noticed and even enjoyed them—would come at a horrible cost to me. What made me feel most at home in this pedophile's world? Far more than Epstein's riches, it was the prior abuse I'd endured on humble Rackley Road.

It's taken me a long time to understand that Epstein and Maxwell solidified their power over me by offering me a new sort of family. Epstein was the patriarch, Maxwell the matriarch, and these roles were not merely implied. Maxwell liked to call the girls who regularly serviced Epstein her "children." She and Epstein once took me to a boat show in Palm Beach and spent the afternoon introducing me as their daughter, just for kicks. As bizarre as that sounds, it felt kind of good to me. Less good, given my history, was that Epstein sometimes insisted that I call him "Daddy" during sex.

While I was hardly equipped to judge, it often seemed to me that Epstein and Maxwell behaved like actual parents. The first time we ate a meal together, for example, they were appalled by my table manners. So Maxwell taught me how to hold a knife and fork, just so, and to fold my napkin in my lap, the way civilized people do. Soon, she'd be telling me how to do my makeup, how to dress, and where to get my hair cut (the celebrity stylist Frédéric Fekkai groomed many of the girls in Epstein's world, including me). Even then, part of me knew she was having her dentists whiten my teeth, or sending me to a waxer to remove my body hair, to please Epstein. But the role Maxwell played in my life sometimes felt like more than that. One day in the fall of 2000, we heard "Yellow," Coldplay's new love song, on the car radio. I loved it and couldn't get the tune out of my head. A day later, Maxwell presented me with the CD as a gift. She also gave me my first cell phone. Of course, it served her to have me on a short tether, for her and Epstein's use. But the gift also felt vaguely protective. I was no expert on mothers, but in those early days, I sometimes imagined Maxwell as mine.

AFTER A FEW days in Manhattan, and many sessions in The Dungeon, we headed for Little Saint James, which was as beautiful as Epstein had said it would be. Surrounded by crystalline turquoise water, the island had three private beaches and had been enhanced with two swimming pools, a helipad, and its own desalination system. In addition to a massive blue-roofed main residence, there were guest cottages painted in cheerful Caribbean colors: light yellow, minty green, coral pink. There was a sundial as big as a horse paddock and a dock where a thirty-five-foot Donzi powerboat bobbed under a thatched roof. Epstein bragged that the boat had cost him $60,000. Down by the beach, Epstein had built several gazebos for massages and whatever else he required. Were it not for what went on there, the place would have been paradise.

On that first Caribbean trip, when I wasn't servicing Epstein, I discovered the rhythms of island life. Because there were no A-list guests to entertain, as there would be on subsequent trips, I spent hours on a floating trampoline, just a short swim from the dock, where I marveled at the colorful fish that swam underneath. The group of us also went scuba diving off Epstein's powerboat. At one point, I swam into a smack of jellyfish and was stung all over my body. My skin was on fire. Maxwell asked our boat captain for vinegar, which was supposed to help with the pain, but none could be found. "Lay down on the deck," Maxwell said. When I was flat on my back, she pulled her bikini bottoms to one side and urinated all over me. I know it sounds gross, but it worked: my agony subsided. On another day, I discovered that Maxwell and I both loved collecting treasures on the beach. "Pirates used to dock here," she told me, as we walked together, scanning the sand for sea glass and driftwood. I wanted to believe she was fond of me.

Epstein continued to cast himself as my mentor. Sometimes we'd sit in his steam shower for hours as he held forth on topics I'd never heard of before: game theory, say, or evolutionary biology, financial derivatives, or the mathematical underpinnings of human language. He also gave me books to read. Many of them were sexual in nature, such as Nabokov's *Lolita* and Anne Desclos's *Story of O*, but his insistence that I read them still felt like a vote of confidence. Frequently, Epstein told me something I needed to hear: that I was smart and full of potential.

At night, Epstein, Maxwell, Tayler, Kellen, and I would gather in front of an enormous TV in the island's main house, sharing bowls of popcorn, watching movies and TV shows. Epstein particularly liked *Sex and the City*, which made him laugh. But cozy evenings like this could turn sexual in an instant. A dark, distant expression would move across Epstein's face, and I'd see it in his eyes: he had to "get off" right then. When that occurred when I was with Epstein and Maxwell, Maxwell would then instruct me to take off my shirt and do whatever else Epstein wanted. In those moments, it was more difficult for me to avoid the truth: that to them, I was nothing but a tool to be used for their pleasure.

Today, I can see how this, too, was an echo from my childhood. I hated the sexual duties that Epstein and Maxwell required of me, but I bargained with myself, just as I had when my father abused me: "Just get the icky part over with so the good parts of life can go on."

Over the years, I've wondered a lot about what made Epstein seem to favor me. As the world has learned from countless others who survived his abuse, Epstein often preferred girls with little to no sexual experience. Many victims have described how he seemed to enjoy watching inexperienced girls suffer the discomfort of being introduced to sex by him, an older stranger. Because I'd been sexually abused before meeting him, I could never give him that satisfaction. I've come to believe, though, that I provided something else Epstein needed—something I'd learned from my previous abusers. I knew how to read a room—or Epstein's face—and to adapt accordingly, becoming what was required in the moment. I could fade into the woodwork, invisible, or I could feign delight. Unlike some of Epstein's other repeat victims, who got jealous or tried to assert a relationship with him, I was detached and never made demands. Long before I'd met Epstein, I'd been trained to accept whatever affection, if any, I could get. Epstein liked that.

While I have no evidence to prove it, I think it's also possible that in me, an abused child, Epstein saw a bit of himself. Only once did I question him about his experiences growing up. I knew him well enough not to directly ask: Were you ever abused as a kid? Instead, I carefully inquired whether he'd had a happy upbringing. Sensing where I was heading, I think, he cut me off almost before I finished my question, making clear that was a topic I should never raise again. Years later, when he was asked under oath if he had been sexually abused as a minor, he would refuse to answer, asserting his constitutional right not to incriminate himself. Maybe I'm wrong, but I've always believed that during his own childhood, he'd experienced some kind of molestation. If that is true, it doesn't lessen the awfulness of Epstein's crimes. But it may help explain them. I know that Epstein was emotionally broken, devoid of any ability to form deep connections to others. But whether he was born that way or was abused in a manner that eroded his capacity for empathy, no one will probably ever know.

ELEVEN

The Bottom of the Pyramid

I know it probably sounds strange to say, but whenever I was in the Caribbean with Epstein, one of my favorite places to hang out wasn't the boat dock or the beach, but the island's big open kitchen. That's because Epstein's personal chef, Adam Perry Lang, was often there. Though Lang would later become a celebrity chef renowned for his barbecue, in the early 2000s he excelled at the healthy fare Epstein required: tofu, fish kabobs, hummus. I liked Lang because he treated me and Epstein's other girls as human beings. Even if I was standing naked in front of him, which was not unusual since Epstein preferred us that way when we were on the island, Lang would look me in the eye, not ogle me. He also snuck me food that was not on Epstein's approved menu.

The first time Lang asked me what I was hungry for, he threw together my favorite food—pizza—as if it were nothing. After that, I didn't even have to ask. When I'd finish attending to Epstein or one of the other guests, Lang would have a cheesy hot pie waiting. I'd jump up on a stool, he'd hand me a beer, and we'd talk for a bit.

This probably doesn't sound like much of a rebellion, but it felt like one to me. Epstein wanted us girls to stay thin, so pizza and beer were strictly off-limits. In this realm, as in so many others, Maxwell was his enforcer. Everyone knew what a stern taskmaster she was when it came to menus and household routines. At each of Epstein's homes, she kept manuals that specified her preferences about everything from coffee (she liked Maxwell House, naturally) to thermostat settings (sixty degrees in the bedrooms, eighty-eight degrees in the pool) to toilet paper (she specified that the end of each roll be folded "into a 'V'"). One night when Lang and I were having a drink, she walked into the kitchen and reprimanded us, but I didn't care. Maxwell had so much power over me; it felt good to have a friendship that she didn't sanction.

It was around this time that Epstein expanded the duties he expected me to perform for him. Already he was requiring me to dress him each morning. First I'd apply lotion to his feet, then scrunch up his socks and then roll them over his toes and heels like a parent would an infant. "You're going to be such a good mother someday," he'd say, as I knelt before him, holding his pant legs open so he could step into them. Now he began asking me to tuck him into his pink satin sheets each night. While "tuck him in" might sound like a euphemism for sex, it didn't always mean that to Epstein. Though my job during the day was to arouse and satisfy him sexually, at night he mostly wanted to be soothed—and then left alone. He liked me to reach under the covers to massage his feet and maybe then his scalp. Only after he fell asleep was I permitted to pull the covers up to his chin and quietly exit his room. I am the only one I know of who was asked to do this for him, and at the time he told me that signified that I was "Number One" among the many girls and servants who attended to him. That designation gave me a proud feeling. Epstein intentionally fostered rivalries between the girls who serviced him, so to be held in his esteem seemed like a prize. Nevertheless, I found the tuck-in ritual, which could take more than an hour, increasingly tedious. Each night I'd emerge exhausted.

It wasn't until we returned to Florida that I realized the bedtime rituals I'd been performing for Epstein had unlocked something in him. Suddenly he was confiding in me. One day we were in the massage room in Palm Beach when he showed me a hidden doorway next to some paintings of naked people stretching. I'd been in that room dozens of times by then but had never noticed a door there. Opening it, Epstein revealed what can only be described as a trophy closet. On the walls, from floor to ceiling, he'd tacked up hundreds of photos of young girls. All of the girls were naked, many of them quite obviously underage, and the images were raunchy, not demure. A stack of shoeboxes in the corner held the overflow. He had so many photos that he'd run out of display space.

I turned to him, speechless. He didn't speak either, but the smug look on his face said, "Look at my conquests. Look at how powerful I am."

Maxwell was seemingly beginning to trust me to some extent, too, but that wasn't good news, because it meant I was assigned a new job: recruiting girls for Epstein. The first time was in the Caribbean. Maxwell, Epstein, Kellen, and I had been ferried over to Saint Thomas for dinner one night, and we were strolling around afterward when Epstein said to me and Kellen, "Why don't you two hit the nightclub here and see if there's anyone interesting to bring back for the evening?" Maxwell nodded her assent. I'd already been told his criteria: recruits were preferably white, with wholesome, "girl next door" looks that made them appear between twelve and seventeen years old. No piercings, no tattoos, and definitely no call girls. But his key requirement, other than looks, was vulnerability. Recruits had to be enough "on the edge," as Epstein and Maxwell put it, that they would submit to sex in exchange for money.

On this night, it hit me: I was being trained yet again. For hours, I tagged along with Kellen as she chatted up girls, floating from one stranger to another with ease, flirting. While we didn't find anyone suitable to take back to the island that night, I now knew the script that I would soon be using myself with shameful regularity: "I work for a billionaire who has a taste for beautiful young girls. He has contacts in the acting, modeling, and art worlds, and he'd love to help you make your dreams come true. Come meet him!"

For months I'd been watching how Maxwell and Kellen constructed their pyramid-like recruitment scheme. In New York City, they reserved afternoons for hunting. At 3:00 p.m., when the high schools let out, they'd be on the street, looking for pretty girls to approach. Maxwell, particularly, was amazing at sussing out what a particular girl might want or need, and she tailored her pitch for maximum appeal. After a girl visited Epstein for the first time, she'd be told she could make double the money if she brought a friend along next time. The incentive to lure another girl into the web was twofold: not only would the procurer make $400 (instead of the $200 she'd been paid the first time), but she'd usually avoid having to service Epstein herself, since the new girl would satisfy him.

It was my fear of disappointing Epstein, not the prospect of doubling my money, that really drove me to take on this new task. I was afraid of making him mad—the way he'd threatened Skydy still loomed large in my head—and I'd seen him sever relationships (if that's the right word for his liaisons) with countless girls. But I was also utterly reliant on him at this point, not only for my rent but also for validation. Some other victims have talked about experiencing Stockholm syndrome—developing positive feelings for one's abuser as a means of surviving. Today I can see that I did this too. I needed to believe that while Epstein was afflicted with an illness—sex addiction—still deep down, he believed in me and had my best inter-

THE BOTTOM OF THE PYRAMID

ests at heart. I needed him not to be a selfish, cruel pedophile. So I told myself he wasn't one.

Once, I asked Epstein if he ever thought he would settle down and get married. He said he didn't believe that love with one monogamous partner was possible, but that love with many was. At the time, I believed that in his unusual way, he was saying that he loved me. And I had feelings for him, too—not love exactly, but I think the right word is fealty. He'd succeeded in convincing me that he was helping me—protecting me from a mediocre life that I didn't deserve. I felt strangely indebted to him.

So I began to do the worst thing I've ever done in my life: I drafted other girls into Epstein's sickening world. I knew it was wrong, but I rationalized my behavior by telling myself that at least I leveled with the girls I approached. Unlike Kellen, whose pitch made an encounter with Epstein seem not just lucrative but fun, I warned each potential recruit that they'd have to strip naked during the massage, and that the rich man they'd be servicing could sometimes expect more intimate physical contact. But the fact that I issued warnings doesn't diminish the ugly truth: when I targeted girls who were hungry or poor, I knew I was exploiting their vulnerabilities. I stooped so low that I even brought Epstein a few friends of mine to abuse. No one ever turned me down—my friends had seen my nice apartment and those who said yes, I think, wanted to believe servicing Epstein would be easy money. But again that's no excuse: that I targeted girls who said yes only proves how good I'd become at spotting those who were the neediest. The faces of girls I recruited will always haunt me. I know their pain, and I will never get over playing a role in causing it.

As 2001 began, Maxwell and Epstein indicated that they had bigger plans for me. "We need to get you a passport so you can fly international with us," Maxwell announced in early January, and soon she told me where to get photos taken and helped me fill out the application form. On the line asking my occupation, she told me to write "masseuse." January 20 was Epstein's forty-eighth birthday, and Maxwell said we needed to make a fuss. As the day neared, I asked Maxwell, "Do you think he'd like a watch or something?" Maxwell scoffed. "He doesn't want *you* to give him a watch," she said, indicating Epstein wouldn't be caught dead wearing a timepiece that a girl like me could afford. If I wanted to please him, she said, there was only one way: "All he wants is photos of you naked."

A few hours later, Maxwell took me out to the patio around the pool and told me to take off my clothes. She posed me carefully, with an almost tender attention to detail. She arranged my hair and placed me in positions that revealed the parts of me she thought Epstein liked best. "Perfect. Beautiful," she said, but she sounded as if she were talking to herself, not to me. I would soon be joining the other girls in Epstein's trophy closet.

TWELVE

"Just Like You Do for Me"

It was around that time that Tony Figueroa, my boyfriend from middle school, stormed back into my life. I was in my Royal Palm Beach apartment one afternoon when I heard a knock at the door. "Who is it?" I asked, and when he answered, I'd have known that voice anywhere. It had been three years since I'd seen last Tony, before Mom shipped me off to Growing Together, and he'd filled out a bit. His black hair was shorter, and now that he was into rap—Tupac, Biggie, Ja Rule—he dressed in oversized T-shirts and baggy shorts that hung off his ass. But he still had those big brown eyes.

"Damn, girl, you finally answered," he said, wrapping me in a hug. "I've been trying to track you down for months." Not wanting Michael to find us together, I suggested we go out for a drink. We spent hours talking, easily picking up where we'd so abruptly left off. It'd been a tough couple of years, I told him, but now I had a good job working for a rich guy in Palm Beach. I was intentionally unclear about my duties. Tony listened, then told me about his own struggles. Neither of us seemed to be in a great place, but it felt good to be sitting across from someone who'd known me for so long. When Tony dropped me off that night, I gave him one chaste kiss, but I had a feeling I'd see him again soon.

For months I hadn't known how to talk to Michael about Epstein and what I did for him, so I said nothing. For some reason, I felt different with Tony. I knew he wouldn't judge me. As we began spending more time together, I filled in the gaps. Tony wasn't thrilled to hear what my "job" entailed, of course, but he didn't blame me for the fucked-up situation. Life had always been hard in Loxahatchee—for him and for me. Weren't we all just trying to get by? Little by little, just as we had in middle school, Tony and I evolved from being friends to being lovers.

When Michael found out that Tony and I were back together, he was crushed. I made that worse because I didn't tell him it was over. Instead, he learned the truth when he walked in on Tony and me one night—not my finest hour. Tony and I weren't in the middle of anything passionate, but still Michael sensed what was up. We had a huge fight—yelling and screaming at each other—and then he left. A few days later, Michael came to retrieve his stuff, and I felt so bad that I let him take all the animals but two: my Chow Chow, Mary-Jane, and a cat named Cougar. Not long after that, Tony moved in.

When I think back on this period, I'm not proud of myself. Even though the adult me knows that the child me was battling just to survive, I wince at how passive I had become. Just like when I was held captive by Eppinger, I was turning more and more to Xanax and other drugs, which were prescribed for me by doctors Maxwell sent me to. Sometimes, when I was really struggling, I took as many as eight Xanax a day. Even then I knew that a girl with more options (and fewer demons) would not be doing what I did for Epstein and Maxwell. And yet I was afraid to break free. Even on days when Epstein was out of town and I had more control over my time, I anesthetized myself by partying hard—drinking, smoking marijuana, and sometimes dropping acid.

"JUST LIKE YOU DO FOR ME"

Epstein strung me along with the promise that he would introduce me to real massage therapists, who he'd pay to let me apprentice alongside them as they worked on his body. In one instance, when the only massage therapist available on a given day was male, I was actually coached by a talented expert. I remember this man's showing me how prolonged pressure in a single spot could unknot even the most stubbornly clenched muscle. "Be patient," this masseur said. "Don't be afraid to slow down and focus." I devoured his advice and tried to apply it to my own life. "Maybe if I'm patient, things will get better," I thought, grateful to be learning.

Except for that single session, however, every other masseuse that Epstein hired to educate me was female, and you can imagine how that went. I remember being in the middle of a session, working beside a woman who seemed to be legit, when Epstein suddenly turned to the woman and commanded: "Take off your clothes." When she obediently complied, I realized the whole "lesson" had been a sham: one of Epstein's sick fantasies, brought to life. Epstein had sex with both of us that day, and when I finally got home, I desperately wanted—no, needed—to get stoned. For months now, I'd been doing my damnedest to justify what I was allowing to happen to me—"If I can only endure it, this could lead somewhere good!" Now, I increasingly needed to be numb to get through the day.

My need to feel nothing only grew stronger when Epstein and Maxwell began lending me out to their friends. The first time, Epstein made it sound as if he were launching me on an exciting new phase of my "massage training." My new "clients," as Epstein described them, were a man and his pregnant wife. Both needed massages, Epstein said. They were staying at The Breakers, an exclusive Palm Beach hotel not far from El Brillo Way, and Epstein had specific instructions for how I was to treat them. "Be gentle with her," he said. "Make her comfortable. But save most of your energy for him." When

Epstein said this, I looked up. Did he mean what I thought he meant? "Give him whatever he wants," Epstein confirmed. "Just like you do for me." Epstein said he was sending me as an emissary, so how I behaved would reflect on him. It was important that I uphold his reputation.

That night I took a taxi to The Breakers. The man—I'll call him Billionaire Number One—and his wife were staying in an apartment in the residential section of the vast property. When I arrived, they promptly showed me to the master bedroom, where I would work on the woman first. As a joke, Maxwell had warned me that I could induce premature labor if I massaged the woman's ankles "in the wrong way." I believed her and, not knowing any better, was petrified that I might hurt the baby. As the billionaire's wife undressed, I realized I'd never seen a pregnant woman naked before. Her midsection was swollen, as if she'd swallowed a basketball, and her belly button protruded slightly. I had no massage table with me, so we went to the bed, where I arranged a nest of pillows to bolster her as I rubbed her with the oils I'd brought. I knew nothing about prenatal massage, but I did my best, avoiding her ankles altogether. After about forty-five minutes, the woman said she was going to go to sleep and asked me to turn off the light. I did so and exited quietly, much as I did each night with Epstein.

The apartment was dark when I emerged, and I had to tiptoe around a bit before I found Billionaire Number One in a sitting-room area, taking off his clothes. There was a throw rug on the floor, and he lay down on it naked, facing up. I asked him to turn over, hoping against hope that a massage was all this stranger was expecting. Working on the floor was more difficult than on a table or a bed, but I was intent on doing a good job. Nearly four hours after I'd arrived at the apartment, I was still kneading the man's muscles when he looked up, groaned, and asked me, "Wouldn't you be more comfortable working in the nude?" I was disappointed, but not surprised. We had sex on the floor, and afterward, he tipped me a hundred dollars. As I left that night, I felt that familiar scooped-out, empty feeling. But I must've been getting used to it because as I sat in the back of a taxi, headed home, the main thing I was thinking about was Epstein: "He'll be happy that I did what he asked."

The next morning, my phone rang. I was to come to El Brillo Way for lunch. When I arrived, I headed to the pool, where Epstein sat on a chaise longue, surrounded by paperwork. "How did it go?" he asked, as if having sex with a stranger were a final exam, or a root canal, or some other everyday activity. I told him I'd done everything that anyone required of me and that his friends seemed satisfied. He grinned then, popped a red grape in his mouth, and walked back to his office. I had pleased him. And I was dismissed.

I NEED A breather. I bet you do too. So I now interrupt our grim chronology to take you to a place that Robbie and the kids and I have gone many times when we needed a fun family outing: Fremantle Prison. You may wonder what could possibly be fun about a prison, but remember, I have two boys and a girl who's as tough as any boy. My kids know that their country of origin started off as a penal colony when the British, responding to overcrowded prisons in England, began sending convicts to Western Australia in 1850. Alex, Tyler, and Ellie are fascinated by the idea that these earliest arrivals were forced first to build the very walls that would imprison them and later to construct several cellblocks, a gatehouse, and a labyrinth of tunnels too. My kids love it when our tour guide asks for a volunteer to be cuffed to the flogging post, where misbehaving prisoners got lashed with a cat-o'-nine-tails, or when visitors are offered the chance to be locked (just for ten seconds) in a pitch-black isolation cell.

"That does my head in," Robbie announces, laughing as he and the kids emerge from this claustrophobic chamber. I never accompany them, preferring to wait in the low-ceilinged hallway outside, hugging my French bulldog Juno, who wears an "Emotional Support Animal" harness on these trips. But through my children, I still experience the thrill.

Fremantle Prison is the Giuffre family's favorite spooky haunted house. All five of us have gone on its Torchlight Tour, which commences after dark and makes my kids all giggle and shiver with its ghost stories about inmates who died inside. No matter what time of day we visit, as we wander around the prison grounds, we shudder at what it was like to live in this stone fortress with no plumbing or electricity. And yet some within those walls found a way to keep their hopes alive—like James Walsh, an inmate who escaped without ever leaving. Locked inside Cell #833 in about 1860, Walsh—who was serving eight years for forging a one-pound note—used the brass buttons of his prison uniform to scrape intricate, classically styled artworks onto every inch of the walls. These detailed drawings were hidden for almost a century, the tour guide tells us. They were only discovered in 1964, when a clumsy prison officer bumped into the wall of the storeroom that had been Walsh's cell, chipping the whitewash and revealing what lay beneath.

When I stand inside Cell #833 today, looking at Walsh's drawings of religious figures, scenes from Roman and Greek mythology, and images of Queen Victoria, I think to myself: "This man's body never broke free of Fremantle Prison, but his soul certainly did." Looking back on my years with Epstein and Maxwell, I sometimes marvel at how I managed to endure how they treated me. But seeing what Walsh accomplished makes me realize: there's something within all of us, even when we're not aware of it, that fights to keep our spirits alive.

EPSTEIN LIKED TO share with me what he insisted were "scientific" justifications for his yearnings for young girls. For example, he would only have sex with girls who had started menstruating. Why? So he could assert that—since they were biologically able to bear children—they were "of age." I was flabbergasted when he said this stuff, but I held my tongue. No matter how young a girl looked, or how sexually inexperienced she was, if she had her period, he felt he could defend his abuse of her as part of the natural order of things. I was never sure who he imagined making this argument to—the girls themselves? his business associates? law-enforcement officers? himself?—but it was clear that he took a certain glee in what he saw as a loophole in society's moral code. The fact that different nations and states define the age of consent differently (in Florida it's eighteen; in New York it's seventeen; in England it's sixteen) only gave him ammunition. He said these inconsistencies proved these laws were arbitrary and meaningless; no one could convince him that sex with minors was wrong, because no one could agree on what a minor was! Epstein also claimed that because women, unlike men, can have multiple orgasms, that meant they were supposed to have multiple sexual partners as well. His logic was loopy, propped up by pseudoscience, but he presented it as reality. I never challenged him. It was easier to pretend to believe him.

Early on, he'd made clear that during sexual encounters, I should appear to be enjoying what he did to me or what he made me do to him. "I want bubbly and energetic," he said. "Nobody wants a dead horse." So when he'd ask me questions about my body's response to him—to describe having an orgasm, say—I would do so, even though most times, I had faked it and had to lie. Of course, sometimes there was so much stimulation from vibrators or sex toys, particularly during the orgies that Epstein liked to orchestrate, that I couldn't help but climax. When that happened, it sparked confusing feelings in me, just as it had in my childhood. Did having an orgasm mean I was a willing participant? I suspected that it did, and that only increased my self-loathing.

A pattern was emerging: during my off-hours, I was so eager to forget what was happening with Epstein that I spent most of the time stoned. I told myself I was just "being a normal teenager," but the truth was that I was self-medicating. Usually it was Xanax, but now I was occasionally taking Ecstasy as well. In general, Epstein disapproved of nonprescription drugs, but when I told him that Ecstasy decreased sexual inhibition and increased pleasure—"it made me want to pet anything furry," I said—he pressured me to take it again, but this time in his presence. I remember he was thrilled when, in that day's session, I acted more enthusiastic than usual. But later, after the drug wore off, I felt even more terrible about myself. Flashes of my own lusty, promiscuous behavior kept popping into my mind, and that made me nauseous and humiliated. For those hours at least, I had become the "naughty girl" he'd told me he wanted the first day we met. *What was happening to me?*

One thing that was happening, and with increasing regularity, was that I was being sexually trafficked by Epstein and Maxwell. The second person I was lent out to was a psychology professor whose research Epstein was helping to fund. This time I flew commercial to Saint Thomas, then was ferried by boat to Epstein's island, where the professor met me. He was a quirky little man with a balding pate of white hair, and from his nervous affect, it seemed he wasn't used to being with women. Alone on the island except for a housekeeper, we spent two days riding Jet Skis and hiking and swimming. The man never asked directly for sex, but Epstein had made clear that was what he expected me to provide. "Keep him happy, like you did with your first client," Epstein had said.

So when the professor asked at one point for "one of your famous massages that Jeffrey has told me so much about," I complied, taking him to a cabana and giving him a rubdown that ended with intercourse. We only had sex once, though. The next night, the man told me he wanted to watch movies instead. I showed him how to use the remote control on Epstein's largest TV and how to turn it off when he was done, and I went to bed. I was glad for the night off, but I remember feeling worried that I'd somehow disappointed the professor in a way that he'd share with Epstein.

The psychologist was only the first of many academics from prestigious universities who I was forced to service sexually. I didn't know it then, but Epstein had spent years campaigning to keep company with the world's biggest thinkers and bestselling scientific authors—among them the physicist who discovered the quark, for example, and the computer scientist who consulted with Stanley Kubrick for his iconic film *2001: A Space Odyssey*. At one point, Epstein would even host the theoretical physicist Stephen Hawking, among others, at a symposium organized around the question "What is gravity?" Epstein had convinced himself that he—a college dropout—was on the same level as degree-holding innovators and theoreticians, and because he funded many of their research projects and flew them around on his jets, he was largely welcomed into their fold. Then Epstein offered some of them a bonus: sex with one of us girls. In the coming months, I would be told to service many men whom I'd later learn were illustrious in their fields. On any given night, Epstein would tell me to wait in the massage room until one of these strangers entered, clearly expecting sex.

Scientists weren't the only people Epstein used his vast resources to win access to—which is how I came to be trafficked to a multitude of powerful men. Among them were a gubernatorial candidate who was soon to win election in a Western state and a former US senator. Since Epstein usually neglected to introduce me to these men by name, or introduce them at all, I would only learn who some of them were years later, when I studied photographs of Epstein's associates and recognized the faces of those I was forced to have sex with.

There were several of these men whose names I knew well, however, because they visited Epstein's homes so frequently.

For example, the French modeling agent Jean-Luc Brunel, an old friend of Maxwell's, raped me repeatedly in New York and on Epstein's island. Brunel, who was then in his fifties, was hard to miss—he favored loud clothing in bright colors and polka-dot or paisley prints. Brunel ran MC2, a modeling agency that Epstein had invested in, and he was known not only for preying on the girls he represented but also for providing girls to other men. Epstein liked to boast that he'd had sex with more than a thousand girls supplied by Brunel. On one occasion, Epstein told me, Brunel sent him three French twelve-year-olds—I think they were triplets—for his birthday. Epstein had sex with them, then put them on a plane back to France. On another occasion, Brunel had a group of "talent" scouts fly to Brazil in Epstein's jet to recruit underage girls off the soccer fields there. They were delivered to Epstein for his use and then returned to Brazil.

Epstein and Maxwell, in turn, gave me to Brunel to use again and again. Sometimes we all had sex together. I'll never forgot how Epstein and Brunel looked at one another as they abused girls side by side. They were truly gloating, taking a mutual malignant pleasure in our misfortune.

Once Maxwell and Epstein had started trafficking me to strange men, I often wondered what they stood to gain. One theory is that they trafficked girls to some of their powerful acquaintances in the hope of being owed future favors. My impression of many of these men is that they didn't know how to pursue women. Awkward and socially immature, it was as if their big brains were missing the ability to interact with other people. By giving them obedient girls, Epstein eliminated their need to persuade or entice potential sexual partners, and they were grateful for it. Another theory—which is supported by the fact that Epstein's houses were all outfitted with video cameras in every room—is that he wanted to record men in compromising positions in order to blackmail them later. I don't know if that is true, but I do know that Epstein kept a huge library of videotapes that had been recorded inside his houses. In the Manhattan townhouse, Epstein himself showed me the room in which he monitored and recorded the camera feeds.[*]

It probably goes without saying that, given what my father and his friend Forrest had done to me when I was a child, being trafficked by Epstein and Maxwell was painfully triggering. To the extent that I saw the two of them as pseudo-parental figures, their disregard for my welfare as they lent me out for sex made me feel a familiar strain of worthlessness. But at times that familiarity was weirdly comforting. This is complicated to explain, but that echo of past hurts was somehow bearable to me because I'd felt it—and somehow endured it—so many times before. It was like finding myself once more in a room I'd lived in for years. I hated that room, but I knew its contours—the shape of its windows, the nap of its carpet beneath my feet, the click of the door lock when it was thrown. I knew I could exist in that room

---

[*] To date, no one has come forward to publicly assert that Epstein blackmailed them with a compromising videotape he'd taken in his homes (though of course that doesn't mean it didn't happen). However, in 2023, the *Wall Street Journal* reported that on one occasion, Epstein did attempt to pressure Bill Gates into participating in a multibillion-dollar charity fund he tried to start by threatening to reveal a past extramarital affair. Gates didn't do what Epstein asked. But that report demonstrated for the first time what many have suspected: that Epstein was capable of such manipulation. Meanwhile, another woman who was victimized by Epstein, Lisa Phillips, has stated that she once asked Epstein why he'd encouraged a friend of hers to have sex with Prince Andrew. His response, she recalled: "It's good to have things on people."

because I'd existed there before. At that point, at least, this made me feel less afraid.

I had other complex feelings. Just as I had as a seven-year-old, the seventeen-year-old me wanted praise from my overseers, and I often got it. Returning from trips to service other men, I'd be greeted not only with money but with something I wanted more. "We're proud of you," Epstein would say, and despite my shame and embarrassment, I'd feel something I thought was contentment. That knot of contradictory feelings would take me years to untangle.

THIRTEEN

Life with "Other-Man"

I've said that Epstein seemed to be placing more trust in me. Now he began requiring me to travel more with him alone, without Maxwell or anyone else. On one trip in February 2001, we went to Zorro Ranch, where we saddled up two horses and rode together for hours. I was still his sexual servant, but this trip, in particular, had a familial feeling. I think it was here that Epstein tried to teach me how to drive in a car that had a manual transmission (I say "tried" because my stop-and-go grinding of the clutch scared him to death. He couldn't wait to get out of the vehicle).

From New Mexico, we flew to Carmel-by-the-Sea, California, where Epstein had meetings. At a seaside hotel, we checked into adjoining rooms, as we almost always did. I didn't know it then, but I've figured it out since: Epstein was in town for the so-called Billionaires' Dinner hosted by John Brockman to coincide with the annual TED conference in Monterey. Brockman, whom *Slate* once called "the literary superagent who seems to represent every scientist who's ever written a bestselling book," had become something of a fixer for Epstein, connecting him with scientists who were doing research that Epstein was interested in. Epstein, in turn, donated money to many of those research efforts and to Brockman's nonprofit, The Edge Group, whose stated goal was (and remains): "to arrive at the edge of the world's knowledge, seek out the most complex and sophisticated minds, put them in a room together, and have them ask each other the questions they are asking themselves." Epstein regularly attended Brockman's Billionaires' Dinner at TED, hobnobbing with a who's who of academia, literature, tech, and show business/entertainment.

During the 2001 conference, when Epstein was busy, I wandered around the picturesque European-style village of Carmel-by-the-Sea. The main street was like something out of a fairy tale, with curved-roof cottages and asymmetrical stone chimneys. As I meandered through the shops, I met a beautiful blond girl with a Southern accent who I guessed was in her late teens. She told me she was on a road trip with her best friend, who was sleeping off a hangover. We smoked a joint together as I weighed whether to ask her to meet Epstein. Finally, I came out with it, describing what Epstein was looking for. Instead of taking offense, the girl said she needed the money. I didn't think much about the consequences she'd face if she did my bidding; I just asked her to come to our hotel that afternoon and told her which door to knock on. At the appointed time, she slipped into my room, and I ran her a bath and told her to wait in the tub. When Epstein returned, I brought him to my bathroom and revealed my "big surprise." When he saw the girl, he looked at me with such gratitude that I knew I'd done well. And that was more important to me at that point than any stranger's feelings. While I knew what I was doing was wrong, I focused only on meeting Epstein's needs. For the rest of her life, that girl would have a horrific night to remember, and I am responsible for that.

The next day, Epstein and I continued on to Los Angeles. On this leg of the trip, the cartoonist, animator, and *Simpsons* creator Matthew

LIFE WITH "OTHER-MAN"

Groening hitched a ride with us on Epstein's jet.* I'm not sure how the two had met, although Groening, too, attended Brockman's dinners at times. I just recall that Epstein required me to massage Groening's feet, which were calloused and sweaty and in terrible shape. I did as I was told, as usual, tempering my disgust with the knowledge that I'd now met the genius who'd invented the dysfunctional family—Homer, Marge, Bart, Lisa, and Maggie Simpson—that had helped me survive my own family. Before we touched down, Groening kindly drew me two sketches that I asked him to sign for my little brother and my dad. I never had any sexual contact with Groening. But in due time, Epstein would force me to have sex with at least two other people in Brockman's circle.

In Los Angeles that night, we stayed with a woman Epstein described as a former girlfriend (which I think meant former abuse victim). A tall blond, she lived in an apartment Epstein said he paid for near the beach in Malibu. Epstein and I went out for breakfast the next day, and he told me another person was going to be joining us: a young woman he'd recruited when she was a teenager. I know this woman's name, but out of respect for her privacy, I won't use it here.

She was now in her early twenties and working in California. Epstein implied to me, maybe falsely, that he'd helped her along in her career. So when Epstein was in town, she felt obligated to be available. On this day, Epstein seemed eager to get the two of us alone together. We headed back to Malibu, where he told our host we needed to use her bedroom. Once the three of us were behind closed doors, he directed the scene, with me and this young woman as his costars. He told us how to touch one another and how to touch him, and each of us dutifully played our parts. We were so different—in our looks, in

---
* Thanks to flight logs that have been made public in various court proceedings, we know the exact date of the flight that Matt Groening was on: February 23, 2001.

our origin stories—but Epstein had forced us to be the same: submissive, resigned victims of his abuse.

I don't know how to reconcile this sordid scene with the worldly reputation that Epstein seemed intent on projecting. This was a man who displayed framed photographs of himself with the Dalai Lama, with the pope, and with members of the British royal family. A photo in his Palm Beach house showed Epstein posing behind the podium of the White House briefing room. This was a man who'd had former president Bill Clinton over for dinner (I was at the table that night) and who'd hosted Al and Tipper Gore as well (again, I was there). More than once, I'd been on Little Saint James when Epstein hosted his friend Leslie Wexner, the billionaire founder of L Brands, which owned Victoria's Secret and Abercrombie & Fitch. (Epstein often told girls, falsely, that he was a Victoria's Secret "scout.") Epstein had managed some of Wexner's money at one time, and Wexner was the previous owner of Epstein's lavish Manhattan home, which by some accounts he'd sold to Epstein for one dollar. I'd met all these people because I was in Epstein's orbit. Can you forgive me for wanting to feel that some of their power and importance might rub off on me? If someone as well connected as Epstein thought I had the makings of someone special, as he often said, I wanted to believe he was right.

Sometimes after Epstein had lent me out to someone with a boldface name, he'd reward me with a solo trip to Zorro Ranch. He knew how much I loved to ride the horses there. I think he also knew the place was so remote, there was no way I could escape, even if I'd tried to. During these trips, I stayed in a cottage in Epstein's little town, since the idea of rattling around alone inside his grandiose "castle" scared me. Every morning I'd get up early and head for the stables, choosing a fresh horse and heading out into the open terrain. In winter I could see snowcapped mountains in the distance, and the brisk air was clean and sharp. In summer I marveled at how big the sky

LIFE WITH "OTHER-MAN"

was. At dusk the heat rose from the dusty earth, refracting the light and blurring my vision. It was rare, but in these moments, I could remember what it felt like to be free.

BACK IN FLORIDA, Tony and I developed a shorthand. Instead of "Jeffrey," we called Epstein "Other-Man." We'd hit on the nickname as a joke, but over time, it became less funny. Mostly Tony accepted that my "work" for Other-Man supported our lifestyle, but thinking about the details of what went on between us also made him angry. While I was on trips with Epstein, which often lasted weeks, Tony would act out, throwing parties and trashing my apartment. More than once I caught Tony with other girls. "But a girl in my situation can't be picky," I thought to myself. Most guys wouldn't have put up with sharing their girlfriends with one other man, let alone many. So I took the bad parts of Tony with the good. When we finished out the lease on the Royal Palm Beach apartment, Tony and I rented a small house in Loxahatchee. After sexually servicing men who were three and four times older than me, it was nice to have someone my age to come home to—someone who knew my name.

I had gotten my passport, as Maxwell had commanded, and now she told me we would put it to use. In March 2001, Epstein, Maxwell, Emmy Tayler, and I boarded Epstein's biggest plane—a Boeing 727 that he (and later the news media) liked to call "The Lolita Express"—at the Palm Beach International Airport. The interior of this plane, whose tail number (N908JE) incorporated Epstein's initials, had been retrofitted and bore almost no resemblance to that of a commercial jet. The seating for up to twenty-nine passengers included velvet-upholstered couches and lounge chairs in various earth tones, all arranged in roomy common spaces. Several private cabins, meanwhile, were equipped with queen-size beds.

"Paris, here we come," Maxwell exclaimed merrily once we all were on board.

Epstein owned an eight-thousand-square-foot apartment on Avenue Foch, near the Arc de Triomphe, in the Sixteenth Arrondissement. But it was being renovated, so we stayed in a hotel overlooking the Champs-Élysées. For three days, we saw the sights, visiting the Eiffel Tower and wandering the narrow streets of the Marais. I was beginning to become interested in art history—particularly paintings—and one day Epstein, Maxwell, and I spent hours touring the galleries of the Louvre. Anyone who overheard Epstein lecturing me on the provenance of the tapestries, or who saw how Maxwell hovered close, like a mother hen, surely assumed I was their daughter.

On March 8, the four of us got back on the jet, but this time, we had guests with us: famed interior designer Alberto Pinto, his sister Linda, and the noted Mexican architect Ricardo Legorreta. Epstein had retained Pinto and Legorreta to remodel Zorro Ranch, and we were all headed to Granada, Spain, to tour the Alhambra, one of the best-preserved palaces of the historic Islamic world. For a few hours, we wandered the palace's patios, gardens, and galleries as the designers gathered inspiration for Epstein's project. Then we flew to Morocco and checked into a hotel overlooking the Strait of Gibraltar and the Bay of Tangier: the El Minzah. The place was rated five stars, with bold Spanish-Moorish decor. But when I entered my room, I found that a monkey had crawled through an open window and relieved itself on my bed. Maxwell called housekeeping, and my linens were promptly changed. Still, Maxwell couldn't resist turning the whole incident into a joke. "Maybe you should leave the window ajar tonight," she teased. "That might be the way to find you a husband before you get any older."

It must've been that same afternoon when, against the advice of the concierge, I decided to walk to the village market and take some photographs. I was in Africa, after all, for the first and perhaps last time in my life. It would be a shame if all I saw was the inside of a hotel. As I set out, I'll admit I was taken aback by how many beggars lined the streets. I soon found myself surrounded by children, many of them tugging on the sleeve of my jacket, their palms outstretched. Some were painfully thin, and I could see hunger in their eyes. I turned a corner, and the crowd around me dispersed but for two young boys just ahead of me. They looked like brothers, and as I watched them kicking a tin can back and forth in the street, I was struck by their joyfulness. They were just as skinny as the other kids I'd noticed, and their clothes were dirty. But when I caught up with them, they spoke to me in English, and their enthusiasm and curiosity won me over. I asked them why they weren't in school, and they said their family was too poor to send them. Maybe it was my own regret about quitting school before graduating, but the way they talked made me sad. The boys seemed to accept that kicking a can in a dusty street was all they could hope for. For a second, I was reminded of myself—so used to unacceptable living conditions that I had stopped even hoping for what I lacked. But then I felt guilty about the comparison. How could I feel sorry for myself, a well-fed, well-dressed American who was staying at the El Minzah? Without thinking, I opened my purse and emptied my wallet, pressing nearly two thousand US dollars into the boys' hands. Before saying goodbye, I handed a disposable camera to a passerby so the brothers and I could pose for a photo. (I'd keep that photo for years, until one of my lawyers asked for—and then lost—it.) When I got back to the hotel, Epstein made fun of me for giving so much money away. But it felt good to try to help someone whose circumstances seemed bleaker than mine.

A day later, the architects and designers peeled off, and our original foursome flew from Tangier to London. We arrived late in the afternoon, and Tayler headed off to visit family (her father was a professor at Oxford University). The rest of us went to Maxwell's pied-à-terre—a white mews house in Belgravia, a short walk from Hyde Park. Epstein and Maxwell were going out to dinner, but I begged off, claiming exhaustion. With the house to myself, I took the opportunity to call my parents and was thrilled to find that both my brothers were there. As they passed the phone from person to person, I strived to paint a glowing picture of their adventurous sister, making good money and seeing the world. After I hung up, however, I felt exhausted and empty. It had been hard work to project positivity when at my core I was struggling. Eager to be unconscious, I took a sleeping pill and fell into bed.

The next morning, on March 10, 2001, Maxwell woke me up by announcing in a singsongy voice: "Get out of bed, sleepyhead!" It was going to be a special day, she said. Just like Cinderella, I was going to meet a handsome prince! Her old friend Prince Andrew would be dining with us that night, she said, and we had lots to do to get me ready.

Maxwell and I spent most of that day shopping. She bought me an expensive purse from Burberry and three different outfits. When we got back to her house, I laid them out on the bed. There were two sexy, sophisticated dresses she'd picked out and a third option that I'd lobbied for: a pink V-necked, sleeveless mini-T-shirt and a sparkly, multicolored pair of jeans embroidered with a pattern of interlocking horses. After I showered and dried my hair, I put on the jeans and top, which left a strip of my stomach exposed. Maxwell wasn't thrilled, but like most teenage girls then, I idolized Britney Spears and Christina Aguilera, and the third outfit was something I imagined the two of them might wear. I told Maxwell it felt more like "me."

When Prince Andrew arrived at the townhouse that evening, Maxwell was more coquettish than usual. "Guess Jenna's age," she urged the prince, after she introduced me. The Duke of York, who was then forty-one, guessed correctly: seventeen. "My daughters are just a little younger than you," he told me, explaining his accuracy. As usual,

LIFE WITH "OTHER-MAN"

Maxwell was quick with a joke: "I guess we will have to trade her in soon."

In contrast to his appearance today—stout, white-haired, and jowly—Prince Andrew then was still relatively fit, with short-cropped brown hair and youthful eyes. He'd long been known as the playboy of the royal family, and as a divorcé (he and his wife, Sarah Ferguson, or "Fergie," had split in 1996) he was holding tight to that role. That night he wore slacks and a light-blue dress shirt, open at the collar, with French cuffs, and elegant cufflinks. When I noticed that Epstein called the prince "Andy," I began to call him that too.

As we chatted in Maxwell's entryway, I suddenly thought of something: my mom would never forgive me if I met someone as famous as Prince Andrew and didn't pose for a picture. Excusing myself, I ran to get a Kodak FunSaver from my room, then returned and handed it to Epstein. I remember the prince putting his arm around my waist as Maxwell grinned beside me. Epstein snapped the photo.

After a bit more small talk, the four of us headed out into the cold spring air. The prince rode with his security detail. Epstein, Maxwell, and I were in a separate car. We went to a restaurant for dinner and afterward to an exclusive London nightclub called Tramp. The prince went to the bar and came back with a cocktail for me. Then he invited me to dance. He was sort of a bumbling dancer, and I remember he sweated profusely. I had another drink, and the prince did too. We then headed back to Maxwell's, again in two cars. On the way, Maxwell told me, "When we get home, you are to do for him what you do for Jeffrey." I knew better than to question her orders. That empty feeling descended upon me again. More and more, it felt like my default state.

Back at the house, Maxwell and Epstein said goodnight and headed upstairs, signaling it was time that I take care of the prince. In the years since, I've thought a lot about how he behaved. He was friendly enough, but still entitled—as if he believed having sex with me was his birthright. I took him first to a bathroom, where I drew him a hot bath. We disrobed and got in the tub, but we didn't stay there long because the prince was eager to get to the bed. He was particularly attentive to my feet, caressing my toes and licking my arches. That was a first for me, and it tickled. I was nervous he would want me to do the same to him. But I needn't have worried. He seemed in a rush to have intercourse. Afterward, he said thank you in his clipped British accent. In my memory, the whole thing lasted less than half an hour.

The next morning, it was clear that Maxwell had conferred with her royal chum because she told me: "You did well. The prince had fun." I nodded appreciatively, as I always did, but in truth, I didn't feel so great. Soon, Epstein would give me $15,000 for servicing the man the tabloids called "Randy Andy"—a lot of money. But while being pimped out to strangers was something I thought I had to endure and had even become used to, it was wearing me down.

When I was sure I couldn't be overheard, I called Tony and told him what had happened. I hadn't wanted to have sex with the prince, I said, but I felt I had to. Our livelihoods depended on it, for one thing, but I also truly believed there was no way for me to free myself from Epstein and Maxwell's grip. While traveling, Maxwell had made me hand over my passport. That night Tony's voice sounded worried. He was scared that I was alone in a foreign country with people so powerful; he said he understood why I felt powerless. Less than four years earlier, Lady Diana had died in a car accident, prompting some conjecture (never proven) that the royal family had somehow been involved. Tony and I had no way of knowing if this was true, but we were sure that I was surrounded by people who wielded vastly more clout than I ever would. After a few more minutes of trying to soothe each other's paranoia, we said goodnight—but not before Tony and I agreed that, especially while I was abroad, I needed to keep Epstein and Maxwell happy.

LIFE WITH "OTHER-MAN"

After we returned to Florida, I took my FunSaver cameras to a one-hour photo developer near my house in West Palm Beach. Thanks to the store's system of marking the back of each print, I can tell you exactly the date I first held the image of me, Prince Andrew, and Maxwell in my hands: March 13, 2001. I showed the four-by-six-inch photo to Tony. At the time, we were both just glad I'd made it home in one piece; we had no idea what a commotion this photo would later cause.

FOURTEEN

Puppets on a String

My second encounter with Prince Andrew took place about a month later, at Epstein's townhouse in New York. By this point, I knew the place well. Its garish decor seemed intended to intimidate, with black-lacquered cabinetry, bloodred carpets, a huge taxidermied tiger, and a custom-made chess set whose pieces were scantily clad women. To me, though, the house's most unsettling design detail was a hidden back staircase whose banister was adorned with a series of carved eyeballs that stared at you as you gripped them, climbing up or down. The message was clear: "We're always watching you."

On this night, which was probably around April 2001, Epstein greeted Prince Andrew and brought him to the living room, where Maxwell and I were sitting. Another one of their victims, Johanna Sjoberg, arrived soon afterward. As always when the prince was around, Maxwell was being a saucy flirt. She told Sjoberg to come with her to a closet, where she pulled out a puppet with a little tag on it that said "Prince Andrew." Maxwell then announced to the prince that she'd purchased him a joke gift, a puppet that looked just like him. She made a big show of giving it to him, then suggested we pose for a photo with it. The prince and I sat down next to each other on the couch, and Maxwell put the puppet in my lap, positioning one of its hands on one of my breasts. Then she put Sjoberg on the prince's lap, and the prince put his hand on Sjoberg's breast. The symbolism was impossible to ignore. Johanna and I were Maxwell and Epstein's puppets, and they were pulling the strings. Later they sent me to a bedroom, where I had sex with the prince for a second time.

As compliant as I was, I have a memory from this period that indicates I was beginning, ever so slightly, to resist. It was nighttime in the Caribbean, and Epstein and I were on one of his boats, having just picked up Sarah Kellen in Saint Thomas. The air was warm and the darkness complete, pierced only by tiny twinkling lights. It would have been peaceful except that as we motored back to Little Saint James, Kellen insisted on blaring music from the onboard CD player. She cued up the song she was looking for—Santana and Rob Thomas's "Smooth"—and started dancing suggestively around Epstein. "Come on! Dance with me!" she told me, pulling me up off the captain's chair where I was sitting. Suddenly, I wanted to shove her overboard. I didn't want to dance for Epstein. I didn't want Kellen to give me orders. Since I'd met Epstein in the summer of 2000, my anger had gone missing. Not anymore. Now the lyrics to "Smooth"—a song I'd once liked—filled me with rage: "If you said this life ain't good enough / I would give my world to lift you up / I could change my life to better suit your mood." I got up and danced because I could see Epstein wanted me to, and I didn't want to invite his wrath by disobeying him. But inside, I was seething. Day and night, my every waking moment was circumscribed by his wants and needs. I was caught in the trap of familiar diminishment. But still, something about Epstein's hold on me kept me docile and acquiescent.

In May 2001, Epstein, Maxwell, and I flew to the French Riviera to attend the model Naomi Campbell's thirty-first birthday party, which was being held on a yacht. That night I wore the same outfit I'd worn when I first met Prince Andrew—the shiny jeans emblazoned with horses, the tight-fitting pink top. All evening, I felt like a stowaway on that crowded boat in Saint-Tropez. For her part, the birthday girl ignored me, and her white-haired boyfriend Flavio Briatore, an Italian businessman and convicted con man, looked old enough to be my grandpa. Conscious that I was one or two decades younger than everyone else, I lowered my eyes and tried to blend in.

It could have been after this party that a friend of Epstein's—I'll call him Billionaire Number Two—caught a ride with us back to La Bastide de Saint-Tropez, the five-star mansion-turned-hotel surrounded by four Provençal farmhouses where we were all staying. On the way, Epstein made it clear that he wanted me to give this fifty-year-old stranger with thinning brown hair a "massage," so when we arrived, I accompanied the man to his cottage. Hoping that I could get away with merely a rubdown, I used my most professional-sounding therapeutic voice and instructed him to undress and lie under a towel. But Epstein must have briefed him about what he could expect, because Billionaire Number Two ignored my instructions and began to undress me. "You really can't give a massage wearing this outfit, sweetie," he said.

After we had intercourse, the man offered to pay me triple what Epstein paid me if I'd come "work" for him. I politely said no and said my goodbyes, returning to Epstein's room, as he'd instructed me to. When I told him about Billionaire Number Two's offer, Epstein was fascinated.

"That's good money. How could you decline?" Epstein asked, amused.

I responded with my own question: "Who would look after you, if I were gone?"

I'll never forget how he gazed at me that night. I wanted to believe he adored me. But what he adored was my loyalty to him. And I was so invested in my role as his caretaker that I told myself he was loyal to me too.

I see now that this was a fantasy, but it was one that Epstein encouraged. For example, he never hesitated to give me advice about my tumultuous relationship with Tony, whom he insisted wasn't good enough for me. One day, after I'd had a fight with Tony, I was giving Epstein a massage when he raised his head off the table and told me: "You know it's not good to massage people when you're angry. Too much negative energy." I hesitated as I tried to evaluate what he meant. Was he just admonishing me, or was he curious why I was upset? Unsure, I tearfully told him Tony had cheated on me again. Epstein paused, and for a second I thought he was going to console me. But instead he laughed. "You can't hold that against him," he said matter-of-factly. "He's only doing what every guy in the world does." I must have looked crestfallen, because he kept talking, taking on the professorial tone that he often used with me. "I'm on your side, which is why I'm going to save you a lot of grief with this one tip," he said. "Never expect a man to be faithful, and you'll never be let down. It's just the way men are genetically imprinted." Then he lowered his head back into the face cradle, and I spent the remainder of the massage even sadder than before. That was classic Epstein: he liked to assert that he was "enlightening" me, making me better by teaching me the ways of the world.

I DON'T KNOW exactly when I had sex with Prince Andrew for the third time, but I do know the location: Little Saint Jeff's. I also know that it was not just the two of us this time; it was an orgy. "I was around eighteen," I said in a sworn declaration in 2015. "Epstein,

Andy, and approximately eight other young girls, and I had sex together. The other girls all seemed and appeared to be under the age of eighteen and didn't really speak English. Epstein laughed about how they couldn't really communicate, saying they are the easiest girls to get along with."

Since I gave that account, the pilot David Rodgers has said in a deposition that a coded notation ("AP") that he made on his flight log for July 4, 2001, referred to Prince Andrew. He said that Epstein, the prince, another woman, and I flew from Saint Thomas that day back to Palm Beach. I guess it's possible that the orgy I remember occurred in the days leading up to that flight, which would mean I was still seventeen. I'll probably never know the date for certain. What I do know, because Epstein told me, is that Brunel, the French modeling agent who was also in attendance, supplied the other girls who took part.

Just four days after Independence Day, on July 8, 2001, Epstein, Maxwell, Tayler, a few others, and I flew from Palm Beach to Teterboro Airport, just outside New York City. I wasn't in great shape. For three weeks, I'd had irregular bleeding, but had tried to ignore it. Now that we were back in New York, I began feeling a tenderness in my abdomen. I lay down for a nap, and must've fallen asleep, because the next thing I knew, I woke up in a pool of blood. Sharp waves of pain racked my body as I crawled to the intercom, screaming that I needed help. I remember Jojo, the butler at the Manhattan townhouse, was so kind, helping me down the stairs as Epstein and Maxwell got a car to take me to New York–Presbyterian Hospital. When we arrived at the emergency room, though, Epstein took charge, lying that my birthdate was in 1982 (I was born in 1983), so I would appear to be eighteen. I was admitted and given some sort of pain medicine, and things got blurry after that. I remember a doctor asking me questions, and when I described my stabbing pain, he wondered if I had polycystic ovary syndrome, which can be painful when the cysts burst. I have hazy memories of my feet in the stirrups, of white papery gowns and bright lights. I also remember Epstein was in the examination room with me, and before the doctor left to write up his notes at one point, Epstein intercepted him. The two men talked quietly in the doorway, serious looks on both their faces, then Epstein sent the doctor away. My sense was that a gentlemen's agreement had been struck between Epstein and the doctor: whatever was going on between this middle-aged man and his teenage acquaintance, the two men seemed to have agreed, it would be kept quiet.

This would be one of many doctors' visits, the specifics of which I tried to blot out. After being used by Epstein and his pals, my body was often in agony. But just as in my childhood, when my frequent urinary tract infections led to countless uncomfortable examinations, in the hospital it was as if my mind protected me by shutting down. That and the fact that I was heavily sedated have always made it difficult to know precisely what happened. Besides, the doctors at New York–Presbyterian talked to Epstein more than to me.

It was only after I was discharged a couple of days later and Jojo ferried us back to Seventy-First Street that I began to piece things together. I had a tiny incision near my belly button, which one of the other girls in the house told me was consistent with a laparoscopic surgery for an ectopic pregnancy. But Epstein told me I'd suffered a miscarriage, which is something altogether different. I've seen the medical records since, and they don't contain the word "miscarriage." They note severe cramping and weight loss ("7 lbs this month"), as well as that I'd reported having sex with the same partner for two years, but they don't definitively describe all I went through. The one thing I remember clearly is that, at one point, a doctor told me I might never be able to have children.

I've already said that Epstein never wore a condom. Neither did the men he and Maxwell trafficked me to. I made Tony wear a condom, at Epstein's insistence, and I was on the pill. But I must have missed a day. After my hospital visit, I had to come to terms with the fact that I had gotten pregnant and lost a fetus without even knowing it was happening. That made me feel even more numb. But there would be no time for grieving. In Maxwell and Epstein's world, the party never stopped.

IN THE YEARS since, doctors and healers who I have consulted have suggested that my body—having withstood so much sexual trauma—was staging a kind of revolt. That idea makes sense to me, especially because around this time Epstein was inventing new ways to abuse me. He'd become interested in sadomasochism, and he didn't care who knew it. When a *Vanity Fair* reporter paid a visit to his Manhattan townhouse, he left a paperback copy of the Marquis de Sade's *The Misfortunes of Virtue* out on his desk for her to see. But he wasn't just reading about it. He'd begun to experiment with whips and restraints and other instruments of torture. At that time, I was the only one of his girls, so far as I knew, whom he subjected to this cruel torment. In session after session, he would play out various fantasies, with me as the victim. I was gagged, and often hog-tied. Epstein liked to put a black leather, metal-studded collar around my neck that continued down my spine, where it attached to a chain that bound my hands and feet tightly together. The backbreaking contortions this contraption forced upon me caused so much pain that I prayed I would black out. When I did, I'd awaken to more abuse.

In the midst of all this, Epstein bought a ticket for me to see a Broadway play: *The Phantom of the Opera*. I'd never been to the theater before, and I was stunned not just by the spectacle but by how much the phantom reminded me of Epstein. A brilliant scholar, magician, architect, inventor, and composer, the Phantom had been born with a deformed face. I'll never forget the scene when he forces a young girl he has abducted to put on a wedding dress. The girl explains that she fears not his physical appearance but rather his inner nature. Even today, when I hear Andrew Lloyd Webber's song "Think of Me," I think of Epstein, the twisted monster who essentially abducted me. Thinking about an imagined future when his prisoner has broken free, the Phantom sings, "Long ago, it seems so long ago / How young and innocent we were / She may not remember me, but I remember her."

I had descended into a deeper level of hell.

As we moved into autumn, the world was going crazy. On September 11, terrorist attacks on the World Trade Center towers shook every American to his or her core. But even before that, I had begun to fall apart. My grandma Shelley had fallen ill, and while I'd managed to see her in Florida right before she died at the end of August, I felt guilty that my obligations to Epstein had long ago turned me into an absentee granddaughter. In October, Maxwell flew up to New York City to host a dinner party for Prince Andrew, who was visiting the United States for the first time since 9/11. Epstein and I stayed behind in Palm Beach, I remember, and that's when he pulled me aside and said he'd noticed how strung out I seemed. There were dark circles under my eyes, and my ribs were visible beneath my skin. I told him I wasn't sleeping well. I'd added cocaine to the drugs I was taking, and that wasn't helping any. Epstein looked disgusted; he said my drug abuse had become unacceptable. He'd always demanded that his regular girls be cheerful and appear to desire him. Me, I was dead-eyed and listless.

"You're not the same girl you were," Epstein said coldly. "You need to clean yourself up." I didn't argue. He said he was going on a trip. "I'll call you next time I'm in town," he said. Then he sent me home.

All I felt was relief, at least at first. This was my chance for a new life, and I tried to treat it as such. I had invested the money Epstein paid me in a car of my own, a used Dodge Dakota pickup truck with a great stereo system, so for the first time I could get myself around. That was good because I needed to make money: Epstein had stopped paying my bills.

I worked briefly in an animal hospital, trying to make good on my childhood vow to learn what it took to become a veterinarian. But I was a mess. I got there late and made up excuses. They fired me. Chastened, I got my first waitressing gig, and while that restaurant didn't keep me on for long, the experience I gained made it easier to find another job. Little by little, the drugs I'd been numbing myself with left my system, and I began to feel more like the old Jenna. At the same time, though, a nagging feeling of worthlessness remained. Amid the awfulness, Epstein's praise had been my main source of self-esteem for so long. Even though I needed the break he had given me, I felt ashamed that I'd caused him to think ill of me.

Tony and I made a vow: we would go back to school. We enrolled at the aptly named Survivors Charter, a place aimed at older students who wanted to get their high school diplomas. I hoped having a common goal would help Tony and me improve our fraught relationship. But if that had ever been possible, I soon found out that it was no longer. Tony had gotten caught more than once stealing everything from DVDs to his brother's truck. I suspected drugs were driving his kleptomania, and at one point, I threw him out, only to take him back in a few weeks later. We were both fighting to control our worst impulses, even as we tried to support each other. But we were unraveling.

In November 2001, my old tormentor Ron Eppinger—who'd pleaded guilty to charges of "smuggling aliens" to the United States for purposes of prostitution—finally received his sentence: twenty-one months in prison, a $6,000 fine, and the forfeiture of a boat and the limousine he'd used to promote his call-girl service. To my mind, Eppinger had gotten off easy. Not that I was surprised. Less than three years had passed since he'd first picked me up in that limo, but it felt like forever. And everything that had happened to me in Epstein's world had only confirmed that certain privileged men existed in a liminal space outside the law, no matter how dastardly their behavior.

During this period, Epstein was keeping busy. Flight logs would later show that he and Sarah Kellen flew to Ohio to attend the funeral of Leslie Wexner's mother, Bella. But while I was unaware of that trip at the time, there was one thing I had figured out: I'd been naive to believe Epstein's claim that I was his special "Number One." Given how abruptly Epstein had sent me packing, and that he hadn't reached out since, it was clear that he was doing just fine without me. In a weird, complicated way, that hurt.

Still, as time passed, those feelings of rejection were replaced by a tentative surge of optimism. No, I wasn't flying on Epstein's jets anymore. I was too busy waitressing for five dollars an hour (plus tips) at T.G.I. Friday's. And that was okay. Even as I faced how disposable I'd been, I was finding ways to establish my own value outside Epstein's world. My older brother, Danny, was about to get married to a great woman named Lanette, and I was happy that I would be able to attend their ceremony. Had I still been on call 24/7 for Epstein and Maxwell, there's no way I could have guaranteed that. After T.G.I. Friday's, I did a few shifts at a restaurant called Mannino's, then I got a full-time gig at a place called Roadhouse Grill. I liked my colleagues and enjoyed how my ability to read customers' wants and needs translated into generous tips.

Then one night after my shift in March 2002, Tony—who'd borrowed my Dodge truck—came to the Roadhouse Grill to pick me up. As he sat at the bar waiting for me, he noticed the jar that held the tip money that the waitstaff had pooled throughout the night. When no one was looking, he helped himself. I had no idea. I clocked out and we went home.

The next day, my boss called and accused me of stealing. I said I hadn't done it, but with a heavy heart I suspected I knew who had. I begged my boss to take what was missing out of my next check, and when he said no, I went over the next day and paid the money back. But still he told me I was fired and that he'd called the police. I was terrified I would be arrested. That's when Epstein called me to check in. His timing was uncanny—eerie even—and almost made me believe he was as all-knowing as he liked to brag that he was. "Come for lunch," he said. "I want to see you." When I arrived, he looked me over, evaluating whether I was still using drugs. Only when he was satisfied that I was clean did he ask me how I was doing. I burst into tears. The tip jar at work, I told him, my words pouring out of me—Tony had emptied it and gotten me fired. What if the police came for us both? Epstein had never approved of Tony, but he said he could easily get the police to back off. He had one condition, however: I had to return to El Brillo Way.

I had no job. My boyfriend was a screwup. So when Epstein turned and led me to the massage room, I followed him. That was all it took. I was back under his thumb.

FIFTEEN

A Bridge Too Far

Epstein once told me that every girl he'd had sex with had benefited in one of three ways: either he gave them money to better their lives or he helped jump-start their career or he married them off to one of his successful friends. All the girls in Epstein's household knew, for example, that in 1994 a former girlfriend of Epstein's—a woman in her twenties—married another man in his social circle. (Several of us had met this man.) More than once, Epstein had brought up his ex-girlfriend's marriage to this man as proof of his largesse, as if he'd arranged it. He told me he'd be willing to do the same sort of matchmaking for me. When he said this, he clearly believed that what he was offering me was a life-changing gift. He clung to the idea that, at his core, he was a generous benefactor. Meanwhile, he also fantasized about improving the human race by fathering children who carried his "superior" genes. Sometimes he'd talk about his plans to use his Zorro Ranch as a literal breeding ground to propagate babies. Who would birth these imagined offspring? The girls he kept in his orbit, of course, and he thought we'd see it as an honor.

Maxwell was a different animal—selfish, certainly, but more fragile than Epstein. Especially after she turned forty, on Christmas Day 2001, the insecurities that lurked under the surface of her outgoing persona emerged. A blazing beauty when she was young, Maxwell was still attractive. But her short haircut—while provocatively stylish for a woman of twenty or so—looked a bit haggard on someone twice that age. Increasingly, it was as if Maxwell was trying too hard. While she still prided herself on being the matron of Epstein's house, she seemed to chafe, more and more, at being seen as matronly.

After I returned to the fold, she started to take these frustrations out on me in brutal new ways. I'd always believed her when she said she wasn't possessive of Epstein and didn't care whom he had sex with. Now, though, she seemed fiercely jealous of anyone to whom Epstein showed affection. Maxwell was a lot of things—glamorous, captivating, boldly sexual in a way that many men found alluring. But she was not a nurturer, and I think she and Epstein could both see that I was. "You have a very maternal instinct," he'd said to me more than once, and now he immediately resumed our nightly tuck-in routine. In response, Maxwell began lashing out at me during our threesomes. For example, she would grab a larger-than-life-size dildo and use it to hurt me. If I complained, she hurt me more. For some time now, she'd teased me that soon I'd be too old for Epstein. If I—an eighteen-year-old—was too mature for him, she had to know that he saw her as downright ancient.

But while her motivations were unkind, Maxwell was right to warn me about the implications of getting older. In the context of Epstein's world, if I wanted to glimpse my future, all I had to do was look at Sarah Kellen. For a few years before I'd met her, she'd serviced Epstein sexually, or so I'd been told. But as she entered her early twenties, she'd aged out and was forced into a new phase of servitude: recruiting others. My sense of guilt about the times I'd recruited girls had been steadily growing. Now I began to worry that if I stayed with Epstein and Maxwell much longer, I'd soon be like Kellen, responsible for luring an unending parade of young girls into a situation that I knew would damage them forever.*

If there was one thing I knew about, it was damage—the lasting reverberation of past trauma. I had been trafficked to dozens of men by this point, and I remembered their faces clearly. There were old men and even older men; nerdy, shy men and boorish, arrogant men. There were men who wanted me to wear outfits and men who wanted to see me naked and men who didn't notice if I was clothed, as long as I touched them. There were men who couldn't get or maintain erections. There were men who behaved as if I were lucky to be with them. There was at least one man who ignored me as I serviced him sexually, preferring instead to focus his eyes upon, and even to fondle, Epstein. Some men seemed grateful for my attention, particularly the septuagenarians, many of whom thanked me afterward, calling me "a good girl." While I appreciated that these ancient men were less brutish than others, I still felt sick when they said that. Their words made it undeniably clear that for them, my childlike appearance was part of my sexual appeal. It is truly impossible to say how many men there were, in part because I didn't keep count, and in part because my interactions with many of them were so similar. Still, I was expected to make all the men happy, even though doing so made me miserable.

Just when I thought things couldn't get worse for me, they did: Epstein trafficked me to a man who raped me more savagely than anyone had before. We were on Epstein's island when I was ordered to take this man to a cabana. Immediately it was clear that this man,

---

* Kellen would later claim that she, too, was a victim of Epstein's. But at Ghislaine Maxwell's trial, Kellen was identified by victims as having booked them for "massages" with Epstein. And at Maxwell's sentencing in 2022, Judge Alison Nathan named Kellen as "a knowing participant in the criminal conspiracy."

whom I've taken pains to describe in legal filings only as a former minister, wasn't interested in caresses. He wanted violence. He repeatedly choked me until I lost consciousness and took pleasure in seeing me in fear for my life. Horrifically, this man laughed when he hurt me and got more aroused when I begged him to stop. I emerged from the cabana bleeding from my mouth, vagina, and anus. For days, it hurt to breathe and to swallow.

Afterward, I tearfully begged Epstein not to send me back to him. I got down on my knees and pleaded with him. I don't know if Epstein feared the man or if he owed him a favor, but he wouldn't make any promises, saying coldly of the politician's brutality, "You'll get that sometimes."

Today I know that Epstein liked to tell friends that women were merely "a life-support system for a vagina." I didn't know that then. Today I know that Epstein made the following chilling distinction: "I'm not a sexual predator; I'm an 'offender.' It's the difference between a murderer and person who steals a bagel." I didn't know that then either. Today I see how little he cared about the girls and women he abused. But for a long time, I couldn't see it. Or maybe I didn't want to see it. My experience being brutalized by the former minister—and the way Epstein glossed over it—changed that for me.

Before the minister's attack, Epstein had me fooled. I thought that Epstein's predilection for childlike girls was a sickness, but that in his twisted way he meant well. After the attack, I couldn't stay a fool. Having been treated so brutally and then seeing Epstein's callous reaction to how terrorized I felt, I had to accept that Epstein meted out praise merely as a manipulation to keep me subservient. Epstein cared only about Epstein.

At that point, I hit bottom. I now knew I wouldn't survive. I saw only two possible options: either someone Epstein trafficked me to would kill me or I would take my own life. About eight weeks or so after my encounter with the former minister, Epstein informed me, as he often did, that he wanted me to service an important friend on one of his jets. Epstein told me what time to be at the private airport in Palm Beach and said I'd only be up in the air for an hour. Taking him at his word, I got Tony and some of his friends to drive me there, then asked them to stay and wait until I returned. I had no idea who I was meeting that day as I climbed the stairs that led to the plane. Then I ducked my head and stepped inside.

"Hello again," said the minister, the man I feared more than any other.

The blood rushed to my head, and I could barely breathe. "Will he kill me this time?" I wondered, and for a dizzy moment, I thought I might faint. The pilot discreetly closed the door to the cockpit, and we took off. For the next hour, I was on high alert, braced for a fatal blow. As it turned out, this second encounter with the former minister was more typical of those I'd had with other men—his only goal was ejaculation. Still, it was the longest sixty minutes of my life as I anticipated the minister once again injuring and asphyxiating me. When the airplane touched down, I emerged in a daze, stumbling back to the car where Tony and his friends were waiting.

I didn't know it then, but my second interaction with the former minister was the beginning of the end for me. My behavior began to change. I'd bump into a beautiful young stranger in my favorite bookstore, realize she'd be perfect for Epstein, and then intentionally leave without getting her number. A new sense of agency was taking hold inside me. While I couldn't yet save myself, at least I could spare one girl at a time.

Then, sometime in the summer of 2002, Maxwell and Epstein pushed me past my breaking point. The three of us had spent an afternoon snorkeling in the shallow reefs around Epstein's island. As we dried off on the dock, I noticed Epstein share a glance with Maxwell before he sat down next to me. He put his hand on my back—a fond gesture that was rare for him. "I hope you know how much I appreciate you for embracing my lifestyle," he began, as Maxwell cozied up next to me too. "Over the past several months, you've shown me a devotion that is difficult to find. The friends I've introduced you to agree: you are a delightful young woman." He took a breath, and I wondered where all this was going. Then he came out with it: "Jenna, I want you to have our baby."

Though I'd heard him talk hypothetically about seeding the human race with his DNA, his proposal shocked me. I remember trying not to flinch as Maxwell joined in with the financial particulars. "You'd have round-the-clock nannies to help you," she said, her voice oddly chirpy. "Jeffrey would buy you a mansion in Palm Beach or New York—your choice!—and you would have a hefty allowance." If memory serves, she floated the astronomical figure of $200,000 per month. But then came the conditions: like a modern-day handmaid, I would have to sign over to Epstein and Maxwell all legal rights to the child. I would have to travel with the child wherever and whenever Epstein wanted. I would have to attest, in writing, that Epstein and I were not a couple, and that the baby would remain with him if we ever had "a falling out." That's how Maxwell put it, as if it were conceivable that the end of Epstein's and my relationship might ever be a mutually-agreed-upon parting. That was laughable to me. Everybody knew that Epstein was the one who ended his relationships with young girls—never the other way around.

Up to that point, the idea of having kids had been a distant dream. I still felt like a child myself sometimes, so it was hard to imagine being a mom. Given what that doctor had told me the year before, I wasn't even sure I could get pregnant again, let alone carry a baby to term.

But still, everything about Epstein and Maxwell's brazen request felt wrong. There was no way I wanted to bring a child into the world for them to raise. What if the baby were female? Was the plan for Epstein and Maxwell to have me bring that little girl up until she reached puberty, then hand her over for them to abuse? I wanted no part of it. Epstein and Maxwell had made so many demands that I had met, ignoring my own feelings in the hope of pleasing them. But this proposal would endanger another person: a helpless child. It was a bridge too far.

Today I'm sad that I found it easier to stand up for an as-yet-to-be-conceived baby than for myself. With perfect clarity, I simply knew that I couldn't agree to their proposal. That said, I also knew I couldn't just tell Epstein and Maxwell no. That was too dangerous. For the first time in more than two years, I began actively seeking a way to escape, buying time by pretending to think over their offer. After a few days, I came up with at least part of a plan. I told the two of them that, yes, I'd have their baby, but first I hoped they would deliver on the promise they'd dangled in front of me the first day we met. At long last, would they help me get formally trained as a masseuse? I politely asked them to consider it.

It was just before my nineteenth birthday when I got my answer. We were on Epstein's island again when Epstein gestured for me to sit on his lap. "First of all, happy birthday," he said, his face close to mine. "We know how hard you've worked, and we agree you deserve something special. So, we are sending you to Thailand." I must have looked confused—I'd assumed if Epstein agreed to get me trained, it would happen somewhere closer to home. But Epstein said that Maxwell had found a school in Chiang Mai, in the northern part of the country, where I could get certified in Thai massage in just eight weeks. I started to thank him, but he wasn't finished.

"Just one more thing," Epstein said. "While you are in Chiang Mai, I will need you to get to know a particular girl." He told me her name—it sounded Thai to me—and said if I thought she met his criteria, he would have her flown to the United States. "So even when I'm far away, I'll still be recruiting?" I asked myself silently. At the same time, though, I realized this might be my only chance for an exit and I'd be crazy not to seize it. So I smiled and gave him a warm hug. It was important to make Epstein and Maxwell believe I was on their side.

Over the next few weeks, Maxwell arranged for me to attend the International Training Massage School, which had a reputation as one of the best centers for the study of Northern-style Thai massage. She bought me a coach ticket and reserved me a room at the Dusit Royal Princess, a four-star hotel. Epstein paid the bill in advance.

I was sent home to Florida to pack and say my goodbyes. By this point, Tony and I had moved in with his parents, so I spent most of my time there, trying to decide what to put in storage and what I should try to carry with me. While I didn't know what the future held, I sensed that I should take with me anything I couldn't live without. I also visited my parents, and my brother Danny and his new wife, Lanette, came to see me off. I remember I took Skydy—then fourteen—aside and told him I'd always be there for him. For those few days, I pretended I was a normal girl preparing for an exotic vacation, not a prisoner plotting her escape.

In mid-September 2002, Epstein and Maxwell arranged for me to return to New York; I'd continue on to Thailand, solo, from there. On the morning my commercial flight was leaving Miami for New York City, I said one last goodbye to my dog, Mary-Jane, and then Tony and I loaded my many suitcases into my Dodge truck. I've never been a light packer, but this time I was even heavier than usual. My luggage held every memento and photo that was important to me. We wrestled my many bags out of the truck, which I was letting Tony use in my absence, and he helped me haul everything to the ticket counter. Luggage finally checked, we headed for security. That's when I broke down, weeping. Tony was mystified. Hadn't I been away for several weeks before? What was making me so emotional? I couldn't explain it, even to myself, but I had an inkling that I wouldn't be coming back. I hugged Tony tighter than I ever had that day and told him how much I'd miss him. "Take care of the pup," I said, as I always did when I was jetting off somewhere with Epstein. Tony said he would, and I gave him one last kiss, then walked away.

For the next several days in Manhattan, Epstein and Maxwell put me to work training Epstein's new "assistant": a Czech beauty named Nadia Marcinkova, who he said would be filling in for me while I was away. Marcinkova was about three years younger than me—the same age I'd been when I'd first met Epstein—and he required that she and I "massage" him together, much like Maxwell and I had done back in 2000. "Follow Jenna's lead," Epstein told Nadia that first session. I could see how hungrily he looked at her then, and this stirred up some feelings in me. All those stories I'd told myself about being needed, about mattering, about being the only one who could take care of him—all that was so obviously untrue. As much as I wanted to disappear from Epstein's life, it stung to be so easily replaced.

On September 21, Epstein and Maxwell were leaving New York on an extended trip to Africa. Marcinkova was flying with them on Epstein's Boeing 727, as were several high-profile guests: the actors Chris Tucker and Kevin Spacey and former president Clinton, not to mention six US Secret Service agents. (Clinton has said the trip was a humanitarian mission that included stops related to the work of his foundation.) Before they left, Maxwell sat me down for a serious chat. Once I landed in Chiang Mai, she said, I needed to immediately track down the Thai girl Epstein was interested in. Maxwell wanted to hear from me regularly about my progress on that. She handed me my travel documents, which included locations of Western Union offices where she'd be wiring me money. I still have the envelope all this came in. On the outside, Maxwell had written the name of the Thai girl and two phone numbers: her own cell phone and that of Jojo, Epstein's New York butler. "CALL MS. MAXWELL!" she commanded, in all capital letters.

"See you in two months," Epstein said before he and Maxwell left. I nodded, and as the door shut behind them, I felt a mix of elation and tension. Freedom like this was rare for girls in Epstein's orbit, but in truth, I felt I'd been trapped since the age of seven. Run. Survive. Run. Survive. That had been my rhythm even before I met Jeffrey and Ghislaine. After more than two years, I was about to break out of the gilded cage they had built for me. Now I just had to keep them from putting me back in it.

Six days later, I boarded a commercial jet headed for Bangkok, buckled my seat belt, and closed my eyes. Everybody knew that Epstein was the one who ended his relationships with young girls—never the other way around. I knew that too. But there's a first time for everything.

Part III

SURVIVOR

Have I been wrong, have I been wise
To shut my eyes and play along
Hypnotized, paralyzed by what my eyes have found

—Natalie Merchant, "Carnival"

SIXTEEN

The Land of Smiles

Picture a wisp of a woman with long blond hair that falls around her face. She is nineteen years old and is traveling abroad by herself for the very first time. She doesn't want to bother you, but will you please take her photograph? She seems friendly, like she would do the same for you. Chances are, you say yes.

She hands you her pocket-size disposable camera. Before boarding a plane to Southeast Asia, this teenager made sure to stock up on Kodak FunSavers, which she tries always to carry with her. Each one has just twenty-seven exposures inside, and she's vowed to use them wisely. Given her situation, it seems smart to conserve resources.

Very few photos exist of Jenna Roberts during this time. But maybe that is as it should be. After all, didn't I come to Chiang Mai to disappear? Later, though, I will wish I'd done more to memorialize this period of my life. During the years I'd spent with Epstein and Maxwell, I'd visited many places people write guidebooks about: London, Paris, Tangiers. But I had a feeling this trip to Southeast Asia would be more meaningful, and I was right. What happened in Thailand would set my life on an entirely new course.

THERE'S SOMETHING ABOUT being up in the air, especially when traveling solo. It's as if the world below ceases to be, and to me that is a relief. No one can touch me. I decide when to sleep, when to eat. My own needs—no one else's—come first. During my twenty-one-hour journey from New York to Singapore and then on to Bangkok and finally Chiang Mai, I wasn't used to these feelings of independence, but I enjoyed them. By my third and final flight, I was tired, but there was no sleeping now. My body was humming, as if jolted by electricity. Could it really be that, at least for the moment, I was free?

I had read that my destination city was surrounded by mountains, so I craned my neck to try to catch a glimpse of them out the window: Chiang Dao to the north, Mae Kampong to the east, and Doi Inthanon—Thailand's highest peak—to the west. Then we touched down, and I spent the next half hour corralling my six overstuffed suitcases. Finally, a taxi delivered me and my luggage to my hotel. I checked in, and a porter unlocked the door of No. 923, leading me into a spacious room with two queen-size beds. Floor-to-ceiling windows looked out on a shimmering swimming pool. I tipped the smiling porter, and he nodded and closed the door. It was still daytime, but I needed to be unconscious. I closed the curtains and crawled into bed.

I wish I could tell you that a few hours later, I awoke, grabbed a FunSaver, and headed out into the sunshine to explore this exotic new place. Instead, my first two days in Chiang Mai I stayed put, eating fried rice and French fries I ordered from room service and waiting for the phone to ring. Just as in that creepy fifth-floor bedroom in Epstein's Manhattan townhouse, I felt as if I were on call and would be punished if I failed to answer. I know that probably sounds ridiculous. There was no one there to reprimand me. Still, I'd lived by Epstein and Maxwell's rules for more than two years. When Maxwell called to check in, I picked up before the second ring.

On my first day of school, anticipation woke me early, and I hired a tuk-tuk—one of those motorized three-wheel cabs—to take me to the International Training Massage School. "What we will teach you here is a powerful massage technique whose origins go back to the days of the Buddha," the head of school, whose name was Chongkol Setthakorn (but he went by John), told us in his orientation lecture. He said the fundamentals of traditional Thai massage—known as Nuad Bo'Rarn—originated about 2,500 years earlier and had been handed down from generation to generation. Thai massage employed principles of both yoga and acupressure, he said, and was based on the theory that the body consists of some 72,000 energy lines—roughly equivalent to the twelve meridians, or energetic pathways, of Chinese acupuncture. We students would learn to breathe alongside our clients, to establish compatibility with them, and to use the weight of our bodies to help them stretch and let go of their stress. John compared the relationship of masseuse and client to a mother who shows love and kindness toward her children. Thai massage could be intense, he said, but fundamentally it should leave both the giver and the receiver refreshed, happy, and energetic.

From the start, I was reminded how much I'd once loved school. It was amazing to feel curious again, even as doing so forced me to flash on the childhood abuse that had interrupted my ability to learn. To hear my instructors speak of wholeness and respect and heaven-sent healing was not just intellectually intriguing, it was what I'd spent years yearning for. Now ITM—which is what everyone called the school—was promising to teach me a set of skills, while also pushing me to grow in a spiritual way. Given how I'd been living, the school's emphasis on psychic release seemed aimed directly at me.

The ITM teachers were great at explaining the basics of Thai massage, which was fortunate, since I had a lot to learn. Unlike what I was used to, this practice made no use of oils and there were no massage tables; clients lay face up, on mats on the floor, while we knelt beside and sometimes over them, leaning into them with all our strength. We learned to use the balls of our thumbs, not the tips, to target pressure points. The goal was to increase flexibility while releasing both deep and superficial tension, all in the hope of letting energy—or qi—flow more freely. We needed both physical stamina and mental awareness to stay in tune with whomever we were working on, feeling for their heartbeat, trying to align ourselves with their rhythms. Hearing all this, I couldn't help but think about how, without words, I'd forged a trusting relationship with my first horse, Alice, and that gave me confidence. If one of the key elements of Thai massage was reading the cadence of another, I just knew I could be good at it.

Classes went from nine in the morning to three in the afternoon, with one break for lunch. Every session started with chanting a mantra, whose syllables (in Pali, a derivative of Sanskrit) were spelled out phonetically on a chalkboard. Then we had an hour of yoga and meditation. Finally, we'd break into groups of three—two students, one teacher—and take turns massaging and being massaged, with instructors modeling the proper technique and students mimicking them. I preferred giving rather than receiving. I didn't like strangers' hands on me, even through my clothes. But I wanted to learn, so I made the best of it.

At first, I spent all my time after school at the hotel. But soon I got bolder. Maxwell was calling me almost daily, but she left a message with the front desk if I didn't pick up. When we did talk, if I heard disapproval in her voice, I simply told her how busy school was keeping me. "Have you tracked down the girl Jeffrey wants you to meet?"

Maxwell asked in every phone call. I told her no, not yet, and then promised I would. But I never did. Every time I ignored her commands and nothing bad happened, I got a little braver. Before long, I was exploring Chiang Mai with gusto.

Not for nothing was Thailand often referred to as the Land of Smiles. Every man, woman, and child I met seemed happy to see me. And as I discovered Chiang Mai's celebrated beauty, the joyfulness of its people made more sense. This vibrant city was bound by a moat and the remains of walls built a thousand years before, and it was crammed full of temples, monasteries, and stupas—dome-shaped structures erected as Buddhist shrines. Good vibes, it seemed, were everywhere. At one of the city's most famous attractions, the Chiang Mai Night Bazaar, vendors lined up along the footpaths, erecting tables and tents to display their goods: touristy trinkets, tooled leather, snacks, electronics, clothing. I'd always loved shopping when I traveled—not just to acquire things but also as a way of interacting with local people. Now I began visiting the bazaar almost every night, walking down the rows of tables, exchanging greetings with the vendors. I knew they were hoping I'd spend some baht at their stalls, but even when I didn't, their warmth felt genuine.

Back in my hotel room, I called Tony a lot at first. I was feeling lonely and nervous about what would come next, and as he had since my middle-school days, Tony served as my sounding board. (Besides, since Epstein was paying the bills, I didn't even consider what those conversations would cost. Years later, phone records unearthed in various legal cases would show that between talking to Tony, returning Maxwell's calls, and letting my family know I was alive, I racked up a phone bill of about $4,000 in under two weeks.)

But it wasn't long before my need to hear Tony's voice waned. Seventy-seven students were enrolled at ITM, and after school, groups of us would gather at the city's lively clubs and rooftop bars. For the first time in forever, I felt free to get to know interesting new people my own age, without being expected to drop everything if Epstein called (or, worse, to recruit for Epstein's use whatever friends I managed to make). After living without autonomy for so long, being in charge of myself felt liberating. When a female classmate of mine complained that her accommodations were crappy, I invited her to stay in my room with me. It may sound like a little thing, but to have the chance to help someone else out of a bad spot, without any strings attached, filled me with pride.

Looking back, though, I see that in addition to enjoying my freedom, I was also behaving recklessly. A few of my fellow ITM students liked to party—smoking pot and trying other drugs—and I fell in with them in our off-hours. I justified this by telling myself I couldn't just quit Xanax cold turkey after using it so regularly. And thanks to Epstein's frequent infusions of cash, which I picked up at a Western Union near my hotel, I could buy anything I wanted. Either I was blind to the dangers of procuring drugs in a foreign country or I didn't care. Probably a little of both. At one point, a male friend and I found ourselves at the wrong end of a dark alley when the drug dealer we thought we were meeting sent thugs to rob us instead. We got away on my friend's motorbike, but the night could easily have ended differently. Even after that, though, I spent little time pondering the consequences of my decisions. It wasn't that I thought I was superior or immortal. I have many faults, but arrogance is not one of them. Instead, I think that a core part of me felt undeserving of self-defense. I'd managed to convince Epstein and Maxwell to let me out of their clutches, at least temporarily. In that way, I had successfully advocated for myself. But still, their abuse—and the abuse I'd suffered before I met them—made me internalize a devastating belief: I wasn't worth protecting.

SEVENTEEN

Bully Basher

I think it was a week into my studies that I met a fellow student named Mathew Olsen. A tall, gentle Australian in his midtwenties, Mat and his best friend growing up had come to Chiang Mai together, he said, partly so Mat could do his teacher training at ITM.

One afternoon as we were finishing our lessons, Mat asked me and another student if we were up for an excursion. He said his best friend, Robbie, was studying Thai boxing at a nearby Muay Thai gym, which was having a competition that night. "It'll be big fun," he promised, writing down the address for me. I said I'd think about it—I wasn't very interested in martial arts. But later, finding myself with nothing else to do, I put on a little mascara and hired a tuk-tuk. "Maybe," I thought, as we wound through traffic, "I can convince the gang to go clubbing afterward." Thinking back now, it's funny to me that those were my highest hopes as I arrived, twenty minutes later, at the address in the Saraphi District.

Looking around the cavernous space, I was searching for Mat when I spotted a lean, dark-haired man with probing brown eyes who seemed to be holding court inside a circle of friends. Everyone—men and women both—seemed to hang on his every word. In retrospect, maybe they had no choice: I was about to find out that to be near this man was to be swept up by his boisterous presence. But even at a distance, before I knew who he was, I felt instantly drawn to him.

A fight began, and I tried to apply what Mat was explaining about Muay Thai—something about it being "the art of eight limbs" because fighters use fists, elbows, knees, and shins—to what I was seeing in the ring. But when I turned my head, my eyes settled again on the dark-haired stranger. Mat must've seen me looking, because he said, "That's my friend Robbie."

Mat has since told me that, at that same moment, he was noticing something strange. Mat knows Robbie like a brother—they went to (and dropped out of) high school together and had been roommates for years. So Mat knows how much Robbie likes to analyze other fighters' moves. Usually during a bout, it was impossible to tear Robbie's eyes away from the ring. But on this night, Mat saw that Robbie was uncharacteristically distracted. I didn't see it, but Mat did: instead of scrutinizing the two sparring partners, Robbie was staring at me.

Robbie insists he knew instantly that I was his soulmate. "I hear a ruckus behind me, and I look around and see this sheila," he'll tell anyone who asks how we met, using the Aussie slang for a pretty woman. "I hadn't had that feeling since I was in primary school. I got these butterflies in my belly, and I was just like, 'She's it: the embodiment of beauty.' Jenna was special. Even before I spoke to her, I just knew." At this point, he usually pauses for effect, raising his dark eyebrows before adding with a laugh, "So I played hard to get."

If only this were a joke. But it's true: whenever I looked Robbie's way that night, he seemed to be engrossed in something or someone else. Robbie says he sensed this was the only way to win me, and while I felt frustrated then, I think he was probably right. Had he come on strong, I would have deflected, batting him away. After so many years of forced intimacy, I could be aloof when I felt pressured. I didn't know how to handle feelings of sincere, mutual attraction. But as Robbie leaned out, I found myself leaning in.

When the final bout ended, and everybody headed to the exits, I knew I needed to make a move. It was that or give up, but something about Robbie made me feel that giving up wasn't an option. So I maneuvered myself to be at Robbie's side as we squeezed through the crowd and out onto the street. "I'm Jenna," I said, smiling. "Want to share a tuk-tuk?" I'll never forget the way Robbie looked at me then, his face close to mine. His gaze was steady and calm, but the lights were on in his eyes. He waited a beat, and then he said what he's been saying to me in one form or another every day since: "Yes."

Remember who I was in 2002: a survivor of sexual abuse who'd spent years obediently performing intimate acts on men and women—some of them repeat abusers, some of them utter strangers—without any true feelings of closeness or affinity or desire. In fact, cutting myself off from my own wishes or wants had been one of my coping mechanisms. Even relationships with my past boyfriends had had a transactional quality. I had never been in love, not once, not with anyone. But now, almost instantly, I was falling in crazy love with Roberto Antonio Giuffre. In the tuk-tuk, I noticed that I liked the way his body felt next to mine—its temperature, its solidity, its warmth. I loved the way he smelled.

I took Robbie back to the Royal Princess that night, but we just hung out with my roommate and eventually he went home. For the next three days, he continued his hard-to-get act, and he was so convincing that I was beginning to think he just wanted to be friends. Here are a few things I quickly learned about Robbie: He was smart. He was funny. He was loyal. The youngest of four children born to Sicilian parents who'd immigrated to Sydney, Robbie—then twenty-six—

had been very religious as a child and attended church frequently with his mother. But at the age of nine, he'd begun to have night terrors in which he believed he was being held down by a terrible force. The dreams scared him so much that he turned away from Catholicism and began to study other forms of spirituality. "I went into the forest and said, 'You know what? No more fear. Fear holds you back,'" he told me, recalling how he began to read up on everything from Islam to Buddhism to shamanism. His studies brought him back, again and again, to a respect for nature, which he said gave him the sense of peace he was looking for. "I've always had a connection to Mother Earth. Put me in the bush with a campfire, and I'm centered. The cycles of the seasons just make sense to me," he told me. "All my reading about different religions gave me a path to follow. You walk your walk. You look back at the sand and see your own footprints. The goal is flow—balance. It's your own dharma."

I didn't know dharma from Parmesan cheese, and I told him so. But he didn't care, and just as importantly, he didn't judge me. He seemed to want to lift me up, not tear me down. A lifelong protector of the picked-on, he'd seen himself as what he called a "bully basher" long before he laid eyes on me, he said. As a kid, he'd made it his business to wait after school to punish those who picked on those smaller than themselves. "I'm a scrapper," he said. "Always have been."

On the third day of our friendship, we met up again at my hotel. My roommate was out, and Robbie and I were getting ready to go to dinner. I was sitting on the floor, and he was on the bed, and when he bent over to tie his shoe, I planted a kiss on him. I wasn't sure what would happen—maybe he just wasn't into me? But he kissed me back. I remember I grabbed hold of him then—and for the first time since I'd embraced my childhood best friend Kyle, I did so purely out of desire, not obligation or desperation.

From the start, Robbie and I had a different connection than any

I'd experienced before. For one thing, Robbie was straightforward. How, he wanted to know, could a nineteen-year-old massage student afford such swank accommodations in a four-star hotel? We were sitting in my room, just the two of us, when he asked that question. And suddenly I wanted to tell the truth. After a lifetime of toggling between two modes—Run and Survive—I wanted more than mere survival, and I was tired of running. Against all logic, something in me already believed this could be a relationship with real potential, a relationship that I didn't want to fuck up. And the more I talked to Robbie, the more I felt that way. I was sick of keeping secrets, of hiding what my life was really like. So I took a deep breath and told Robbie that I worked for a rich, powerful man who sexually abused me; that this man had a female partner who enabled and orchestrated an army of young women and girls to service him; that he and she lent me out to their friends, some of whom had hurt me beyond measure; and that I was deeply afraid of them.

As I spewed all this awfulness, Robbie's face constricted. "Where is your family?" he asked pointedly. "Can't they help you?" I told him they couldn't or wouldn't—I had never been sure which. I remember that Robbie had a knowing look on his face then, like he could intuit what I was leaving out. "I had a rough childhood," I stammered. The way Robbie locked eyes with me then, as if to say, "You're not alone anymore," told me I didn't need to reveal any terrible details to be understood. At least not yet. Robbie sensed we'd have plenty of time to get into all that.

At first glance, Robbie and I were complete opposites—me, the slight, fair-haired waif, him, the muscle-bound athlete whose body was covered in a silky carpet of dark fur. But we fit together. I felt like a different Jenna when I was with Robbie. I'd never met anyone like him. When we made love for the first time, he asked me something no other person had ever asked: what I did and didn't like in bed. As it turned out, there were lots of things I didn't like, things that reminded me of past, nonconsensual encounters. But I didn't share that with Robbie yet. I still believed that my role was to focus on my partner's pleasure, not my own.

My understanding of loving and feeling loved was extremely limited. For so long, I had only been seen as "good" if I did what was required of me, no matter how painful or upsetting. Now here came a man who claimed he didn't require me to do anything. He wanted me to be myself, he said. I didn't admit it to Robbie then, but it had been years since I knew who "myself" was. Part of me was stuck in time, as if still a little girl. I knew I felt safe when I was with Robbie, though, and I hadn't experienced safety since I was six years old and sitting atop Alice.

Robbie asked more questions about Epstein and Maxwell. How often did they check in on me? How soon was I expected to return to the United States? I remember I was crying as I told him I wasn't sure how I could ever break free from Epstein and Maxwell's web. But Robbie shook his head. "You don't have to live that way," he said, taking my hand. "Come back to Australia with me." A week into knowing each other, he dropped down onto one knee and proposed. "You won't be rich," Robbie told me, "but I will work hard to support you. I'll never hurt you. Never betray you. I'll be here for you and always love you. I'll have your back until we die." I'd never thought I'd hear those words from anyone, and as I told him yes, happy tears ran down my cheeks. "I love you, too," I said.

Some people, when they hear our story, marvel at how quickly we moved after that. After all, it's no small task to plan a wedding, especially in a country whose language you don't speak. And then there's the fact that we barely knew one another. But Robbie and I shared a belief that we had been destined to meet and be together. Fueled by that certainty, we found a seamstress to sew me a simple white halter dress and to tailor a dark olive suit for Robbie—I picked the color to match the green flecks in his eyes. I bought him a necklace with a Buddha pendant. He gave me a "Thai gold" ring that had sapphires arranged in the shape of a heart (it would eventually turn my finger green, but it was all we could afford). And on October 16, 2002, just ten days after first laying eyes on one another, we hired a translator named Charlie and stepped aboard a tram that would take us to the top of a mountain. Our destination: Wat Phra That Doi Suthep, the glorious temple where we'd be married.

Doi Suthep, as the temple is known, is a holy place marked by gilded pagodas, statues, and shrines. According to legend, it exists because in the fourteenth century AD, a monk named Sumanathera had a dream that he was supposed to go to the city of Pang Cha to look for a relic. He followed the premonition and found what many believe to be the Gautama Buddha's shoulder bone. When the reigning king of Thailand heard of the discovery, he had the monk bring it to him. Half the bone, which had split in two, was placed on the back of a white elephant, which was then set free. The elephant made its way up the steep, 3,400-foot Doi Suthep mountain, stopped at the summit, trumpeted three times, and dropped dead. Seeing this as a good omen, the king ordered that a temple be built there in the year 1383. My favorite part of the legend was that the Buddha's shoulder bone was said to have magical powers. Among them was that the bone was able to vanish.

On my wedding day, I was determined to do the same. At least when it came to Epstein and Maxwell, I no longer wanted to be seen. When he'd asked me to marry him, Robbie had given me the chance to achieve that goal. We were two people from two different countries who'd met in yet a third country and fallen in love, almost overnight. For days, we'd been swept away by one another, as if there were no one else on earth but us. Today we would become husband and wife.

As the tram ascended, I looked at my reflection in its glass windows. My new dress fit perfectly; my hair was mostly up, with a few tendrils falling around my face; and I wore a crown of baby's breath and small yellow and purple flowers. The vision made me cry again, overcome by the idea that I might be in control of my own life at last. Confused, Robbie asked if I was having second thoughts. Not at all, I reassured him. "But until you," I said, "I thought weddings were for other people, not for me." I felt like I was inhabiting a dream.

When we reached the mountain's summit, we each tied seven strings around one another's wrists, as Thai brides and grooms do. Each string signified something we hoped for: long life, enduring love, friendship, fertility, prosperity, sustenance, freedom. When we exchanged vows inside the temple, kneeling in front of a monk who wore flowing orange robes, they told us we were the first Westerners ever to do so. Mat, our only witness, used one of my FunSavers to take our picture.

After the short ceremony, we descended into the city again. We called our parents—Robbie's in New South Wales, Australia, mine in Florida—and after they recovered from their astonishment, each one of them wished us well. Robbie took me out for ice cream, then we headed back to the Royal Princess. Opening the door to our room, I saw nothing but rose petals—on the threshold, strewn from the doorway to the bed, and arranged in a heart shape on the coverlet. Robbie had asked the hotel to turn our room into a bridal suite, and, boy, had they pulled it off. When we flung ourselves on the bed, sending the rose petals flying, I had never felt so tethered to another human being. I only hoped I could make Robbie happy.

Our wedding day was almost over when I realized I had one more call to make. Robbie had made clear that he needed to hear me tell Epstein and Maxwell goodbye. He wanted that for himself, he said, but also for me. I had a right to assert myself, he said—to choose my own path. Robbie believed it would be good for me, and for us, if I said so out loud. I agreed with him in principle, but still I hesitated. Even with eight thousand miles between us, I was afraid of them. Finally, I dialed Epstein's cell phone. I felt a churning in my gut as I waited for him to answer. Would he yell? More likely, he'd threaten. I knew he would stop paying my way at the Royal Princess—Robbie and I were prepared for that. But could I truly sever my ties to the powerful people who'd ruled my life for more than two years? I still wasn't sure.

A few tense moments passed before Epstein picked up. "Hello?" he said, and his voice—that smug Brooklyn growl—sounded impatient.

"I fell in love and got married, Jeffrey," I blurted out. "I'm never coming back."

There was the briefest pause. "Have a great life," he said. Then a click—Epstein had hung up on me. We wouldn't speak again for more than five years.

EIGHTEEN

Honeymooners

*L**ook, if you had one shot or one opportunity / To seize everything you ever wanted in one moment / Would you capture it or just let it slip?* In the soundtrack of my life, no song better fits the start of my new life with Robbie than Eminem's "Lose Yourself," which was released just days after we married. At the beginning of our relationship, still so new to one another but already completely attached, we must have listened to that song a thousand times. "You better lose yourself in the music / The moment, you own it, you better never let it go," Eminem warned us, and we listened. "You only get one shot, do not miss your chance to blow / This opportunity comes once in a lifetime," Eminem rapped, and I believed him. Robbie was my one shot, my true love, a gift I had never imagined I'd receive.

The day after our wedding, we'd moved out of the Royal Princess and found cheaper accommodations. I also let the massage school know I was withdrawing. I'd loved my brief interlude with ITM, and I had completed two of its five levels of instruction, but I didn't have enough of my own money to continue. Besides, Robbie wanted to take me on a honeymoon. I think we spent three more days in Chiang Mai. Then, after a quick luggage edit (Robbie said I could only take three of my six suitcases), we set off by train. We were headed to Vientiane, the capital city of Laos, four hundred miles or so to the east, to get my passport stamped. Robbie was hoping that if we pinched our pennies, we could travel around Thailand for a few months, but my student visa was set to run out in just a few weeks. If I left the country, even briefly, and then entered again, Robbie had been told, the clock would restart, and I'd have more time to explore. So while Vientiane was hardly a romantic destination, that's where we needed to go.

When we arrived, tired and sweaty, it was late afternoon. Robbie had warned me that the place was far from picturesque, but I was still appalled by the sight of children squatting and urinating in the streets. Soldiers were everywhere, just waiting to enforce the 9:00 p.m. curfew. We were so obviously tourists, with Robbie somehow carrying my three suitcases and his own big backpack, and I knew we stuck out like sore thumbs. So once we got proof of my visit to Laos stamped in ink on my passport, I told Robbie I wanted to get out of there. We took a boat back across the Mekong River, found a cheap hotel, and slept in Thailand that night.

In the morning, we got on another train. Our next stop, about eight hundred miles south, was Surat Thani, a transport hub where we'd catch a bus (and later, a ferry) that would deliver us to our ultimate destination: Ko Pha-Ngan, an island that Robbie and Mat had visited when they first arrived in Thailand. This magical place, one of three islands off the southeastern coast in the Gulf of Thailand, was renowned for its monthly Full Moon Party: an all-night celebration, tied to the lunar calendar, that attracted throngs of tourists. But Robbie promised me the island was also the perfect place to spend one-on-one time—beautiful, peaceful, affordable.

Sitting on a bench in the crowded, rusty ferryboat that took us from the mainland to Ko Pha-Ngan's Thong Sala Beach, I was transfixed by the view. The ocean was an unbelievable shade of luminescent blue, and above it, like frosting on a cake, was the lighter blue strip of the sky. A Thai man next to us was carrying a rooster that he had trained to "sit" on command. Every time the rooster sat down, I burst out laughing. Robbie held me tight with one powerful arm. I was happy.

Stepping onto the dock on Thong Sala Beach, we were immediately surrounded by locals, all of them tugging at our sleeves, each more determined than the next to lure us to stay in the hotel he or she was there to represent. One young man handed Robbie a printed business card that said Two Suns Resort. On the card, handwritten in English: "I can get you anything you want." Robbie looked at me and grinned. Two Suns would be our place. For less than six dollars a night, we rented a private bungalow a hundred feet from the ocean. The resort was run by a family who cooked all our meals. I was still shy about eating new foods. Epstein's strict diet regimens had made me hyperfocused on remaining thin, and even the blandest Asian delicacies—pad Thai noodles, say—seemed off-putting. But Robbie was encouraging, and for him, I tried to be brave. Thai beer was cheap, and the sun was hot. Truly, we were in paradise.

As we lay around on the sand, Robbie and I began really getting to know one another. He told me about his parents, Antonina and Frank. His dad had once worked painting and refurbishing fishing boats, but now the family ran a catering business in Sydney. Robbie told me about his older siblings—two brothers, Gaetano (who everyone calls Guy) and Frank Jr., and a sister, Angela. Robbie had dropped out of high school because he was bored, he said, though he'd later finished another year through a correspondence course. At seventeen, he'd moved out of his parents' house and lived for a few years with a Korean woman who became his fiancée despite her parents' objections. "I stayed longer than I needed to," he said of that relationship.

Indeed, while he'd never lacked for female companionship, Robbie tended to be a one-woman man, not a player. He said he'd always prided himself on having close women friends, and he was often the "bloke" who gave these "sheilas" romantic advice. My new husband had strong opinions, I was learning, but also understood that people moved at their own pace. To be a bully basher, you must have a sixth sense for spotting vulnerability, but Robbie's response—the polar opposite of Epstein's—was to help, not to hurt.

Robbie asked more about my family and my upbringing, too, and bit by bit, I divulged the ugliest parts of my childhood. As I described what my father and Forrest had done to me, and what my mother had failed to do in response, I saw anger in Robbie's eyes. All families have their difficulties, his face said, but this was beyond the pale. "Where were your brothers?" he demanded, clearly imagining how he would have reacted if his sister had been so mistreated. I explained that Danny was sent away to boarding school and that Skydy was a kid, too small to defend me. And besides, neither of them knew, because I'd never told them. Robbie just shook his head, then opened his arms wide to envelop me in a hug.

At one point, I asked Robbie if he believed in God. "God is like the wind," he said, explaining how reading about paganism had taught him to see God in nature. "Can you see the wind? No. But you can feel it when it brushes your cheek." Did I believe in God? I couldn't answer that. I'd always been comforted by the idea of reincarnation because it promised that my piss-poor excuse for a life was not the only one I was going to get. But God? I wasn't sure. Hadn't Forrest, one of my earliest abusers, invoked God to manipulate me—just as the counselors at Growing Together had done? In my experience, God had been wielded by others to get what they wanted. Still, meeting Robbie at the very moment I needed him most seemed the best evidence I'd ever had of the existence of something divine.

Lying in the sand on that pristine island, exchanging stories about our lives and our beliefs, we covered a lot of ground in a short time. For example, we talked about how Robbie's spirituality dovetailed with his interest in fighting. He'd grown up watching *Monkey Magic*, a wacky, cult Japanese TV show that played on Australian TV every Sunday night. From the moment he discovered the show—whose title character is an ape, a skilled fighter and the king of his tribe, who achieves enlightenment through martial arts—Robbie was fascinated with the Buddhist concept of satori: the sudden comprehension of one's true nature. "The nature of Monkey was . . . irrepressible," said a voice-over in the show's opening montage, and Robbie could relate. That his spiritual awakening owed such a debt to a badly dubbed 1980s TV series could be seen as funny, he knew. But hey, he said, you take your illumination wherever you can find it.

"Martial arts is not just about fighting," he told me. "It's a way of thinking—a way of life." Robbie was fascinated by the idea that through intense physical conditioning, you could prepare yourself for anything.

"One of my teachers was all about controlling your punches," Robbie told me. "You were not allowed to land a hit. You had to stop an inch away from your opponent's face. Instead of dominating them with force, you blocked their blows and let them wear themselves out. We used to take broken bottles and scrape up our shins so that after a while, we couldn't feel anything. My body got conditioned to the point where if someone hit me, I'd just look at them and smile."

I'd never set foot inside a boxing ring, but I understood at least a version of what Robbie was talking about: shoring yourself up to increase the odds of your own survival. I'd spent my life blocking the blows of others, wishing they'd tire of abusing me. And at least for a while, I'd gotten good at blotting out feelings while keeping a smile plastered on my face. Robbie's experience helped me look at my own from a different vantage point. I flashed on the mantra I'd learned at ITM—the Pali prayer in which we asked to attain "the knowledge of all nature." Was this how I would do that? Not just knowledge of the world around me, but of my internal self? I sensed that I was beginning a process that would not be easy.

One thing, though, could not have been easier: hanging out with Robbie. Being with him never felt like a chore. Despite our differences, we seemed to move at the same rhythm. He introduced me to an Australian rock band called Powderfinger, and I fell in love with their biggest hit, whose lyrics—"My happiness is slowly creeping back / Now you're at home / If it ever starts sinking in / It must be when you pack up and go"—described to a tee the feeling of pining for a lover who's far away. I told Robbie I never wanted to be far away from him.

One night I told Robbie there was something I needed him to help me do. First we went to a bar in Ko Pha-Ngan, so I could sip a little liquid courage. "I think I've told you that Jeffrey Epstein prohibited tattoos," I said, taking a swallow of Thai whiskey. Robbie nodded. He had a yin-and-yang symbol on his right shoulder that I'd admired, but he knew I didn't have any ink. "Well, there's a tattoo parlor next door. And I need you to come with me and hold my hand." A few minutes later, I told a Thai tattoo artist what I wanted and where I wanted it and then lay face down on a table. Soon, I had a blue butterfly—to symbolize the freedom of flight—and the words "In Love With Robbie G" on the small of my back. (Actually, the artist misspelled Robbie, using only one B. To this day, in my phone, my husband's contact number is filed under "Robie.") In my mind, my new tattoo accomplished two goals: first, declaring my commitment to Robbie for all the world to see; and second, guaranteeing that I would repulse

Epstein, who shunned tattooed girls. As I told Robbie, only half-joking: "This is an insurance policy. Because now Jeffrey wouldn't want me, even if he could make me come back."

We must've been at the Two Suns for about a week when Mat showed up for a visit. Back in Chiang Mai, Mat had at first been worried when he heard how quickly Robbie and I planned to wed. He thought Robbie's parents would kill him for not somehow slowing us down. Robbie had always had a way with the ladies, Mat knew—"I don't think I've ever known him to be single," he'd tell me later. But Mat could see that Robbie's and my connection was deeper than those he'd witnessed before. So Mat had stood up for us at that mountaintop temple, and now he had arrived to make sure all was well.

You know how you can learn a lot about people by the company they keep? From ITM, I already knew Mat had a kind way about him. But to see Mat and Robbie together showed me a different side of my new husband. They teased each other relentlessly, but with affection. Mat had had a rough upbringing after his parents divorced. He'd left his mother's home at fifteen and moved to Sydney in search of his father. After he and Robbie met, Robbie's family had eventually taken Mat in. They'd been friends ever since.

We were on the beach drinking beer when Mat turned to Robbie with a serious look on his face. "Do you think it's a coincidence, Rob?" he asked.

"What are you talking about?" Robbie said.

"Petra," Mat said, and I watched Robbie's mouth drop open. Robbie is a talker—it's usually hard to get a word in edgewise around him. But now, he was mute—and his tan, brown face had gone a little pale.

"Who's Petra?" I asked. Mat looked at Robbie and, after getting a nod of approval, turned to me. "You know by now that Rob is a searcher," he began. "Well, about two years ago, we heard about a psychic named Petra who lived out in Campbelltown—that's west of Sydney. Friends told us she was the real deal." Mat was reluctant to go see her, he said, but not because he doubted her powers. He had an aunt who could see the future, so he knew such people existed. For a variety of reasons, however, he didn't want to know what life had in store for him. Robbie, though, was gung ho. He couldn't wait to track Petra down.

"So what did Petra say?" I asked.

"She said Rob would travel a long distance," Mat said, "to meet a blond-haired, blue-eyed girl who would be his Only One." I couldn't believe it. I turned to look at Robbie, who was shaking his head.

"I'd forgotten, mate," he stammered, clapping Mat on the shoulder. Then he took a deep breath and turned back to me. He was still processing the memory. "There's more to this story," Robbie said. "Right before Mat and I left for Thailand, another good mate of mine asked me to be the best man at *his* wedding. When I told him I'd already bought my ticket to Bangkok, he tried to persuade me to push the trip back a month. But I said no. 'I don't know why,' I told him, 'but I've just got to go now.' So now I'm realizing why: if I'd come a month later, I wouldn't have met you."

This was like a fairy tale, I thought, as Robbie took my hand and held it. "I told you I believe in us, baby," he said. "I believe we are meant to be."

Apparently, though, we were also meant to face adversity together. Robbie and I had befriended a charming nineteen-year-old Canadian, one of several travelers from all over the world who were staying at the Two Suns. After Mat said goodbye, promising to reconnect with us soon in Australia, we invited the Canadian to join us one night to party inside our bungalow. We thought he was terrific until the next morning, when we discovered most of our money was gone. Robbie ran outside half-dressed and raced to the raised structure where the

Canadian had been staying, but on the way, he encountered two Irish women who told him the guy had booked it out of there just after sunrise. We were out more than $2,000; we had only $200 or so left.

Months later, Robbie would say that the robbery was a blessing. "It was time to get out of holiday mode and come down to earth—to get back into real life," he'd say. But in that moment, we panicked. The robbery meant our honeymoon was over, obviously. But worse than that, while Robbie had already bought his return ticket to Australia, I had no ticket to fly, and now we couldn't afford to buy one.

Robbie called his parents. I'm sure they were wondering—who *was* this woman who'd bewitched their son, and who was now stranded with him, nearly penniless, on a remote tropical island? But they stepped up to help us, as they would do so many times in the coming years, paying $800 for my flight to Sydney and sending a little more money to tide us over until we got there. We packed up and told the Two Suns goodbye, retraced our steps from our honeymoon paradise to Bangkok, and then checked into a dingy, dirt-cheap backpackers' hotel to await our departure.

There was one glitch in the plan: Robbie's parents had not been able to get me on his direct flight, so we'd be traveling separately. My flight would leave a few hours earlier than his did and would connect through Singapore. Realizing this, I was filled with dread. I'd come to rely on how secure Robbie made me feel. The next day, as Robbie walked me to my gate at Bangkok International Airport, I didn't want to let go of his hand. "I'll see you on the other side of the world," Robbie said, grinning. I tried to smile, too, but I didn't completely succeed. We kissed goodbye, and I got on the plane.

It turns out I was right to be nervous. When I landed in Singapore and tried to make my way to my connecting flight, customs officials descended upon me. If I was not an Australian citizen, they wanted to know, why did I only have a one-way ticket into the country? Where, they demanded, was my travel visa to Australia? (I had no idea I'd needed one. Maxwell had always handled those matters for me before.) I was almost hysterical with fear. If they sent me back to Bangkok, I didn't know what I'd do. I thought of the time, back in Florida, when Tony stole the tip money and got me fired, and I'd had no choice but to go crawling back to Epstein. Was this going to be like that—a brief escape followed by a pitiful return to purgatory? In my despair, I yearned for Robbie, who by this point was somewhere above the South China Sea. But I was going to have to figure this out on my own.

I don't think I've ever been more persuasive. It helped that I was telling the authorities the truth: that I'd just married an Australian citizen. I showed them the seven strings around my wrist. Where was the marriage license? they wanted to know. Of course, I didn't have one (later, we'd end up having to get remarried in Australia to make our union legal). But I pulled out several of the photographs Mat had taken with my FunSaver, feeling grateful that I'd hurried to get them developed. The customs officials looked at the photos, then back at me. And then a miracle: they let me get on my connecting flight.

Eight hours later, I arrived in Sydney and stepped into the terminal feeling both exhilarated and anxious. Robbie's parents were coming to meet us, and since I'd landed before Robbie, I would need to introduce myself. Coming out of the baggage area, I saw an older couple behind a rope—a wiry, white-haired gentleman and a stout, broad-shouldered woman whose round face was framed by an auburn pixie cut. They looked like the people that Robbie had described. I took a deep breath and headed toward them, forcing a smile.

"I'm Jenna," I said, extending my hand, which Nina and Frank each shook, nodding politely. Then we just stood there together, not talking, waiting for Robbie. I'd soon learn that Frank spoke little

English, but I didn't know that then. So the silence made me worry they already disapproved of me. Finally, after what seemed like an hour but was only a few minutes, I glimpsed Robbie walking toward us down a long hallway. Relief washed over me. Slipping under the ropes separating us from the passengers-only area, I sprinted until I was in his arms. We'd made it. Together. Now, our new life could truly begin.

NINETEEN

Down Under

When I picture myself during my first few days in Australia, I have to laugh. I am standing behind the stove in my in-laws' kitchen, learning how to make coffee the Italian way, one strong cup at a time. I pour water into a tiny silver percolator, then spoon finely ground coffee into the sieve-like reservoir through which hot water will soon flow. It's a cozy scene, except for what I'm wearing: a skimpy undershirt and Daisy Duke cutoff shorts with my thong underwear protruding from the waistband. To see me, you might think I'm trying to show off my body, but that isn't right. While in Epstein's employ, I'd been encouraged to wear clothes that made me look even younger than I was. Now, no longer Epstein's captive, I was a wife—a grown woman. But I still felt—and dressed—like a teenage girl. I didn't have the slightest idea how an adult version of me should look.

When I moved into Frank and Nina's house, that was just the beginning of what I didn't know. I had never loaded a dishwasher, for example, or scrambled an egg or separated laundry into darks and lights. I'd never opened a bank account or filed income taxes or made a good cup of coffee—the list went on and on. Sometimes the weight of my ignorance overwhelmed me. What is adulthood, I wondered, and will I ever master it? What is it to be a wife? It would take time for me to figure out the answers.

Our first weekend in Australia, Robbie took me camping in Hunter Valley, north of Sydney, with a group of his friends. The place is one of the country's major wine regions, but we had so little money that Robbie decreed we were there to rough it and enjoy the natural beauty, not to sip Shiraz. I was good with that until I saw where we were sleeping: a ramshackle shed. That weekend was quite an introduction to my new country. Yes, we saw a few Aboriginal cave paintings, but the weather was freezing and the only kangaroo we spotted appeared to have been dead for months.

A few days after our return, I fell terribly ill with some sort of flu. When I spiked a fever, Robbie was at work—he'd gotten a construction job. I felt awful: clammy and hot. I didn't want to be a pain in anyone's ass, and—especially since I'd just learned the Aussie phrase "having a whinge" (complaining for no reason)—I was determined to be stoic. But when Robbie's dad discovered how sick I was, he swung into action, whipping up his special *zuppa di lenticchie*, or lentil soup. I was too weak to get out of bed, but Frank propped me up on my pillows and then sat beside me, feeding me spoonfuls until I was full. Later, as I passed in and out of a sweaty, delirious sleep, he returned every few minutes to cool my forehead with a damp cloth. When my fever broke, Frank brought me coffee that was creamy from the raw egg he'd stirred into it.

After I'd recovered, Frank sat with me and showed me how to peel a prickly pear, teaching me to avoid the nettles, which will embed themselves like fiberglass in your fingers if you aren't careful. He didn't say much, just as Robbie had warned that he wouldn't, but in those first weeks that I was in Sydney, Frank gave me more nurturing than I ever got from my own father.

The women of the Giuffre clan were more skeptical of me. Robbie's mom, especially, is blunt and quick to call out wrongdoing, and at first she was suspicious of this skinny American who'd crash-landed on her doorstep. Then, just before Christmas, Nina took me to the home of some of Robbie's aunties, or *zia*s. It was cannoli-making day, and I was being drafted to help. I knew nothing about making cannoli, of course, but I quickly figured out the assembly line: pounding out the dough, then rolling it thin and wrapping it around bamboo poles that we dipped into a fryer, taking care not to burn them. Then we stuffed the crispy shells with three kinds of fillings: ricotta, vanilla cream, and chocolate. We must've made three hundred cannoli that day, and when I returned home, I had ricotta in my hair. But I'd passed some sort of test. The *zias* were proud of me.

Married life took some getting used to. I couldn't get a work permit until we were legally married, which we would accomplish in January 2003, but already, Robbie was working all the time, trying to make good on his promise to provide for me. I helped out when I could with the Giuffre family's catering business—hauling steam trays, doing dishes, waitressing when needed. I liked keeping busy and contributing to this family I'd just joined. But at the same time, I was struggling to come to terms with my new existence.

Robbie's and my sex life, for example: I was fiercely attracted to him, but I still sometimes had trouble letting myself fully enjoy being with him in bed. Before Robbie, I'd been a sort of zombie when it came to sex—going through the motions, keeping my true self under a psychic lock and key. I had also been trained to do things that Robbie found downright weird. I remember the first time I jumped out of bed right after we made love, only to return with a warm, wet washcloth. When I tried to clean Robbie up, like Epstein had required me to do, my husband took hold of my wrist. "You don't have to do that," he said gently. "That's not right. Lay down with me instead." I did as he asked, and I never brought a washcloth to bed again. But while this should have been a relief, it also left me confused. That act, however demeaning, had been expected of me for so long, and I'd been praised for it. Now that I wasn't doing it anymore, I was unsure what to do with myself instead. It was difficult just to relax.

"What do you like—and not like—in bed?" Robbie had asked soon after we met. Now, little by little, I began to acknowledge that there were things I wasn't comfortable with. For example, I wasn't wild about giving blow jobs—too many memories of unwelcome hands pushing on the back of my neck, forcing me to swallow. And receiving oral sex only reminded me of my dad. This was a lot for Robbie: hearing how much my past abusers had ruined for me, and also for him. When he first realized how much I was effectively removing from the menu of our intimate life, Robbie looked a little stunned. But then he made it okay. There were lots of ways to make each other feel good, he told me, as we lay around in bed. "I want you to feel loved," he said.

I did feel loved, most of the time. But then my past would intervene. I didn't want to think about the Billionaires, the former minister, and all the others. But sometimes during sex, a contorted face would pop into my head, and I'd remember. This was awful in myriad ways—experiencing flashbacks in the first place, obviously, but also trying to shield Robbie from knowing it was happening. I wanted both to protect him and at the same time to keep him from knowing how damaged his new wife really was. But whenever Robbie got an inkling that I was trying to hide something, he felt as if I were shutting him out. We were a team, he said. We needed to deal with these things together. I knew that made sense, but at times, that kind of wide-open togetherness was more than I could handle.

DOWN UNDER

While we were still living with his parents in Sydney, Robbie—knowing how much I missed Mary-Jane, the Chow Chow I'd left in Florida—bought me a Jack Russell terrier. I named him Champion (Champ, for short), and he gave my days structure. Like any dog, Champ needed to be walked, which got me out of the house. But his unrelenting Jack Russell brain also demanded that I engage with him constantly. I couldn't just retreat into my own memories—Champ wouldn't allow it. Being driven by the needs of others was familiar to me, but with Champ, that was a healthy impulse.

Robbie and I had always planned to move out of his parents' home eventually, but Champ's arrival hastened that decision. Frank and Nina were from the old country, so they believed animals should be kept outside. My need to have Champ on my lap, at the table, in our bed, made them crazy. So in early 2003, Robbie and I moved into our first apartment in Parramatta, a bustling, artsy, multicultural neighborhood. The walls of our tiny two-bedroom second-floor walk-up were thin—I remember our lovely Indian next-door neighbors had a new baby, whose cries we heard at all hours. I'm also sure they heard Robbie and me fighting. Too often, usually after drinking too much, we'd go at it hammer and tong—why didn't I clean the house, he'd yell, when he was working so hard? Why couldn't he come home earlier, I'd scream, when he knew I was so lonely? Sometimes he'd call me on his lunch break, and I'd just be waking up. "What are you doing, just faffing around?" he'd ask, using Aussie slang for wasting time. "Jenna, you are acting like a child." That made me angry. But the truth was that in some ways I still *was* a child.

A perfect example: We were so poor that at first we couldn't even afford a sofa. But Robbie scrimped and saved, and one morning before he left for work, he gently nudged me awake. "I know how much you love shopping," he said, stroking my face. "Go out today and buy us some furniture." He handed me a thousand dollars in cash. "This won't get us much—you'll probably need to go to a secondhand store. But it'll be a start."

That night, when he came home, I proudly showed him what I'd bought for us: an Xbox game console.

"Jenna, are you kidding?" Robbie said, trying not to laugh or explode, or both.

"I thought it'd be fun," I said. "It comes with two controllers, so we can play together."

"But we have nowhere to sit, Jenna. What were you thinking?"

I felt embarrassed and defensive. "What I was *thinking* is that all you do is work," I fumed. "I was just trying to bring some laughter into the house." What I didn't say, because I was ashamed to admit it, was that the thought of going to a furniture store alone had paralyzed me. I didn't know how to shop for furniture because I'd never seen anybody do it. I was afraid of doing it wrong. So I'd blown all our money on something I knew how to buy—a toy.

The fact was that I was unprepared to run a household. One morning I came into the kitchen and encountered the hugest spider I'd ever seen, just enjoying itself on the wall next to the sink. I can deal with many things that make other people squeamish: worms don't scare me; snakes are a breeze. But spiders? Ever since Forrest and my dad took me to see *Arachnophobia* with them, I've been deathly afraid. So I called Robbie at work and said I needed him to come home. "I'm sorry, sweetie," he said, sounding distracted. "I can't leave."

"But it's looking at me," I pleaded, risking a glance at the spider's many eyeballs.

"Is it a huntsman?" he asked.

"What's a huntsman?" I practically screamed. Robbie explained: The huntsman spider, also known as the giant crab spider, looks a little like a tarantula, but bigger. And, of course, one of the

Me, as a six-year-old first grader, around the time I got my first horse, Alice. These days in Loxahatchee, Florida, were among my happiest.

My mom, Lynn, my little brother, Skydy, and me.
I could spot Mom's fiery red hair anywhere.

Me as a teenager, right around the time
I met Jeffrey Epstein and Ghislaine Maxwell.

Jeffrey Epstein and Ghislaine Maxwell in 2005.
I saw them less as boyfriend and girlfriend and more like
two halves of a wicked whole.

Prince Andrew, me, and Maxwell in Maxwell's London townhouse in March 2001. I asked Epstein to take our picture with my disposable camera.

This May 2001 photo of Naomi Campbell's thirty-first birthday party, held on a yacht in Saint-Tropez, captures me in the foreground (Maxwell, wearing a light blue top, can also be seen). In August 2019, this photo was discovered and published in both British and American newspapers, confirming my assertion that I'd traveled with Epstein and Maxwell. Later, I'd meet a fellow Epstein survivor who said seeing me in this photo prompted her to go public with her own story.

Me, sightseeing in New York City, during my years living under Epstein and Maxwell's control. I was determined to document my travels, as I never knew when they would be cut short. Epstein took the photo with my camera.

Robbie and me on our wedding day, October 16, 2002, just ten days after we met. We were married by a monk at a Buddhist temple on top of a mountain in Chiang Mai, Thailand.

Me with our youngest child, Ellie.
Having a daughter was one of a few developments
that would prompt me to step forward
publicly and hold my abusers to account.

Every year since my oldest son was born,
we've gotten a family Christmas portrait taken with Santa.
My kids don't believe in St. Nick anymore, but I still insist on doing it.
I believe in saving happy memories when you get the chance.

Me, age thirty-four, holding a photo of my teenage self during my years with Epstein. This image accompanied "Perversion of Justice," journalist Julie K. Brown's series in the *Miami Herald* about Epstein and Maxwell's sex-trafficking ring and the shameful deal the US government made that protected them from prosecution.

After Epstein's death, Judge Richard M. Berman invited Epstein's victims to a hearing in Manhattan federal court on August 27, 2019. Sarah Ransome (at left) and I were among twenty-three Survivor Sisters, as we call ourselves, who attended and spoke. Also pictured: my lawyers Brad Edwards, Sigrid McCawley, and David Boies.

places on the planet that the huntsman spider thrives is Australia. The monster I was having a staring contest with looked as big as a dessert plate.

"It's a huntsman!" I said, hoping that would motivate Robbie to come save me. But he just laughed. "Darling, you could sleep next to that spider," he said. "It's ugly, but it won't hurt you." Well, that did nothing to reassure me. So I hung up on Robbie and called his dad, who came right over with a broom. "I'll kill it for you," he said valiantly. "I'll kill it dead." And soon the huntsman was no more.

I wish my own father had treated me with similar care. Sometime in this period, I got Dad on the phone. He and my mom had separated. They were headed for divorce. They'd sold the Rackley Road house where I'd grown up, and my mom had moved to Colorado. But Dad was still living in Florida, so I asked him to get my Dodge truck back from Tony and then sell it for me. I was hoping it would fetch several thousand dollars. I also asked Dad to pawn or sell everything in a storage locker I'd rented. Among other things, the locker contained a chandelier and a few antiques my grandma Shelley had left me. Dad agreed and said he'd wire me the proceeds. But this was *my* father, so I guess I shouldn't have been surprised that when I went to collect the wire, all he'd sent me was $500, a fraction of what he'd likely been paid for my things.

That was a problem for a lot of reasons, not least of which was that I was still kicking an expensive habit—Xanax—that I used to help blot out my trauma. Back in Laos, I'd dumped most of my supply in a toilet, because I feared that being apprehended with drugs might get us thrown in jail. But I still had a small stash, and it was running out. Not that I admitted this to Robbie. While I'd been honest with my husband about the range of damaging experiences I'd endured, I think he expected that the farther away I got from those incidents, the better I'd feel. Instead, the opposite seemed to be happening. Memories I'd tamped down for years were now coming up, unbidden, in vivid detail.

Disturbing images would pop into my head during the day—the black leather, studded collar Epstein had choked me with; the greedy, cruel look on the minister's face as he watched me beg for my life. I was haunted by nightmares—my abusers looming over me, about to pounce, and me unable to get away. Frequently I was jolting myself awake, with my side of the bed soaked in sweat. I hated waking Robbie up, so I'd just cuddle closer to him. "You okay?" he'd mumble. "Yeah. Just another one of those dreams," I'd say, as he wrapped his arms around me and dozed off again.

Nevertheless, I was not yet willing to acknowledge how much pain I was in or how much I'd relied on antianxiety meds in the past. The truth was that my Xanax pills had been like life rafts for me, and getting off them revealed how quickly I was sinking.

One day Robbie came home from work and found me sitting on the floor in the corner of our apartment, surrounded by blood and broken glass. I had been cutting myself—not trying to kill myself, but instead using the clarity of inflicting my own pain to quiet my raging demons. Robbie took one look at me and called his mother. He told me later that he could just tell by the look in my eyes that this was a "mom moment." When Nina arrived, she swooped in like a bosomy angel, kicking the shards of glass away and taking me into her arms. She must've held me for an hour, rocking me, telling me it would be all right. Then she took me to the bathtub, stripped off my clothes, and tenderly washed me as if I were her own child. Once again Robbie's parents were giving me what I'd been missing since I was a tiny girl.

I would have understood if Robbie had felt angry about how utterly I was falling apart. But he was more sad than mad. Sometimes he'd reference the roller coaster that we were riding together by joking that when we first got married, he didn't know me from a bar of soap. But he was usually hugging and kissing me when he said something like that. He constantly told me how lucky he felt to have found me. Still, I knew he was frustrated. And so was I.

Often I felt as if I were moving two steps forward, one step back. As I put distance between my abusive past and my nonabusive present, I could at times feel waves of peaceful energy and hope. But then that serenity did something I wished it wouldn't. It was as if my feeling safe cleared a path for some of the most awful memories—ones that I'd locked away for years—to come to the forefront of my mind. When you're fighting for survival, you don't process trauma; you bury it. Well, now that I was surrounded by love, all that ugliness had decided it had been buried long enough.

Memories of Epstein tortured me. He'd been so particular about how girls looked: always reed thin, with small breasts and narrow hips. The eating disorder I'd developed in childhood was only encouraged under Epstein's roof, where us girls were always on a diet. By contrast, the Giuffres not only love to eat; they love to feed each other. "I'll cook for you, sweetheart, and you'll eat everything I cook," Robbie promised, when he discovered that my diet consisted of three things: pizza, buttered toast, or nothing. It would take years, though, for Robbie to win that battle.

At Robbie's recommendation, I tried to read a few spiritual books that he swore held some answers. I saw immediately why he liked *Way of the Peaceful Warrior: A Book That Changes Lives*, Dan Millman's 1980 autobiographical novel that endorses meditation, mindfulness, compassion, and acceptance. It started off with a quote from a collection of Buddhist scriptures—"Warriors, warriors we call ourselves. We fight for splendid virtue, for high endeavor, for sublime wisdom, therefore we call ourselves warriors."—that made going into battle sound like a sacred act. I also tried to read *Illusions: The Adventures of a Reluctant Messiah* by Richard Bach, the *Jonathan Livingston Seagull* guy. That one was just too woo-woo for me. I told Robbie, "These kinds of books love to talk about seeing colors and auras and rainbows, but I'm just trying to figure out my next step."

I drew more comfort from being outside. Robbie's dad had a huge fig tree in the backyard that he was very proud of. In the late spring, the fruit was abundant, not to mention delicious. But more resonant to me was how the tree changed with the seasons. Sometimes there were so many figs that they fell on the ground, creating a fruit carpet that squished underfoot. Other times the tree looked almost naked. Whenever we visited Robbie's parents, I took a moment with that tree—it became a symbol of resilience for me.

When we'd arrived in Australia, I'd insisted upon an unlisted phone number. Even with my new last name, I suspected Epstein and Maxwell could find me if they wanted to, and I wanted to take every precaution. And those precautions were working, at least for the time being. Still, while I had no direct connection with Epstein, he intruded. One day I walked by the living room as my mother-in-law was watching television. There, on the screen, was an actress who'd once been one of Epstein's victims, like me. Now there she was on Nina's TV. "How do you know her?" Nina asked, seeing my stunned face. I didn't know what to say, so I turned and left the room.

Then, in March 2003, *Vanity Fair* magazine published a lengthy profile titled "The Talented Mr. Epstein." I don't remember exactly when I first read it, but I do recall being shocked by its gushing tone: Epstein was described as "good-looking," "charming," "very generous," and "like a king in his own world"; his Manhattan townhouse was like "someone's private Xanadu." There was a reference to Epstein's love of women ("mostly young") and a description of his "complicated past"—a reference to some of his questionable financial dealings. But the article said many people had commented that "there is something innocent, almost child-like about" him. "Oh, is that what you call it?" I asked out loud. "Innocent?!" Then I threw the magazine across the room.

TWENTY

Welcome to the World

I loved it when Robbie called me his "missus." There was so much fondness in the way he said it. I liked how proud he was when he told people I was his. But the truth is that the first few years of our marriage were tough on both Robbie and me. He chalks that up mostly to a single fact: I didn't trust anyone. I hate it when he says that, because it makes me sound harsh, but he isn't wrong. In my core, I knew that men were selfish, women were duplicitous, and anyone could be cruel. I knew these things like I knew that dogs have fleas; it was a fact that I'd had proven to me again and again and again. People couldn't be relied upon.

At my worst moments, even Robbie wasn't safe from my near-nihilistic belief system. I was suspicious and sometimes outright accused him of not having my back. A voice inside me still warned: "Don't let your guard down, or you'll get hurt." So I told him I thought that he didn't understand me, that he never could, and that I didn't believe I could truly count on him. Those words hurt him because they weren't true, so he'd blow his stack. Robbie had a temper. While he tried to keep himself in check when I provoked him, either by accident or on purpose, there was no denying his anger was there. And yet somehow after we fought, we always came back together. What bound us to one another was stronger than all the forces and flaws that threatened to divide us.

In 2005, we escaped the bustle and noise of Sydney and moved to Blue Bay on the central coast. I loved how peaceful it was there. We could walk from our house to the beach, which Robbie and I made a point of doing every day. Robbie was apprenticing to become a bricklayer. I was working as a receptionist for a company called Employment Training and Recruitment Australia, which coached unemployed people on how to find jobs, helping them polish their résumés and ace their interviews. I'd actually been hired there after I went to them for help. My office was walking distance from our apartment, so we only needed one car. We still had little money—at times I waitressed at night to help pay our bills. But Robbie and I were getting along, and once in a while, I'd wonder what it might be like if we could have kids. I had never forgotten the doctors who'd told me becoming a mother was highly unlikely. At different points in my life, I'd been told that one of my fallopian tubes was blocked, and I had polycystic ovaries, among other problems. When I'd told Robbie that, however, he'd joked that my eggs had never seen sperm like his before.

"They have hatchets on 'em!" he'd boasted, before giving me one of his big bear hugs. "Don't worry, Jenna. Why don't we leave it up to fate?"

In July 2005, we went out and had what Robbie calls "a big slosh" night at our local RSL club, which is a peculiarly Australian institution. The Returned and Services League was founded in 1916 after World War I, and its clubs were created as gathering points for returned military and their family members. We loved the RSL near us because the food was great, the cocktails were strong, and the prices were relatively cheap. We ordered lamb shanks and played a little keno in the casino, and both of us were drinking like camels. By the time we got home, we were so tipsy that it seemed too difficult to climb the stairs to our apartment. So we lay down in the grass in front of our building and took turns pointing out stars and constellations we thought we knew the names of. My head was spinning, and we were laughing and rolling around on the lawn when suddenly I said, "You know, I haven't had my period in two months or so. That's a little weird."

Robbie lifted his head up. "Hatchets!" he said, then flopped back down.

The next day, I bought an at-home pregnancy test, which came back positive. I didn't believe it. After two more said the same thing, however, I went to the doctor, who took some blood and pronounced me seven weeks pregnant. Still doubtful, I wasn't convinced until the doctor performed an ultrasound and I saw the baby's tiny heart beating. Robbie was thrilled—we'd beaten the odds! Maybe one of those seven strings we'd tied to our wrists on our wedding day (and left there until they disintegrated) had worked its magic on our fertility. Or maybe the doctors who'd evaluated me five years before had made a mistake. Either way, we were going to be parents, and we couldn't have been more elated. We went out for breakfast to celebrate—I have a photo of me sitting on Robbie's lap afterward, grinning my face off. Then, when we got home, we called our families and announced: "We're having a baby!"

I loved being pregnant. I was empowered by the idea that I had something—someone—bigger than myself to live for. Right away I started assembling a baby book. On the "Parents to Be" page, I affixed photos of me in a bikini, my belly protruding, and of Robbie and me laughing, our arms around one another. Right away I began singing the "Alphabet Song" to my tummy, along with "Itsy-Bitsy Spider," because I'd heard music was good for a baby's brain.

WELCOME TO THE WORLD

One afternoon right around my due date, Robbie was still at work when I felt a sudden dampness in my underwear. I was scared—was something wrong? In a panic, I called a friend, who immediately came over and ferried me to the hospital. It turned out I'd just lost my mucus plug—a gross-sounding thing that I'd never heard of before. But my water hadn't broken yet. Robbie's bricklaying job was an hour and a half away, but he would have plenty of time to get to the hospital: I had about twenty hours of grueling labor ahead of me.

One Thursday in February 2006, at 7:34 p.m., Robbie and I welcomed our first child, an eight-and-a-half-pound boy we named Alexander Anthony Giuffre. I was over the moon about him and felt great physically, so we brought him home the next day. In his baby book, I would soon record his top-percentile Apgar-test scores, his eye color (blue-green), and his hair color (light brown). On the page marked "Welcome to the World," I wrote, "Alex came out just perfect."

About a week after I gave birth, we moved closer to Robbie's parents, to a little house in Bass Hill, just west of Sydney. Now we began calling them simply Nonna and Nonno, which is Italian for grandma and grandpa. Meanwhile, it turned out that one of *my* grandmas, Shelley, had left me not just furniture but also a little money when she passed. I used it to fix up a baby-blue nursery with a Winnie the Pooh motif—a Pooh bear carpet and stickers of Piglet and Eeyore on the walls. Robbie refurbished a white crib—a hand-me-down from his sister, Angie—and I hung a frilly white curtain around it. I wanted Alex to feel loved.

We were nervous parents at first. Alex was hungry all the time, but he fussed a lot, and I worried he wasn't getting enough nutrients from breastfeeding. It turned out Alex had colic, and he woke half a dozen times a night for the first two months. Only Robbie could get him to stop crying, by turning him face down and pressing his palm into poor Alex's distended belly. Exhausted and worried about not meeting Alex's needs, I was constantly asking Robbie's mom and sister for advice.

But wow, how happy Alex made me. "You are truly a special boy," I wrote in his baby book when he was one month old. "You have no idea what you mean to your Father and I, and what you have done to bring such closeness to the family." At nine weeks old, he smiled. "I love being your Mummy!" I wrote.

Watching Alex grow was like medicine for me. I adored every inch of him, but there was something else, too: Alex made me feel essential. He depended on me. And the simple fact that I mattered so fundamentally to him gave my life purpose in a way nothing else had before. Every parent knows how healing it can be to give your child something you didn't receive as a child. Sometimes it felt that by tending to him, I was tending to the child I'd been, giving myself the love I'd needed. By keeping Alex safe and warm and fed and happy, I also got to experience all those feelings—as the grown-up mom that I now was, but also as the affection-starved little girl that I used to be.

In August 2006, when Alex was five months old, I was surprised to discover I was pregnant again. I'd thought that while I was breastfeeding, that couldn't happen. My doctor just shook his head when I told him that old wives' tale. Having been born five years apart from each of my brothers, I liked the idea of my kids coming so close together. Still, a second pregnancy was a lot to handle. Becoming a parent had put me on a steep learning curve, and I was just barely keeping up. I also worried about money, which we never had enough of. Robbie was overjoyed, though. We'd figure it all out somehow, he said.

In addition to changing our lives in a thousand other ways, Alex's arrival made me think a lot about the importance of family. I wanted my son to feel connected to his relatives in a way that I didn't. Robbie's extended family was there for us, for sure, but I found myself missing my parents—or at least the parents I wished I'd had. In

Alex's baby book, I'd written: "Remember, Alex: Friends come and go but your family is forever! We must always look out for each other and create memories together. Most important thing in life: Family." And then I'd drawn a heart. But I felt like a hypocrite: while Robbie's parents were around all the time, mine had never come to visit, and I talked to them infrequently. Now I began to wonder how I could make things okay between me and my mom and dad.

"I've had too much hate towards them," I told Robbie. "The past is the past. We have a happy family now. I want to let go of my hate." An idea had been percolating in my head: I knew Mom, who is afraid of flying, probably couldn't handle a sixteen-hour trip, but I was thinking of inviting Dad to come meet Alex. "I want to give him another chance—a do-over," I told Robbie. My husband was reluctant. "I mean, what kind of man does to his daughter what he did to you?" he asked. But seeing how much reconciliation mattered to me, he gritted his teeth and said okay.

In September 2006, Dad arrived, and my mother-in-law insisted on making a huge breakfast feast to welcome him. As we headed over to their place, just a few blocks away, I was fretting, worried that Dad would embarrass me. And he did, the moment we walked in Nina's door, by announcing that he wasn't hungry. "I already had McDonald's this morning," he said, which basically guaranteed Nina wouldn't like him. You don't tell the Giuffre clan that you won't eat their food. We stayed an hour, then headed back home.

After that, we didn't take Dad out much, but the rest of the weeklong visit went okay. My dad, however, was still my dad. There's a photo of him in Alex's baby book, holding a beer bottle to my infant son's lips. "You and Grandpa Sky sharing your first brewsky together," reads the caption I wrote, making the best of it. Today, though, I see the inappropriateness of my dad's behavior, as well as how triggering it was for me. Forcing an adult beverage on a baby, even in jest, isn't the same as forcing adult sexuality on a child—but it's rooted in a similar logic. Adults have the power to manipulate small children, who don't yet have the capacity to make their own choices. Sometimes it seemed as if my dad enjoyed doing things that were taboo, if only to watch others react in horror or chagrin as he pushed past boundaries. But I so wanted for us to be a tight-knit family that I let it slide.

Maybe that's why it meant so much to me that, in contrast to my dad, the man I'd married was proving to be a devoted father. For example, when Alex was seven months old, he was suddenly determined to learn how to walk. He would use a coffee table or a chair to hoist himself to a standing position, then look around for help. That's when Robbie figured out how to loop a rolled-up bath towel under Alex's arms like a harness, to show our son what walking felt like. Together, we often took Alex to Homebush Bay Aquatic Centre, where we could soak in the whirlpool, and to Featherdale Wildlife Park, which is home to the world's largest collection of Australian wildlife. Alex loved to go to Featherdale to pet the kangaroos and wallabies.

In early 2007, we had a scare about baby number two. During a routine ultrasound, doctors observed that our unborn baby might have a tiny hole in his heart. I remember the doctor counseling Robbie and me about what that would mean for our family—perhaps several surgeries, with no guarantee of success—and he suggested we consider aborting. "You're young and healthy," he said. "You can just try again." But we were several months along—I felt as big as a house—and our baby in utero had already won a place in our hearts. "Think about it," the doctor urged us, but Robbie and I told him no. This child was ours, and we would love him or her no matter what. Having been told (wrongly) that I wouldn't ever have kids, I felt that any child that I carried inside me was a gift.

WELCOME TO THE WORLD

Alex was taking a nap one afternoon in 2007 when the phone rang. When I picked up, I would have known the British accent on the other end of the line anywhere. "Hi, how's life?" Maxwell cooed, and my heart lodged in my throat. For five years, not a day had gone by that I didn't think about the possibility of Epstein and Maxwell somehow tracking me down. Now all my old fears came racing to the surface. Maxwell was exactly as I remembered her—breezy, charming, pushing an agenda. After a little chitchat, she zeroed in on the purpose of her call. "I can't believe this but, after everything he's done for all those girls, Jeffrey's being investigated," she told me. "Have you been contacted?" I told her no. I knew nothing about any inquiry and had no intention of trying to find out. Maxwell said that I'd be "taken care of" if I refused to cooperate with investigators. "So long as you don't say anything, everything is fine," she said, even implying I might be investigated, too—as if we were all in this together. "If you need legal help, we're here to help you." All I wanted to do was slam the phone down and rip its cord out of the wall. But I was afraid that if I expressed hostility, Maxwell would see me as her enemy and punish me. I was eight months pregnant, with a one-year-old and a husband who was at work from 6:00 a.m. to 7:00 p.m. As my grandma Shelley used to say, there are times to kick the hornet's nest and times not to. This was not a time for kicking. I promised I wouldn't speak to anyone. "I've started a new life, Ghislaine," I said. "I just want to be left alone."

I hoped that was the end of it. But a few days later, Epstein called. He said hello and tried to make nice at first, as if we were dear friends who'd somehow fallen out of touch. Never good at pleasantries, though, he added abruptly, "I'm having my lawyer tape this conversation." (I would later learn that Epstein had assembled a veritable army of high-profile lawyers to defend him from the allegations: Gerald Lefcourt, Roy Black, former US solicitor Ken Starr, and other well-known men.) I don't remember which lawyer this was, but after he introduced himself, he explained that an investigation into Epstein was ongoing and that it was based on allegations made by women who'd worked as strippers and prostitutes or who were drug addicts. I didn't need a translator to grasp his not-so-subtle point: the accusers had no credibility, and anyone who turned against Epstein was a skank who would be discredited. Just as in my call with Maxwell, threatening energy zinged through the phone line and hung in the air. I suddenly needed to sit down, so I did, resting the bulky landline telephone on my protruding stomach. When Epstein pressed me—"Have you talked to anybody? Are you going to?"—I was determined to reassure him. I knew in my bones that if I didn't give him the answers he wanted, he would hurt me and my family. "Look," I said, "like I told Ghislaine, I'm not saying anything to anyone."

Epstein repeated some of Maxwell's crap about wanting to "take care" of me if I needed legal advice or anything else. "I don't need your help, Jeffrey," I told him nonchalantly, trying to mask the terror overtaking me. "I'm a mom now. I'm happy. I don't want anything to do with this." I remembered how he used to boast about having law enforcement in his pocket. Now that he and Maxwell had found my phone number, I was sure they also knew Robbie's and my street address.

"Jeffrey, I have to ask: where is all this coming from?" I said before we hung up. I guess I was trying to sound as if I were on his team. But I was also curious. After so many years of surrounding himself with young girls in public, at parties, in airports, and all over the world—after so many years flaunting his predilections and boasting of his superiority—Epstein had made some sort of misstep. Even as he deflected, ignoring my question, I couldn't help but wonder what it was.

Only a few days passed before the phone rang again. The man on the line told me he was with the FBI and that I'd been identified as a victim of Jeffrey Epstein's. I braced myself for an interrogation, but nothing could have prepared me for how immediately explicit his questions were. "Have you ever had sex with Epstein?" he asked. "Has Epstein ever ejaculated in front of you?" The man kept going in this vein, saying photos of me had been found in Epstein's Palm Beach house. But was the caller really an FBI agent, I wondered, or was this one of Epstein and Maxwell's minions, testing my loyalty? How had this "agent" located me? "This isn't a good time," I managed to say. "I have nothing to tell you. Goodbye."

It would be a long time before I found out what, specifically, had led law enforcement to begin looking into Epstein. But while I had little sense of what was happening on the other side of the world, I knew this: Epstein had barged back into my life, and I had a feeling he wasn't going to disappear anytime soon.

TWENTY-ONE

A Person of Interest

Two years before Epstein and Maxwell tracked me down in Australia, the stepmother of a fourteen-year-old girl had called the Palm Beach Police Department and said she suspected that her child had been molested by a wealthy Palm Beach resident. (It was March 14, 2005, and across the world, I—oblivious to any goings-on in Florida—was about to get pregnant with Alex.) The concerned woman told police she'd learned about the incident from another mother who overheard the girl tell a friend that a forty-five-year-old man had paid her to have sex with him. The stepmother said she didn't know the name of the man, but she thought she knew the date, about five weeks earlier.

Today, reading the eighty-seven-page incident report filed by the officers who investigated that first allegation, I recognize so many echoes from my own life. Echo #1 was that the girl appeared to have been recruited by an older female, a community-college student who picked up the fourteen-year-old in her truck and drove her to the man's mansion. "Supposedly, the man has a lot of money and often has young girls come over to his house," the report says. "The man starts with a massage. If he likes them, he keeps them around and does more." (Thinking about what "more" meant gave me Echo #2.) The report says the incident in question led to the girl getting into a fight at school with a classmate who accused her of being a prostitute. Sometime after that, the report says, the girl was involuntarily admitted to a juvenile-education facility "because of disciplinary problems that recently escalated." (There was Echo #3; soon, so many more echoes emerged that I stopped counting.)

When the police interviewed the girl, she said the student who'd recruited her was named Haley Robson. She said that Robson told her on the way to the man's house that if the man asked her age, she should say she was eighteen. The girl recalled that the house they went to—two stories and painted pink—was on a dead-end street. When they arrived at the gate, the incident report says, the man was not there, but the girl and Robson were welcomed into the kitchen by an assistant who said the man would return soon. The girls were offered something to drink. When the man did return, the fourteen-year-old said he introduced himself as Jeff. The girl recalled that Jeff had "a long face, and bushy eyebrows, with graying hair." At this point in the interview, the incident report notes, the girl "became upset and started to cry."

The girl said a young blond woman she believed to be Jeff's assistant took her upstairs. She "recalled walking up a flight of stairs, lined with photographs, to a room" with a massage table at its center, the report says. There was a mural of a naked female in the room, as well as several nude photographs of women on a shelf. The assistant told the girl Jeff would be there in a second, and she left. Soon, Jeff walked in wearing only a towel and told the girl to take off her clothes.

Jeff was stern when he told the girl to undress, she recalled. She didn't know what to do because she was alone with him. She took off her shirt, she said, but left her bra on. Jeff told her to take off everything. She took off her pants but left her thong underwear on. Jeff dropped his towel then, exposing himself, and got on the massage table face down. He told the girl to get on top of him, straddling his body, and to start massaging. Her exposed buttocks were touching Jeff's bare buttocks. Jeff "was specific in his instruction to her on how to massage, telling her to go clockwise," the report says. At some point, Jeff flipped over and masturbated. He told the girl she "had a really hot body." Later, Jeff used a purple vibrator to massage the girl's vaginal area. Then he went to the bathroom, where she believed he masturbated again. When he returned, he gave her three hundred dollars. Before she left the house, he asked her to leave her phone number.

Two days after interviewing the fourteen-year-old victim, police officers showed her a photograph of Jeffrey Epstein in a photo lineup. She immediately recognized him as "Jeff." The Palm Beach police initiated undercover surveillance on 358 El Brillo Way and began secretly collecting and analyzing the contents of its trash cans. Among the items police would eventually find in Epstein's garbage: carbon copies of handwritten phone messages that chronicled a steady stream of girls who'd been coming "to work" at the house; a receipt for a 2005 Amazon purchase of three books about sadomasochism: *SM 101: A Realistic Introduction*; *SlaveCraft: Roadmaps for Erotic Servitude—Principles, Skills and Tools*; and *Training with Miss Abernathy: A Workbook for Erotic Slaves and Their Owners*; as well as numerous sex toys, including a purple vibrator that looked identical to the one the fourteen-year-old girl told police Epstein had used on her.

Over the next thirteen months, investigators tracked down more than thirty victims—each one seemed to lead them to at least one more—and interviewed them. The incident report obscures their names, but not their ages. "REDACTED also stated she was sixteen years old when she first went to Epstein's house." "During a sworn taped statement, REDACTED stated she met Jeffrey Epstein over a year ago. She was sixteen years of age." "REDACTED advised that when she was fifteen or sixteen years of age, she was taken to Jeffrey Epstein's house." An employee said Epstein routinely received two or three massages a day from different girls. Asked how old the "masseuses" appeared to be, the employee said he "felt they were very young." The man recounted how they ate "tons of cereal and drink milk all the time"—"like his own daughter who is in high school."

Almost every girl interviewed told a similar story: on her first meeting with Epstein, he'd say that he only wanted her to do things she was comfortable with. But over time, if a girl returned to the house, Epstein would push her to go further and further sexually. First, he'd ask for his nipples to be pinched, hard, then he'd masturbate, then he'd try to fondle them and use sex toys on them. The incident report says he would pay them more if they brought their friends to him. He would pay them more to have intercourse with him and sometimes would force girls to have sex against their will. And he would pay them more to participate in threesomes with him and an assistant, Nadia Marcinkova (the girl I'd been forced to "train" before I left for Thailand).

A particular line in one of the victim interviews jumps out at me, the echo too loud to ignore (and the threat still terrifying, even after all these years): Epstein had told at least one girl "that she could not tell anyone what happened at the house or bad things could happen."

On October 20, 2005, police executed a search warrant on Epstein's Palm Beach mansion, right under the noses of a New York decorator and an architect, who were there planning a renovation. Police officers noted that it appeared Epstein knew they were coming—it seemed computers had been removed from desks. Still, the incident report says officers seized the photographs of naked females that so many of the girl victims had described, as well as the incriminating message pads that included notes to Epstein like this one, written after a call from his friend Jean-Luc Brunel: "He has a teacher for you to teach you how to speak Russian. She is 2 x 8"—sixteen—"years old not blonde. Lessons are free and you can have 1st today if you call." Officers also seized a high school transcript of one of the alleged victims; a bottle of peach-flavored Joy Jelly sexual lubricant; two hidden cameras placed inside clocks; and several penis- and vagina-shaped soaps, which were displayed prominently in the bathrooms.

In February 2006, investigators requested a grand-jury session in which all the girls who had been interviewed would be called to testify. The goal: to seek an indictment against Epstein. But the incident report indicates that there were forces protecting Epstein from being brought to justice: the report notes that a lawyer for Epstein met with the state attorney's office and provided information about the main victims, including their MySpace profiles, where some mentioned alcohol and marijuana use. Afterward the grand jury was postponed. Translation: a smear campaign was underway.

So was a campaign of intimidation. The incident report notes that the father of the original victim "stated there has been a private investigator [at] his house photographing his family and chasing visitors who come to the house." Detective Joseph Recarey, who was then leading the investigation, soon reported that another victim told him she was "personally contacted through a source that has maintained contact with Epstein. The source assured [the victim] she would receive monetary compensation for her assistance in not cooperating with law enforcement." The victim stated she was told, "Those who help him will be compensated and those who hurt him will be dealt with."

The grand jury was rescheduled to convene over three days in April 2006, and Detective Recarey served each victim with a subpoena. But on the eve of the proceedings, not a single victim had been told when or where to appear. Outraged, Recarey went to the state attorney's office to confront the two prosecutors assigned to the case. In the incident report, he states that one of them said that Epstein had been offered a deal: plead guilty to one count of aggravated assault with intent to commit a felony and receive five years probation—no jail time. "Epstein would have to submit to psychiatric/sexual evaluation and no unsupervised visits with minors," the report says. While Recarey was present, the prosecutor answered a phone call from one of Epstein's lawyers, who said his client would accept the deal. Epstein's lawyer then requested that the grand jury be canceled.

Recarey couldn't believe what he was hearing. "I explained my disapproval of the deal and not being consulted prior to the deal being offered," the detective wrote in the incident report. Still, later that day, someone in the state attorney's office called Recarey, he wrote, "to officially notify me of the cancellation of the grand jury. He requested I contact the victims that had been served to appear, to notify them of the cancellation." Recarey told that person he wouldn't do any such thing; since the state attorney's office had made that decision, he said, someone there could handle contacting the victims.

Recarey was pissed off—the incident report makes that clear. On May 1, 2006, in apparent defiance of the prosecutors, he prepared three arrest-warrant requests and submitted them to the Crimes Against Children unit of the state attorney's office. The one for Epstein sought a warrant for four counts of unlawful sexual activity with certain minors and one count of lewd and lascivious molestation. The one for Epstein's assistant, Sarah Kellen, sought that she be charged with "four counts of Principal in the 1st degree Unlawful Sexual activity with certain minors and one count of Principal in the 1st degree Lewd and Lascivious Molestation." The third arrest-warrant request was for Haley Robson. It sought her arrest for lewd and lascivious acts on a victim under sixteen years old.

In July 2006, Jeffrey Epstein was arrested on only two state felony charges: procuring a minor for prostitution and solicitation of a prostitute. He was allowed to post a $3,000 bond and go home. The state attorney, Barry Krischer, had finally convened a Palm Beach County grand jury, but presented evidence from just two victims. The grand jury returned a single charge of felony solicitation of prostitution, to which Epstein pleaded not guilty in August 2006. That was the last straw for Recarey's boss, Palm Beach police chief Michael Reiter. Disgusted with the way Krischer and his prosecutors had botched the case, Reiter took his department's findings to the FBI.

I knew exactly none of this in 2007, when Epstein and Maxwell called me out of the blue. I'd had just five years away from them, and I wasn't done recovering. Soon, though, my family and I would be swept into their maelstrom yet again.

TWENTY-TWO

"He's a Tyler!"

During the first few months of Alex's life, I found my footing as a mother. I saw my job as keeping Alex healthy and safe in our well-protected den, and with every passing day, I got more confident that I was up to that task. But after Maxwell and Epstein's back-to-back intrusions, that confidence crumbled. The thought of the two of them tracking my family's location kept me up at night. Just like that, my former abusers had stolen my peace of mind. With Robbie away at work each day, I stopped leaving Alex alone, even for a minute—when he napped, I sat in the rocking chair in his room, keeping watch. Robbie was worried, too—not only about the danger Epstein and Maxwell posed but also about my fragile psyche. He made the decision that we would stay with his parents in Sydney until our second child was born. We all had to cram into one of Nina and Frank's guest bedrooms, but we made it work.

The next few months were a blur. Robbie organized a surprise baby shower. I got started on a second baby book, pasting in ultrasound photos and the obligatory bikini pic of me, the beaming, rotund mother-to-be. Then, in April 2007, fourteen months after Alex's birth, I went to the hospital in Sydney and had another baby boy. He had strawberry-blond hair, just as I'd had as an infant. And for all the doctor's warnings, the pediatric heart surgeon wasn't needed after all—our new son appeared completely healthy. Relieved, as well as overcome with gratitude, Robbie and I could finally focus on choosing a name. We'd been considering several, but now, Robbie looked into our second son's dark blue eyes and exclaimed, "He's a Tyler!" And that was that.

Tyler Shane Giuffre, who smiled for the first time when he was just a few days old, brought happiness into our hearts again. I had my hands full with two kids, and we were on a tight budget, since Robbie was the only one working. But we more than made the best of it. After we moved back home, when Tyler was three months old, we got a kitten, whom we named Sophie, who joined Champ in our ever-growing menagerie. We kept up our weekly outings to Featherdale National Park, where, at four months old, Tyler pet his first koala bear. At night I held my boys close as I read them *Curious George* and *One Fish, Two Fish, Red Fish, Blue Fish*. When I needed a break, I let them watch *Sesame Street* and *The Wiggles* on TV, and Tyler developed a fixation on *Thomas the Tank Engine*. At eight months old, Tyler started crawling, and soon I was finding train tracks everywhere I went. I'd be cleaning the house when I'd stumble over a vast toy transportation hub. "Boys?" I'd call out to my sons. "How am I supposed to vacuum around this?!"

In April 2008, when Tyler turned one, I answered a prompt in his baby book—"Describe a typical day"—like this: "Not much changes around here. We eat, sleep, poop, play and do it all over again." But there was something else I didn't write down: I was beginning to worry about my youngest boy. Something wasn't right. I just sensed it. Tyler was crying all the time. As he learned to walk, we'd jokingly called

"HE'S A TYLER!"

him the Drunken Master, because he wobbled and fell a lot. But it wasn't funny anymore. At times, it seemed he had trouble focusing. At other times, like when he wanted to run straight into a swimming pool or attempt some other dangerous activity, I couldn't distract him from his goal, no matter what I did. More than once, I'd had to jump fully clothed into bodies of water to save Tyler, even though I had been watching him like a hawk. (How many cell phones had I ruined that way?) One friend recommended I put Tyler on a leash. I balked at the thought, but eventually I gave in. A leash was the only way to keep him safe.

At this point, Tyler was almost completely nonverbal. He'd indicate something he wanted with his eyes, or by yelling when you touched it. Someone told me it wasn't uncommon for second children to talk later than firstborns did—something about the younger one letting the older one speak for them. But when Tyler began banging his head on the floor, I went in search of help. "It feels like he just wants to be heard, but he can't get the words out," I said, guessing at what I thought my second son was feeling. More than one doctor brushed off my concerns, treating me like a helicopter parent. But I didn't give up. "Please," I said again and again. "I just know there's something wrong."

I enrolled Alex in a preschool near our home in Chester Hill, so I would have more time to focus on our youngest. Soon I was ferrying Tyler from speech therapy to occupational therapy, and Tyler and I became regulars at a sort of "Mommy & Me" for nonverbal kids—he'd play with other children, I'd sit with the other parents (mostly moms) and trade stories about what was and wasn't working for us. Some moms swore by special gluten-free diets for their kids, which I dutifully tried. Cooking a whole separate meal for Tyler was a hassle, but I was willing to do anything to make his life better. In Tyler's case, at least, special diets seemed to make no difference at all, so I eventually abandoned that. But there was nothing I wouldn't try. I took him to an alternative healer who practiced iridology, which looks for clues about a person's health by studying the irises of their eyes. We'd gotten him a helmet to protect his head. But he still got blood blisters from all the headbanging. Often he awoke in the middle of the night screaming, and he was utterly dependent on pacifiers to calm him down.

On one particularly hard day, another mother handed me an essay that she said had helped her. It's called "Welcome to Holland," by Emily Perl Kingsley, and as I read it—sitting in a parking lot, with Tyler screaming in his car seat behind me—it made me laugh and cry at the same time.

"When you're going to have a baby, it's like planning a fabulous vacation trip—to Italy," it begins. "You buy a bunch of guidebooks, and make your wonderful plans. The Coliseum. The Michelangelo David. The gondolas in Venice. You may learn some handy phrases in Italian. It's all very exciting. After months of eager anticipation, the day finally arrives. You pack your bags and off you go. Several hours later, the plane lands. The flight attendant comes in and says, 'Welcome to Holland.'"

Holland is not what you signed up for, the essay—which Kingsley, a writer for *Sesame Street*, composed after her son was born with Down syndrome—explains. "I'm supposed to be in Italy," you protest. "All my life I've dreamed of going to Italy." But there's been a change of plans, and Holland is where you must stay. So you do. "The important thing is that they haven't taken you to a horrible, disgusting, filthy place," the essay says. "It's just a different place." Holland is slower paced and less flashy than Italy, but it has windmills and tulips and Rembrandts. Sure, everyone you know is "coming and going from Italy. They're all bragging about what a wonderful time they had there. And for the rest of your life, you'll say, 'Yes, that's where I was supposed to go. That's what I had planned.' The pain of that will never,

ever, ever, ever go away . . . because the loss of that dream is a very, very significant loss.

"But . . . if you spend your life mourning the fact that you didn't get to Italy, you may never be free to enjoy the very special, the very lovely things . . . about Holland."

This made a lot of sense to me. I had initially felt sad that Tyler's behavior as a toddler wasn't like Alex's. But that was just me torturing myself with thoughts of Italy. I loved Tyler, and he'd taken us to Holland. I resolved to embrace where my second-born child actually was, not my fantasies of where another child might have been.

Certainly, life didn't get easier right away. It was around this time that a cop car rear-ended Robbie, leaving him with three bulging disks. Suddenly my husband was almost completely unable to help me with the boys—he couldn't bend over and pick either of them up without feeling excruciating pain. At times I was so tired at the end of the day that I'd fall asleep midway through a Dr. Seuss book. One day at Robbie's parents' house, Alex was in the backyard, picking figs from the tree and putting them in a bucket. I went in the house to wash my hands, but I must've dozed off on the couch for a minute, because when I woke up, he'd eaten the entire bucket of figs. I won't spell out for you exactly what that many figs can do to a three-year-old's digestive tract. You can imagine that for yourself. But the point is that I was tired. Many days, Robbie would come home from work to find one boy breastfeeding, the other in an automatic swing set that we called the Nap-o-Matic because it put babies right to sleep, and me in the middle, at my wit's end. I'd shoot my husband a death stare that said, "You're going to die a horrible death for doing this to me."

Robbie kept urging me to talk to a therapist, as I was still having nightmares. I had consultations with more than one doctor but didn't feel I clicked with them. Then a terrific counselor who was helping me with Tyler pulled me aside one day. "How are *you* doing?" she asked, and the warm way she looked at me made tears pop into my eyes. This woman—her name was Elizabeth—would prove pivotal, not just for Tyler's well-being but for mine. She and I became close, and for the first time I started to examine, in detail, the events of my childhood. Elizabeth helped me understand how extremely damaging sexual abuse is for children. It wasn't just about sex, though that part of one's life was obviously impacted. It was about how being so fundamentally betrayed often made a person feel deserving of betrayal. Through that lens, I began to make space for the girl whose worst experiences I'd sought to erase—all those bad things that had happened that my rational brain knew weren't my fault but that my emotional brain still felt shame about. Elizabeth also helped me examine another part of my past that filled me with guilt. When I recruited other girls to suffer as I was suffering under Epstein, she reminded me, I was caught in a system I couldn't control. I still blamed myself—I probably always will. But Elizabeth was the first to tell me about the importance of self-forgiveness.

Around this time, Robbie made us an appointment with Petra, the woman who'd foretold our lifelong bond. He'd reconnected with her somehow and asked if we could both come see her. Driving to meet her for the first time in October 2008, I didn't know what to expect. A woman with feathers in her hair and a scarf wrapped around her head? A mystic with cloudy eyes and a whispery voice? As it turned out, when we knocked and she opened the door, I saw that Petra was just a normal-looking woman in a floral skirt. She appraised me knowingly, then waved us into her modest home, indicating we should sit around her circular dining table. "So how are you?" she asked, and I could hear she had some sort of Eastern European accent. We told her we were well—our two growing sons filled our lives with happiness. She nodded and reached for a pack of cigarettes. Fishing one out, she put it in her mouth, lit it, and said in her thick accent, "So, how is

"HE'S A TYLER!"

your little girl?" Robbie and I looked at each other, then back at her. "What little girl?" Robbie asked. Petra turned her gaze away, concentrating as if she were fine-tuning her mental reception, then said, "You will soon be pregnant with a girl." I couldn't help but smile. I'd hoped we'd someday have a daughter. And Petra had been right before.

Just after Tyler's second birthday, I discovered I was pregnant. I would get bigger this time, which I know many women do as they have more children. But looking back, I see that I was growing in lots of ways—stepping into my own power, both physically and mentally. I've read that carrying a baby to term takes about the same endurance as climbing Mount Everest. Well, I'd climbed that mountain twice now and was in the midst of doing it a third time. Despite Epstein and Maxwell's unwelcome intrusion, building my own family with Robbie and handling all the joys and struggles that came with parenthood was helping me regain my self-confidence. Which is partly why I now began thinking that we should move to the United States. We'd spent so much time with Robbie's extended family, which I loved, but it only made me miss my brothers more. I nurtured fantasies of an extended reunion where all our kids could get to know each other. I began to lobby Robbie, and while he was skeptical at first, eventually he agreed that we could apply for tourist visas. I was so excited that I began selling what little furniture we owned to prepare for the trip. But I had to change course when our visa applications were denied. Apparently, we had to prove that we had enough money in the bank to support our two children during the period we were in the United States, and our net worth was too low. We were staying put, at least for now.

As EXPECTED, MEANWHILE, Epstein's shadow still loomed over our lives. In 2008, I'd received a letter from the US Department of Justice that said I was being contacted because I was "an identified victim of a federal offense." There was an ongoing investigation into Epstein, the letter said, and apparently scores of women were receiving these letters. The letter included the name of a lawyer I was encouraged to contact. I thought this meant that Epstein was finally going to be prosecuted. But that was wrong. Unbeknownst to any of his victims, a year earlier, in September 2007, Epstein had entered into a secret nonprosecution agreement with the government, which canceled a trial that had been tentatively set for January 2008. And in June 2008—more than two months before I would hear from the DOJ—Epstein had made an unprecedented plea deal. As part of that deal, the government had agreed not to punish his associates and conspirators, both unnamed and named—a list that included Sarah Kellen, Nadia Marcinkova, and two assistants named Lesley Groff and Adriana Ross. Finally, in return for his pleading guilty to two state charges—procuring a child for prostitution and soliciting a prostitute—Epstein was sentenced to eighteen months in prison.

I only learned of the nonprosecution agreement after I contacted the lawyer—his name was Robert Josefsberg—the DOJ had recommended to me. He and his daughter, Amy, who was also a lawyer, interviewed me for months, and during that time, I foolishly thought they were preparing me to testify against Epstein. "Oh, there's no trial," they finally explained. "The government made a deal. But there will be restitution. What you need to decide now is: what's your number?"

I didn't want money. I wanted justice. I told that to the Josefsbergs, but they said it was too late. I was outraged—an emotion I'd soon discover I shared with so many of the countless women and girls Epstein had harmed. While I'd initially been afraid to testify in public, I'd soon realized I had to if I wanted to hold Epstein accountable. It was time for me to stand up, I now knew, and once I'd made that choice, I had warmed to the idea. But the Josefsbergs now said filing a civil lawsuit against Epstein was the only avenue left open to me. So I stepped back from revealing my name to the world. In May 2009, I filed suit under a pseudonym: "Jane Doe 102." My suit alleged that Epstein had "a sexual preference for underage minor girls" and made clear that I was one of them. The filing described my first encounter with Epstein and Maxwell and accused them of "sexually assaulting, battering, exploiting, and abusing" me. It said I believed I'd been recruited by Maxwell from Mar-a-Lago in 1998, when I was fifteen years old (I was mistaken about my age; later, employment records obtained by other attorneys of mine would show I'd begun working at the spa one year later, in 1999). My suit said I'd been forced to satisfy Epstein's "every sexual whim" and that I was also "required to be sexually exploited by Defendant's adult male peers, including royalty, politicians, academicians, businessmen," and others. As a result of all this, the suit said, I had "suffered, and will in the future continue to suffer, physical injury, mental anguish, humiliation, confusion, embarrassment, loss of educational opportunities, loss of self-esteem, loss of dignity, invasion of her privacy, separation from her family, and other damages." As I reread my lawsuit now, two lines stand out: "Plaintiff has suffered a loss of income, a loss of the capacity to earn income in the future, and a loss of the capacity to enjoy life. These injuries are permanent in nature."

IN JULY 2009, Epstein was released from jail after serving only thirteen months; he was placed on house arrest for a period of another year. It would later be revealed that for most of his jail sentence, he'd been allowed to go "on work release" to the office of a nonprofit he'd newly created called the Florida Science Foundation. As delineated in a handwritten addendum to the nonprosecution agreement, he was permitted to visit this office up to twelve hours a day, six days a week. He continued to molest girls there, and after he got out of jail, he dissolved the foundation. After that, his period of house arrest was equally lax: he was allowed frequent trips to New York and getaways to his private island. No wonder he showed no signs of being chastened by his time behind bars. In late 2009, Epstein kept up his self-justifying narrative in a twenty-two-minute conversation with George Rush, the gossip columnist for the *New York Daily News*. Rush taped it and, much later, described Epstein's spiel to *Vanity Fair*. "It was just kind of this self-serving rationale for how he had been tormented by the lawyers for these girls, whom he characterized as these preexisting prostitutes and strippers who'd already been indoctrinated into the sex world," Rush said. "You got the sense that he could adopt many masks. He played up his working-class roots on Coney Island, and how he understood that this was a good story that sold newspapers, and how everybody hates a rich guy. He basically said, I get why this is a good story for you, but I think a better story would be how these con artist lawyers are abusing the legal system . . . He showed little remorse and no pity for his victims."

Had anyone asked me, I could've predicted that Epstein would remain free of remorse. I'd sure never seen him have any. But at least I didn't have to witness his self-satisfaction firsthand. My only contact with Epstein at this point was through lawyers. In November 2009, I agreed to a confidential settlement. The terms: my lawsuit against him would be dismissed; we would both keep the settlement secret, and Epstein would not contact me again; and while he was not admitting that he'd violated any federal statutes, he would pay me $500,000. That was the number I'd named, and I've since been told it was far too low. I'd chosen the amount after looking at the average home prices in our neighborhood. Later I would learn that at least one victim was paid ten times what I was, but back then, I simply didn't know to ask for more.

There are those who've criticized Epstein's victims for entering into confidential settlements with Epstein because, they assert, that allowed him to sweep his problems under the rug. People are particularly judgmental about our receiving money from him. My response to that is anger. The DOJ—not Epstein's victims—made the secret deal that ultimately let Epstein off the hook in 2008: Alexander Acosta, the US attorney for the Southern District of Florida, approved the non-prosecution agreement behind closed doors without consulting with (and while actively misleading) Epstein's victims. Afterward, those of us whom Epstein had abused were told that was the end of it—Epstein wouldn't be prosecuted, no matter how much we wanted him to be. We were also told that extracting money from him was the only way to punish him. (Remember that it was the DOJ that connected me with a lawyer so I could sue.) But here's the real reason I'm angry at those who judge victims who settle: all that legalese in our lawsuits about pain and suffering and mental anguish—those things are real. And getting treatment for them costs money.

When I settled with Epstein, I had a little money for the first time in my life. After years of scrimping—of buying secondhand furniture, driving used cars, and xeroxing baby photos instead of ordering extra prints—Robbie and I could now buy our first house. We found a brick three-bedroom in the suburb of Glenning Valley, about two hours north of Sydney. Epstein had taken what was left of my childhood. But now a tiny fraction of his immense fortune was going to ensure that my children grew up in their own home.

TWENTY-THREE

My Very Own Princess

Convinced by Petra's prediction that our third child would be a girl, I set about decorating a nursery I'd dreamed of creating since I was a child. One wall was painted watermelon pink, and the crib was surrounded by fairies and teddy bears. In contrast to Alex and Tyler, who'd slept in borrowed bassinets and worn hand-me-down clothing, this baby had a mom who had the ability to splurge. Walking into a baby store near our house, I told the salesclerk I was looking for "everything princess."

In January 2010, seven days after my due date, we left Tyler and Alex with Robbie's parents and headed to the hospital so they could induce labor. The next morning, at 2:54 a.m., Ellie Grace Giuffre was born. She had a lot of dark hair and bright blue eyes. When the midwife placed her in my arms, I burst into tears. My daughter was just that beautiful to me. Three days later, we came home from the hospital, and in February, we moved into the new house we'd bought on 50 Bundeena Road. At the age of twenty-six, I was now a homeowner and mother of three, with all my kids under the age of four.

Ellie came into the world determined to take charge. When she got hungry or tired, she didn't cry, as most babies do. She screamed in a way that sounded as if she were giving orders. "You've definitely taken after the Giuffre side of the gene pool," I wrote in her baby book. "Aye Aye Aye you're 95% Sicilian, I'm sure of it! The loudest, most head strong baby, just like Daddy." I breastfed her for just three weeks before it was too much on top of taking care of her older brothers, but that was okay with her. From the start, she was eager to grow up. Even as an infant, it seemed, she wanted to be seen as equal to her older siblings. When I put all three of them in the bathtub together, and Tyler and Alex would help me wash Ellie's hair, she held court. She'd sit in the middle, not even half their size, and use her brothers' much-bigger bodies to bolster herself, but if she set her sights on a particular bath toy, they both knew better than to deny her. When we'd batted around ideas for what to name her, I'd read that the Greek origin of Ellie meant "shining light." That fit. She was impossible to ignore. I'd been eager to have a princess, but my daughter behaved like a queen.

I know all parents think their babies are beauties, but Ellie really was one. She had impossibly long eyelashes and an impish smile, and as I held her in my arms, I realized I felt different becoming the mother of a girl. I adored my sons, but their births hadn't sent me on a trip down memory lane. Ellie's did. Looking at her, I could picture myself as the vulnerable girl I'd once been. I knew what could happen to Ellie because it had happened to me. From the start, having a daughter changed me, awakening something fierce down deep inside.

I began talking to Robbie about wanting to do more to stop powerful men like Epstein from victimizing others. Ever since I'd met the lawyers who'd filed my civil claim against him, anger had been building inside me. For so long, I'd tried to forget—to throw my memories in the back of the garbage can in my head. "I wanted to move on with my life—to move past those memories," I told Robbie. "But you know what? They won't go away. And now Epstein has gotten away with everything, and I'm pissed off." I wasn't sure what, exactly, one woman could do. But just as I'd discussed with the Josefsbergs, I was now talking to Robbie more and more about my stepping forward in some public way. We knew too well what some daughters were forced to endure. What could *we*, the parents of our own daughter, do about that? I remembered how Ruth Menor, my childhood mentor, had started her nonprofit Vinceremos with just one horse. Could I create something like that, but for people like me? Sometimes after the kids were in bed, Robbie and I would whisper our fears and hopes to each other before falling asleep. Increasingly, I was feeling I needed to play a more active role in holding those who had abused me accountable.

At the same time, I was trying to heal the rift with my father. I know that may sound counterintuitive, or even insane—that at the very moment I was pondering how to be more assertive in taking on predators, I was reaching out to the first man who had preyed on me. I now know that it is common for survivors of abuse to try to "fix" their pasts by continuing to engage with their abusers. But I didn't know that then. All I knew was that I wanted things to be okay with my dad—and with my mom too.

Just before his granddaughter turned three months old, in March 2010, my dad came to Australia for a second time to meet Tyler and Ellie. But this visit was rockier. Knowing my dad was good at fixing things, I suggested he and Robbie build a deck around the tiny pool in our backyard, and that kept the peace for a few days. Robbie's birthday was coming up, and I was determined to get him a small fishing boat because he'd told me how much he'd loved fishing as a kid. So I asked my dad for help picking out the right boat. So far, so good.

But then Dad started crossing little lines. I tended to avoid his touch, but he would come up to me in the kitchen while I was cooking and try to hold my hand or would insist on dancing with me. Robbie was seething. "I wouldn't do that with my daughter," he said, through gritted teeth, when we were alone. I didn't defend my dad but asked Robbie not to make a big deal of it. Then, one night, my dad started showing us sexually explicit photographs on his phone. The people in the photos appeared to be adults, but the images were still disturbing. Seeing my father smirking and trying to get me to look, Robbie completely lost it. "Why are you showing naked pictures to my wife?" he demanded, and when my dad got huffy, Robbie went off. "I know you're a fucking pedophile, and you need to get out of my house." Were it not for me, standing in the middle, they would have hit each other. Robbie was screaming, and my dad was screaming back, refusing to retreat. Finally, I took hold of my dad's arm and dragged him to the front door. "Robbie, please calm down!" I begged. "I will get rid of him." Somehow I got Dad in the car and drove him to a lake, ten minutes from our house, where I knew there were cabins for rent.

I booked Dad into a cabin and told him to stay put. I probably should have slammed the door behind me as I left for home, but I didn't. Instead, I promised to visit him again before his flight back to the United States. I paid to change his itinerary, since he was leaving before he'd planned, and of course paid for the cabin too. I guess I still was trying to prove that I was a good daughter. Even then, I needed his approval. Only after Dad finally left did Robbie and I breathe easier.

To commemorate Ellie's birth, Robbie had gotten a new tattoo on his ribs—an affirmation, he said, of the family we'd built. I'd watched him design it for months. At the top, just under his left armpit, were the words "Twin Flame," because we were a team, he said. Two large figures, a man and woman, embraced below—"yin and yang," he explained—and they were surrounded by fire. "The flames signify the intensity of our love," Robbie told me, "but also the hardships that test any relationship that is based on the truth." At the bottom of his rib cage, right above his waist, he'd added in beautiful script, "In Love With Jenna G."

Life went on. Every once in a while, I'd be reading the news or watching TV when I'd stumble across a name or a face that I recognized. Numerous other well-known men who Epstein and Maxwell had forced me to service sexually would pop up in my newsfeed. Almost as disorienting was when I'd see a photo in the newspaper of some other boldfaced name who hadn't abused me but whom I clearly remembered meeting. Bill Clinton would be in the news—traveling to Haiti with George W. Bush, say, to coordinate recovery efforts after a terrible earthquake—and I'd flash on the hard-to-believe fact that once, in what felt like a former life, I had actually met this man who'd served as commander in chief.

Unbeknownst to me, meanwhile, a journalist named Sharon Churcher had begun trying to determine the identity of Jane Doe 102, the pseudonym I'd used in my civil suit against Epstein. First, she reached out to a Florida attorney named Brad Edwards, who was representing several of Epstein's victims. Edwards had figured out my identity because my name appeared repeatedly on various pieces of evidence he'd collected. He also knew from his sources that I'd been lent out for sex with others. In his 2020 book, *Relentless Pursuit: My Fight for the Victims of Jeffrey Epstein*, Edwards wrote that he believed that because I'd traveled extensively with Epstein, and had been trafficked broadly by him, I "held the key to unlocking another level of Epstein's depravity." He wanted to speak with me, so he passed along the few leads he had to Churcher. "If some dogged reporter was willing to take a chance traveling across the world to knock on her door," he wrote, "I was happy to share what I knew."

Churcher, who worked for the British tabloid newspaper the *Daily Mail*, was nothing if not dogged. First, she tracked down Tony Figueroa, who was then living in Georgia. Tony told her my father's name and where he thought Dad resided in Florida. My father had temporarily returned to California at this point, but Churcher eventually found him. She called and left a phone message, which Dad then passed on to me.

Discovering that a reporter wanted to hear my side, after all this time, was at once validating and terrifying. Robbie and I had been talking for months about what my role could be if I shed my anonymity and spoke out against Epstein and Maxwell. More and more, I thought I was ready. I had done so much healing, and I thought other victims of sexual abuse—those hurt by Epstein and Maxwell, of course, but also by others, too—might benefit from hearing what I'd experienced and how I'd survived. Also, I was furious about how small a price Epstein and his crew were paying for what they'd done. And yet I hesitated. I'd worked so hard to build a life that wasn't tied to Epstein and Maxwell. I was still afraid of them and the other abusers they had enabled. Unsure whether I could go through with an interview, I sent Churcher an open-ended email.

"Hi Sharon," I wrote on February 4, 2011. "My Father, Sky Roberts, informed me of your call and I thought I'd send you my contact details so we can get in touch."

Churcher called right away, and from the start, she has said, my voice sounded "shaky but determined." We were speaking off the record, and I warned her I might never switch from off to on. She said she understood, even as she kept pressing me. She asked about how I'd been recruited into Epstein's world and probed for other details about my experience with Epstein and Maxwell, but it was clear she was particularly interested in which of their friends I'd been forced to have sex with. In my lawsuit, I'd referred to Epstein's "adult male peers, including royalty." Because Churcher worked for a British tabloid, anything royal was catnip to her. Who, she asked, was that a reference to? Prince Andrew, I said.

"Do you have anything to back this up?" she asked.

"I'm not sure," I replied, "but I think I still have a photo of him and me together."

That was all Churcher needed to hear. She booked flights from her home in New York to Sydney. From there, she rented a car and drove ninety minutes to our front door. She's said she didn't sleep during the entire twenty-four-hour journey because she worried I wouldn't be able to find the photograph I'd mentioned. But her jet lag evaporated when I greeted her at my front door with an envelope that I'd stashed in one of our bookcases. Inside were several snapshots from my time with Epstein and Maxwell. The photo of Prince Andrew with his arm around me was among them.

Churcher had asked me over the phone to write down what I could remember of my time with Prince Andrew, and I gave those handwritten pages to her when she arrived. Then she and I sat outside in the backyard and began talking. I was still on the fence about whether I would give her permission to use the material I was sharing, but I figured I'd tell her what I knew, and she could tell me what interested her most. While much of the chronology was disturbing to talk about, it felt good to lift the veil on so much that had been hidden. Churcher had brought about forty photos of various men in Epstein's circle, and she asked me which ones had abused me. I have always been a visual person, by which I mean that my mind attaches to images more than it does to words. Being presented with these photos, then, felt surreal. Some of the men were utter strangers to me, but my abusers' faces I recognized instantly, as if I'd seen them yesterday, and I pointed out several.

Churcher acted like a friend who cared about me. I felt as if I could trust her. On one of our days together, I remember we went to the Crowne Plaza hotel in Terrigal, where Churcher was staying, and met up with a photographer, Michael Thomas. He took about thirty frames of the Prince Andrew photo, front and back. He also took several portraits of me posing at a nearby park. Still, however, I wasn't sure I would give my permission for the *Mail* to publish either my story or my likeness.

Robbie and I saw both the pros and cons of letting the *Mail* run my story. It galled us how Epstein had gotten off nearly scot-free. But we both knew our lives would change forever if I revealed that I was Jane Doe 102. I told Churcher that I had already seen shady characters hanging around our house and that I believed Epstein had sent them to intimidate me into staying silent. The stalkers had had the desired effect: I was scared. I didn't want to let Epstein win, but I couldn't decide what to do.

Then I stumbled upon a photo of Epstein walking in New York's Central Park with Prince Andrew. Another British tabloid, *News of the World,* had taken the photo after a days-long stakeout, and on February 20, 2011, they published it for the first time under the headline "Prince Andy and the Paedo." Soon the photo was being reprinted around the world—including in the former British colony where I lived: Australia. I was of course revolted to see two of my abusers together, out for a stroll. But mostly I was amazed that a member of the royal family would be stupid enough to appear in public with Epstein. When Maxwell had first arranged for me to have sex with Prince Andrew in London in 2001, Epstein was still largely concealing his predilection for young girls behind closed doors or on his private island. But by 2011, everyone knew that Epstein—though he'd gotten off with a light sentence—was a convicted sex offender. Seeing this new photo of Prince Andrew at Epstein's side made "Randy Andy" seem even more arrogant to me.

The Central Park photo had been taken during a four-day visit Prince Andrew had paid Epstein at the end of 2010. The prince stayed at Epstein's Manhattan townhouse, where Epstein had even thrown the prince a party, which I also read a squib about. A powerful publicist named Peggy Siegal had helped wrangle the guest list, which included CBS News anchorwoman Katie Couric, the comedienne Chelsea Handler, the talk-show host Charlie Rose, the *Good Morning America* coanchor George Stephanopoulos, the director Woody Allen, and Allen's wife (the daughter of his former partner, Mia Farrow), Soon-Yi Previn. It seemed that being a sex offender had not eroded Epstein's social cachet one bit.*

The one-two punch of the photo in Central Park and the details of that A-list party knocked me off the fence I'd been straddling. I told Churcher I'd go on the record. Her first article based on our interviews ran in the *Mail on Sunday* on February 27, 2011, under the headline "Prince Andrew and the 17-Year-Old Girl His Sex Offender Friend Flew to Britain to Meet Him." That article made clear that I was Jane Doe 102 and accused Epstein of trafficking me to several unnamed men—"a well-known businessman (whose pregnant wife was asleep in the next room), a world-renowned scientist, a respected liberal politician and a foreign head of state"—but stopped short of explicitly including Prince Andrew in that list. I'd told Churcher all the details of my time with Prince Andrew, but the *Mail*'s lawyers worried they'd be sued if she included them. Instead, Churcher repeated my lawsuit's claim of my having been trafficked to "royalty," then described everything about my first meeting Andrew in London *except* the sex. I guess

---

* Only later would it become clear that Epstein had been shunned by at least one powerful person he'd previously wooed: Donald Trump. In their 2020 book called *The Grifters' Club: Trump, Mar-a-Lago, and the Selling of the Presidency*, journalists Sarah Blaskey, Nicholas Nehamas, Caitlin Ostroff, and Jay Weaver reported that Trump ended Epstein's membership at Mar-a-Lago and banned him from visiting in October 2007, after Epstein hit on the teenage daughter of another member. That was a month after Epstein had entered into the secret nonprosecution agreement with the government but eight months before he made a plea deal.

she figured the *Mail*'s subscribers could read between the lines. Churcher also noted I'd met the prince a second time in Manhattan and a third time in the Caribbean. Alongside the article, the *Daily Mail* published the photo Epstein had taken of the prince and me.

I accepted $160,000 for the use of that photo and agreed that I wouldn't talk to anyone else for three months. Later, after the *Daily Mail* syndicated the photo, I received about $4,000 more. Today I understand what I didn't then: that taking money from a tabloid publication for an interview or for use of a photo discredits the story even if it's entirely accurate. The fact that I received that *Daily Mail* payment has been used against me repeatedly to undermine the truth of my story. I've been cast as a person who made things up for profit, when in fact I naively thought that being paid for telling your story was typical. I've never been paid for an interview again.

Reading that first story Churcher wrote was hard for me. On the one hand, the tone of the piece sometimes made me sound as if I loved being in Maxwell and Epstein's rarefied world. I was quoted talking about the jewelry Epstein bought me—"Diamonds were his favorite"—and I was described as "delighted" (a word I'd never used) to be asked to travel with him. At one point, Churcher quoted me as having said, "I was a pedophile's dream"—which is a spicy soundbite, I guess, but something I would never say. On the other hand, though, it felt good to be standing up for myself. I'd told the story of how Maxwell recruited me at Mar-a-Lago, and I'd made it clear that she was a key player in Epstein's sexual pyramid scheme. Calling out Epstein and Maxwell after so many years felt a little like flinging open the windows to air out a musty, foul-smelling room. I hoped it might do some good. Speaking about the recent photograph of Epstein and the prince in Central Park, I'd told Churcher: "I am appalled. To me, it's saying, 'We are above the law.'" Talking to Churcher was my first attempt to try to bring these people back down to earth with the rest of us.

Several days later, the *Daily Mail* published a second story based on my interviews with Churcher. The headline: "Teenage Girl Recruited by Paedophile JE Reveals How She Twice Met Bill Clinton." Right away, the article noted that I had never been "lent out" to the former president. But I guess the *Mail* found it newsworthy simply that I'd witnessed Epstein and Clinton together. "Jeffrey had told me that they were good friends," I'm quoted as saying. "I asked, 'How come?' and he laughed and said, 'He owes me some favors.'" The story also named other well-known acquaintances of Epstein's, including Senator George Mitchell, then President Obama's Middle East peace envoy, and Ehud Barak, then Israel's defense secretary. Barak's spokesman confirmed to Churcher that Barak "did attend several small functions in Mr. Epstein's home in New York." The story also mentioned that I'd met Al and Tipper Gore while in Epstein's company, as well as Naomi Campbell and Donald Trump. The article was something of a grab bag of random facts, but it featured some of the portraits Churcher's photographer had taken of me, next to a stock photo of Clinton.

After the two *Daily Mail* stories ran, on March 9, 2011, Maxwell issued a statement through her publicist denying "the various allegations about her that have appeared recently in the media." The statement called the allegations "abhorrent and entirely untrue." Epstein remained silent.

THE BRITISH TABLOIDS are fiercely competitive with one another, so despite the fact that Churcher had omitted my married name from her reports, soon other reporters tracked me down. Paparazzi too. (In fact, the media frenzy was so crazy that after Churcher's first story broke, Robbie and I had to get out of town, taking the kids to stay in a rented bungalow farther north.) They still found me, eventually, but I told everyone, No, thanks, I'd had my say for the time being. Churcher and I were still in touch, though, and she urged me to consider writing a book about my life. The idea appealed to me, and somehow, while running around after our five-year-old, our four-year-old, and our one-year-old, I managed to start writing a draft. Eventually, I completed a 139-page typewritten manuscript I titled "The Billionaire's Playboy Club," in which I told some but not all of my story. I didn't reveal that my father had abused me, for example. And I fictionalized parts of the narrative because Churcher told me if I did so, I couldn't be sued. That was entirely false, I now know, but this accounts for why some details in the manuscript—which was never published but which later became part of the public court file—do not align with what actually happened. (I wrote that my third encounter with Prince Andrew, for example, occurred at Zorro Ranch, not where it actually occurred: the Caribbean.) I changed those details on purpose, thinking (wrongly) that I was protecting myself.

Some critics have used my 2011 manuscript—just as they used the fact that I accepted payment from the *Mail*—to imply that I was telling my story (or exaggerating and making things up) to profit from my misery. Instead, my goal was and has always been to try to free myself of some of the memories that haunted me, while also focusing attention on the wrongdoing of my abusers. Just as the teenage me had when I was journaling at Growing Together, the adult me felt better when I grabbed hold of the memories that ricocheted inside my head and got them down on paper.

BACK IN 2007, Palm Beach police chief Michael Reiter had taken his department's findings about Epstein to the FBI. As I've said, I soon heard from someone I thought might be posing as an agent, but I heard nothing more after I hung up on him. Now, four years later, the

Daily Mail's stories about me led the Bureau straight to my door. On March 17, 2011, the FBI interviewed me for the first time about Epstein at the US consulate in Sydney. The meeting lasted several hours; I wanted to help the investigators, but it was a stressful experience. It was difficult for me to talk about all that I'd experienced in one sitting; I got through it, though sometimes tearfully. Like Churcher, the FBI agents showed me photographs of men's faces and asked me if I recognized any of them or had been trafficked to any of them. Again, I identified several men who had abused me. Robbie insisted on being by my side during the interview, which was both a plus and a minus. As always, he made me feel safe, but when I described being passed around from man to man to man, my husband got almost as upset as I was. At one point, as the line of questioning got more and more detailed, Robbie completely lost it, lashing out at the federal agents. "You sick perverts," he yelled. "Do you *really* need to know every fucking thing that happened in each and every room?!"

I tried to calm him down. "Robbie, they have to ask all their questions," I said. But when I mentioned even tiny details Robbie hadn't yet heard, he was gutted. You may wonder why I'd kept things from him. But the truth was that at a certain point in our marriage, he'd said he didn't want to hear more about my time with Epstein. Now, though, he felt blindsided. "Why didn't you tell me those things before?" he asked when we got home from the consulate. "Because I don't want you to know every awful fact," I told him, stroking his head. "When you close your eyes and go to sleep or when you look at me across the kitchen table or when we are making love, I don't want you to see some of the things I see." Robbie was fuming. "I don't need you to protect me," he said. "I need you to be straight with me." But I was adamant. "Robbie, at the end of the day, I'm your wife. And I'd like to remain your wife." By which I meant: if you let me leave out some things, we will both be happier.

The day after the interview, two FBI agents came to our house, where I handed over twenty photographs taken during my time with Epstein and Maxwell. The photo with Prince Andrew was among them. I also gave them the massage certificates I'd received in Thailand from ITM. The FBI would later send me a compact disc with digital copies of all these items, but I would never get any of the originals back.

TWENTY-FOUR

A Small Dent

Even as a toddler, Ellie was a character: mischievous, hilarious, stubborn, and strong as an ox. At eighteen months old, she'd wandered off while we were exploring an animal sanctuary called Walkabout Park in New South Wales. I looked everywhere for her and was becoming hysterical when I finally found her, fearlessly chasing kangaroos. I called her my own miniature Tarzan.

I was inspired by my daughter. More and more, I wanted to set a courageous example for her and for my boys too. Through Churcher, I'd heard that Brad Edwards, the Florida lawyer who'd helped Churcher find me, had filed a lawsuit challenging the legality of the federal government's nonprosecution agreement with Epstein. Edwards believed that the agreement, which promised that Epstein and his coconspirators would not be federally prosecuted if he pleaded guilty to state charges, had violated the Crime Victims' Rights Act of 2004. The CVRA asserts that crime victims have the right to meaningfully confer with prosecutors in cases brought against those who've victimized them. Epstein's victims had not only *not* conferred with prosecutors, we'd been kept in the dark completely. Churcher said Edwards had filed his 2008 suit against the US attorney's office on behalf of two unnamed women. If I wanted to join as "Jane Doe 3," she said, Edwards would probably be interested. So I called him.

Edwards was thrilled to hear from me. In his book *Relentless Pursuit*, he described how he felt: "Finally, someone from Epstein's inner circle wanted to talk, and wanted to help." In our first conversation, he explained to me that the CVRA suit was seeking to invalidate Epstein's nonprosecution agreement so that one of the most dangerous child molesters in human history could finally be charged and tried for all his crimes.

All along I'd known that I was just one of many victims hurt by Epstein and Maxwell. But in the nine years since I'd escaped their grip, this idea had remained abstract—thousands of these girls and women probably existed, but I didn't think I'd ever know their names, let alone meet them. Now, Edwards said he was working closely with some of those women, and he offered me the opportunity to join them. Churcher had told me that Epstein had already made sixteen out-of-court settlements with other victims, much like the one I'd agreed to; more were likely in the works. As I talked with Edwards, I wondered if at least some of us could band together.

On April 7, 2011, I had a phone call with Edwards and another lawyer, Jack Scarola, who said he was representing Edwards in another lawsuit.* The three of us introduced ourselves, and Scarola asked me to describe the basic chronology of my time with Epstein. He asked about my level of sexual experience when I first met Epstein and about how I was recruited. He asked me what I was paid by Epstein

---

* Epstein had filed a bogus lawsuit against Brad Edwards alleging that he and one of his victim clients, as well as a law partner, had formed a criminal enterprise and conspiracy to defraud Epstein. That suit, and Edwards's countersuit alleging malicious prosecution, would later be settled out of court in 2018.

and about how soon Epstein had begun trafficking me to his friends. I answered to the best of my ability.

"Are you able to name some of those people for me?" Scarola asked.

I demurred. "No, not at this stage. I just—some of these people are really influential . . . I don't want to start another shitstorm with a few of them. . . . I don't know if I want to. I'm really scared of where this is gonna go."

Scarola said he understood. "Why are you providing this cooperation?" he asked.

"I'm out to help the bigger picture," I answered. "I think that this has gone on long enough." Referring to Epstein, I said, "It's a big slap in my face that he can get away with hurting me so bad, let alone so many other girls, and laugh about it."

At the end of the call, Scarola said, "Okay, Virginia, is there anything else that you would like to add?"

There was. As the mother of three children, I felt it was my duty to stand up to predators like Epstein and Maxwell, I said. I mentioned Ellie in particular. "I would put my neck on the line to make sure she never has to go through what I had to go through," I said. Joining Edwards's CVRA case, I said, was "what I would want somebody to do for my daughter or my sister or my friend." In the end, I said, I was just trying to do the right thing. "That's what I feel like I'm doing," I said. "I'm making a small dent in this big world we live in."

I HAD RESOLVED yet again to find a new therapist. In September 2011, I met with a psychologist in her seventies named Judith Lightfoot. I liked her immediately. Her intake notes (which have been made part of my court file, so I now have a copy) provide a snapshot of what we covered in that first session. Lightfoot asked me about my relationship with my mother. Based on my answers, she circled both "distant" and "non-existent" on a preprinted form. She asked the same question about my connection to my dad ("non-existent") and my brothers (Danny: "distant"; Skydy: "v close").

According to Lightfoot's notes of what I told her, I'd been "entrapped" from age thirteen to age nineteen, and I suffered from flashbacks and anxiety. When I said that I'd been raped by an older man and that I'd then been sexually trafficked, I could tell Lightfoot had never heard of Epstein (she spelled his first name "Geoff"). But she didn't need to know who he was to understand how much he'd hurt me. I told her about our first encounter and how he and Maxwell had made me undress and perform sexual acts. I also told her how they'd trained me "how to please a man." At one point, Lightfoot asked me how I defined my purpose or the meaning of my life. My answer: "To be the best—do no harm." By the end of the session, she had concluded that I was suffering from PTSD, but she told me she believed she could help me reframe some of my thinking about past traumas. At the end of the intake form, she wrote, "Remarkable young woman—supportive therapy needed."

I felt fortunate to have found a therapist I trusted, and increasingly I was feeling optimistic about life. Partly that was because I'd discovered something that was really helping Tyler: Floortime therapy. I loved the teacher. She put effort into really seeing Tyler, not just scrutinizing me as a mother, which I appreciated. Sometimes our sessions were an hour, other times we were there all day—whatever it took to get Tyler talking. "He's a person," this teacher kept saying of my son. "He deserves to be respected." Previously, I'd been guessing at what he wanted—and then handing it to him if he nodded or smiled. Now I abandoned that approach and instead got down on the floor to play with Tyler at his level. If Tyler wanted a toy I had in my hand, my job was to get him to express his desire verbally—to help him see the link between talking and getting what you want. "You just need to find your words," the teacher told Tyler. She was kind but not coddling. She treated him as if he was capable.

When I first insisted that Tyler say the word for a piece of Lego or a ring of keys before I gave it to him, there were tears of frustration—mostly his, but sometimes mine too. But little by little, over many months, Tyler transformed from a frustrated, nonverbal child to a thriving chatterbox. We got Tyler weaned from his pacifiers, and his tantrums subsided. He still lived in his head some of the time, but now he was becoming precociously articulate.

For so long, I'd thought I'd lost my second son. Now, Tyler had been found. He started preschool at a sweet little place called Noah's Ark Learning Centre, and he began to make friends. In April 2012, when he turned five, we threw a party for twenty-five kids at our house—so many that I thought I needed two clowns, not one, to entertain them all. Alex hated clowns, so he spent the day inside moping. But Tyler was thrilled, especially when he saw the cake. He'd asked for a "hammerhead shark cake," which was so specific that I'd had to download a photo to take to the bakery, just so they could get it right.

The joy of bonding with my sons made me miss my brothers. I thought again about returning to the United States. I truly believed what I'd written on the final page of Tyler's baby book: "Family is what matters most!" But how could I make my family a priority when they were so far away?

In addition, I wanted to be more available to help Brad Edwards. The lawyer and I had kept in touch, and I saw him as a hero. Working initially with a survivor of Epstein's abuse named Courtney Wild, Edwards had been among the first lawyers to begin piecing together how Epstein and Maxwell had enticed girls to recruit other girls. Wild had been fourteen years old in 2002, when she was first molested by Epstein at his Palm Beach mansion. Six years later, she'd walked into Edwards's office, and they'd been a team ever since. Edwards seemed tireless and meticulous. Had I lived in the United States, I would have already joined forces with him. Now that felt like the next move I wanted to make.

Robbie and I talked about it. We knew we could get visas this time, as we had more money in the bank. Robbie was torn—he loved our life in Australia, but he also wanted me to be happy. My brother Danny assured him he'd have no trouble finding work in the States. Finally, Robbie said yes. So at the end of the summer in 2013, we sold our house and began the process of packing our things and saying our goodbyes. We weren't leaving for good, we told our friends and Robbie's family. But America beckoned, and I had work to do.

TWENTY-FIVE

Back in the Sunshine State

On our eleventh wedding anniversary, in October 2013, Robbie and I moved our three kids and two dogs—Champ and Bear, a hundred-pound Alaskan malamute we'd gotten just after Ellie's birth—from Australia to Titusville, a city of about forty thousand people in east-central Florida. Titusville is probably best known for its proximity to the Kennedy Space Center, and it's less than an hour from Orlando. At first we stayed with my brother Danny, his wife, Lanette, and their daughter, Sara. Then we bought our own house on half an acre nearby.

Our new house had two stories, with a screened-in porch and a two-car garage. But my favorite part was the backyard; dominated by a gargantuan oak tree, draped in Spanish moss, it backed up to a canal. Every day, I'd take the kids down to watch the turtles and feed the ducks. Robbie and I made friends with our neighbors, a retired minister and her husband. And our location was ideal: I was a three-hour drive from Brad Edwards's Fort Lauderdale office and just ten minutes from Danny. Soon my little brother, Skydy, and his girlfriend moved in with us for a while, which I was thrilled about. It was amazing how quickly we fell back into our old teasing routines (I'd call him Stupid Head, he'd call me Sissie). It felt good to have my family around me again.

We enrolled the kids in school, and for a moment, it seemed they couldn't have been happier. I began looking for work as a bartender and briefly took a job at a closed-down restaurant that someone was trying to reopen. That's about the time we discovered that the local schools were terribly overcrowded. Our kids kept coming home and talking about how they weren't allowed to ask questions in class; the teachers were struggling just to maintain control. I took a leap of faith: we'd try homeschooling. I threw myself into keeping the kids engaged. We'd go to the beach or explore the local tidal pools. We were regulars at the nearby Manatee Observation Deck, where we watched those huge mammals eat seagrass. Some days I'd play classical music in the kitchen until the kids finished their lessons. Other days would be all Eminem, all the time. Alex in particular loved Eminem. Even at seven years old, he'd run around the living room rapping. "I'm not afraid," he'd squeal, and I'd echo him, just as in the song. "To take a stand," he'd call out, and I'd repeat it.

Moving back to the Sunshine State also put me nearer to my dad, who had come back to Florida from California. He now lived in a triple-wide mobile home in Summerfield, about a hundred miles to the east. I tried to see this as an opportunity: for all Dad's faults, I wanted my kids to know their grandpa. Robbie was down on the idea, but I promised him I could manage my father. "He has good qualities," I said. My husband was skeptical, but he went along with my plan at first. For a while, I thought I was making it work—taking the kids to visit Dad and letting them see the playful, fun side of him. Alex loved being a passenger when my dad fired up his riding lawnmower and took it for a spin around his yard. Tyler was transfixed by Dad's PeeWee 500 minimotorcycle. When we bought Ellie her first horse—a cantankerous animal we called Angel, although she was anything but—we kept her in Dad's barn. I was flooded with memories of how Dad and I had bonded over horses, and I wanted Ellie to love horses too. When we got a second horse, Copper, he also stayed at Dad's.

At this point, I asked Brad Edwards to be my lawyer, and as I got to know him, I began to feel as if he were my third brother. Brad had been locking horns with Epstein for years, and man, did he have stories to tell. Once in a court-ordered mediation session, Epstein had tried to be buddy-buddy with him, suggesting conspiratorially: "We should just start breaking the shit out of all these glasses"—he waved at several drinking glasses laid out on a table—"and make everyone think we're killing each other." Brad believed there was a part of Epstein that enjoyed the cat-and-mouse game of being investigated; he wanted the world to know what he'd done (but only if he still got away with it). Whenever anyone zeroed in on his culpability, however, Epstein would turn snide. Brad told me that when he'd deposed Epstein in 2010, he'd specifically asked him if he knew a woman named Virginia Roberts. Epstein's response was to ask condescendingly if Brad would spell my name. Facing more questions about me, Epstein at one point invoked the Fifth Amendment to the US Constitution, which guarantees that an individual cannot be forced to provide information that might incriminate him or her. But when Brad asked Epstein, "Is it true you asked Virginia Roberts to have sex with numerous friends of yours?" Epstein couldn't resist a smug response. "Are you kidding?" he asked, his voice full of disdain.

Much of my early work with Brad and his associate, Brittany Henderson, was a bit like piecing together a puzzle. Like Sharon Churcher and the FBI before them, they assembled an even larger rogues' gallery of faces to help me identify the men I'd been trafficked to. Again I didn't recognize many of the men. But others, it was as if I'd preserved their faces in an airtight vault in my head—one that had been waiting to be unlocked. The former governor of a Western state. A respected US senator. And so many scientists. As I've said, usually when I was trafficked to these men, Epstein didn't introduce us or tell me their names or their titles. Some critics have insinuated that there's no way I could remember these men, given the Xanax and the alcohol that I sometimes relied upon to survive in those years. But to them, I say simply this: When a man has been on top of you, his face just inches from your own, you remember him. You may not remember the exact day, date, or time that the man abused you, but his face stays in your mind, even when you wish it wouldn't.

For example, I told Brad and Brittany that I recognized Marvin Minsky, the prominent MIT cognitive and computer scientist. It hadn't been hard for my lawyers to find Minsky's connections to Epstein. In mid-April 2002, five months before I escaped Epstein's clutches, the two men had hosted a gathering of twenty scholars in the field of artificial intelligence on Little Saint James. The goal of the three-day conference, called "The St. Thomas Common Sense Symposium: Designing Architectures for Human-Level Intelligence," was to contemplate building a computer resourceful enough to have what the group called "common sense." Minsky had published a paper about it.

This could have been when I was trafficked to him for the first time. I'm not sure of the date. What I do know is that Minsky was in his seventies then, precisely fifty-six years older than me (we shared a birthday). And I remember what happened: Epstein sent me to a cabana on the beach and told me to service the man inside. I will never forget Minsky's bald head, and the way his face seemed to have shriveled like one of those folk-art dolls whose heads are dried-up apples. Throughout my time having sex with Minsky, I could hear the waves lapping outside the little room. I tried to focus only on that sound.

Another prominent man I recognized from his photo was a heralded statesman. He was the oldest person Epstein ever trafficked me to, and I have memories of servicing him in both New York and Palm Beach. I remember this man didn't talk to me much. He also had trouble getting a full erection, so we did not have intercourse. I performed oral sex on him instead. I had no inkling of this man's stature (I assumed he was just another scientist). But I knew the man was important to Epstein, because Epstein made a memorable fuss about how gently I was to attend to him. When I was with this man, I never succeeded in getting him to ejaculate, but he enjoyed being touched. Afterward, I massaged his chest, working my way up to his head, and gave him a scalp massage.

For months now, I'd been continuing my sessions with Judith Lightfoot over the phone, and the psychologist had encouraged me to start journaling again. When I told her I was still having recurring nightmares—in one, Epstein sat in a chair, watching me, as I endured something painful—she had an idea. I was to transcribe my worst dreams, ideally right after I woke up from them. Then, when I'd filled up the green spiral notebook she knew I was already scribbling in, I should burn it. Lightfoot believed that recording my worst memories and then destroying what I'd written might help keep my predators' faces from breaking through my subconscious mind each night. Robbie agreed. He'd always believed in the power of ritual. Soon my notebook was full, and Robbie was building me a bonfire in our backyard.

"Honey, let's put an end to all that evil," he said, on the evening we'd chosen to light my worst torments on fire. The kids were in bed, and it was dark in the yard. The orange light of the blaze reflected off both our faces. I was ready. Holding the notebook in my left hand, I used my right to rip out each page. First, I read what I'd written aloud; then, I threw that page into the flames. Eighty-five pages later, I was done. "These men are only in my nightmares," I said over and over. "They no longer own me." I could only hope that was true.

BACK IN THE SUNSHINE STATE

In July 2014, Brad and I prepared to fly to New York to meet the famed litigator David Boies. Boies's firm, Boies Schiller Flexner, was considering joining forces with Brad on his CVRA lawsuit, but before it did so, Boies wanted a face-to-face meeting. Robbie and the kids stayed in Florida—I booked them into a fancy resort in Fort Lauderdale so they could relax while Mom did her job "fighting bad guys." More and more, I was talking to Alex, Tyler, and Ellie about the wrongs I was trying to right. The details, of course, were too much to share, but I wanted them to know that I believed it was important to stand up to bullies but that, at times, that would mean I would have to be away from them.

When Brad and I arrived in Manhattan, we were four hours early for our meeting, so we had lunch and wandered around the Upper East Side. "You know, we're pretty close to Epstein's mansion," Brad said at one point. "Do you think there's anyone still working there who might talk to you?" I said the only person might be Epstein's New York butler, Jojo Fontanilla. I remembered him fondly—he'd helped get me to the hospital that time in 2001, just before I turned eighteen, when I felt as if I were being torn in half. Brad held up a tape recorder with a remote microphone that he'd brought. If we pinned the mic to my blouse, he suggested, maybe I could gather a little intel. "You could just knock and see if Jojo is there," Brad said. "Want to give it a try?"

I nodded obediently. I so wanted to play a meaningful role in Brad's campaign to make Epstein pay. But as we got closer, I started to feel sick. It was a beautiful mild day, but my palms were sweating. Standing on the corner of Seventy-First Street and Fifth Avenue, I gathered myself, breathing deeply in and out. "I can do this," I told Brad. "I'd do anything to push this case forward." But while bringing pedophiles to justice was an honorable goal, I hadn't fully realized how hard it would be to return to the epicenters of my trauma. I had been acting tough for Brad because I wanted him to believe I was worth including in his campaign. But I could feel my panic rising, and I realized, "I can't keep pretending I can lock these feelings away." Burning my nightmare journals was a good start, but clearly I needed to find more ways to process my worst fears.

As we neared the front door, Brad said it was probably best if he waited across the street. He gave me the recording device, and I turned into the entryway where Epstein's brass initials, JE, were affixed to the wall and headed up the steps toward his massive front door.

Robbie says sometimes my balls are bigger than my brain, and this was an instance that proves, yet again, that he is right. What was I doing returning to this place where, treated like a piece of meat, I had suffered so much? I wanted to be brave—to have my mere presence assert: "I'm no longer your victim. You didn't break me." But now I was nauseous; I could hear my heart beating in my ears. What if they let me in? What if someone inside somehow hurt me again?

I rang the bell, and after a moment, a blond, curly-haired girl who looked nineteen or so answered. I asked for Jojo and gave my name. "He was my driver for a while," I said. "I just wanted to catch up and see how he's doing." The girl closed the door and returned a moment later. Jojo wasn't there, she said. I'll never know whether that was true or whether he was just afraid, as I was. Epstein's employees were all required to sign nondisclosure agreements, and they all knew, as I had known, that there were consequences to disobeying the boss. But while I was relieved to walk back out to the street, at the same time, it stung to get the brush-off. I'd thought that Jojo's heart might be big enough to at least say hello.

When I rejoined Brad where he was waiting, he could see I was upset. But the look on his face said he was proud of me. "You were willing to go into the lion's den, Virginia," he said. Looking back, I'm not sure this exercise was worth the trauma it caused me. But I was determined to be helpful, even to my own detriment.

It was time to go see Boies in his seventh-floor office on Lexington Avenue, near Fifty-First Street. We checked in with the receptionist, and a few minutes later, Boies himself walked through the glass doors behind us. After we all said hello, Boies led Brad and me and another lawyer, named Stan Pottinger, into a large conference room.

I'd heard Boies was a big deal. He'd taken on Microsoft in a landmark antitrust case, represented Al Gore in the wake of the 2000 presidential election, and stood up for the National Basketball Players Association during the 2011 NBA lockout, among a zillion other high-profile cases. But for whatever reason, I wasn't nervous in his presence. As he took his seat at the head of the table, I started in, thanking him for considering helping us. As for my own motivations, I told him, "I've stayed silent for too long, but not anymore. I'm here to help stop Epstein once and for all."

Boies asked me several questions in his methodical way, and I told him my story. I said my goal was to undo Epstein's nonprosecution agreement, and Brad chimed in about how he planned to make that happen. When we were done with our spiel, Boies said, "It appears obvious Brad has everything well under control. Where do you see me fitting in?"

It was Brad's turn to talk. "Epstein should be in jail," he remembers saying. "My goal is to put him there. He will do anything to stop me. He has a powerful team behind him and unlimited resources to go after me, and Virginia, and anyone who stands up to him. . . . We're going to need a heavyweight legal team to counter their attacks." We needed Boies's reputation, his clout, and his firm's resources and expertise. "There will be plenty of room for you," Brad promised.

Boies didn't hesitate. "Okay," he said. "Then I'm in." I didn't know it at the time, but this was a transformative moment, not just for Brad, but for me.

Later that night, Brad and I flew back to Fort Lauderdale, and I rejoined Robbie and the kids. It had been a successful trip, but I was bone tired. Over the next several days, Robbie would tell me I seemed to have regressed, as if by briefly reentering Epstein and Maxwell's world, I'd reverted to the mindset I'd had when I was their captive. Back home in Titusville, I slept a lot, and Robbie said I didn't seem able to communicate with him or the kids. I apologized, but in truth, I wasn't aware of how I was acting. I wanted to be strong—to be a fighter—but part of me was leveled by the effort that required. I guess it made sense: I'd been diagnosed with PTSD. And indeed, I felt shell-shocked, like a soldier who goes back into battle before fully recovering from an earlier ambush.

Other parts of my life, too, were sapping my energy—my attempt to make peace with my dad, for example. I'll never forget the day Robbie, me, the kids, and my dad went to the Busch Gardens amusement park in Tampa. Usually, Robbie wouldn't allow me to be alone with Dad—it was an agreement we'd made that we both felt was for the best. But Robbie hates roller coasters, and Dad and I love them, so on this day, the two of us headed off to get in line for the biggest one, which famously went through a lion's pen before it did twelve upside-down curlicues in the air. It was starting to rain, and the line was moving slowly, when suddenly Dad turned to me and put a hand on my shoulder.

"I'm sorry for what I did to you," he said, and he sounded like he meant it. "I'm sorry for what I let Forrest do to you. It was wrong. You were just a kid. You're my baby girl. I always want you in my life. I'm so sad that I put you through everything that you went through." I remember we were half-standing under an awning then, and it was raining harder, so when I started crying, I wasn't sure if Dad could see it.

In the days that followed, I felt almost high: Dad had acknowledged what he'd never been willing to before. It didn't make up for the damage he and Forrest had done to me, but it was still validating. I wanted that to mean a door to reconciliation had opened for the two of us. But then I began to think seriously about my father. He now had several grandchildren, three of them little girls—my Ellie, then Sara, the daughter of my older brother, and my younger brother's newborn daughter. Even as I had allowed my kids to spend time with Dad, I'd watched over them like a hawk and never left them alone with him—especially Ellie. I wouldn't take the risk that Dad might hurt her in the way he'd hurt me. Now, all at once, I realized: my brothers didn't know to take those precautions because I'd never told them what Dad had done to me. I needed to break my silence about Dad.

"We need to have a sit-down," I told my brothers. I think I met with them separately—that's what they remember, too. I told them what Dad had done to me when I was seven, eight, nine, ten, and eleven years old. Neither one of my brothers wanted to believe me at first, but they could see in my eyes that I couldn't be making it up. By the end of the night, all of us were in tears.

My revelations caused things to change. First, my older brother confronted Dad. "You've got some pretty heavy charges on you in this family," Danny said. My dad just looked at him with a mousy expression that Danny would later describe as "really weird, embarrassed, but perverted." Dad neither confirmed nor denied what he'd done—to Danny or to Skydy, who raised the topic soon afterward, when our dad disappeared with Skydy's daughter while at a Tampa Buccaneers game. Skydy was furious. "Don't ever walk away with my kids again," he told Dad, adding, "and you know why, right?" Dad's response: a blank stare.

Danny told me later that he felt he'd seen a monster inside Dad for the first time—that's the word he used: *monster*. After Danny told our dad he would never see his granddaughter Sara again, Dad showed up at the workplace of Danny's wife, Lanette, and cornered her, blocking her exit. He told her he knew where Sara went to school. "You can't take her away from me!" he threatened. My older brother was so worried that Dad might try to snatch Sara that he called his daughter's school and told them that Dad should never be allowed to pick her up ever again. And that was the end of Dad and Danny's relationship. To this day, they do not speak.

Of course, Dad was mad at me too. Why was it taking me so long, you are probably wondering, to expel him from my life once and for all? That was definitely what Robbie wanted, but I was having trouble setting a firm boundary. I'd warned my brothers, telling them what Dad was capable of. Wasn't that enough? Then came a telephone call so disturbing that I will never get over it. I remember I was standing on our back porch in Titusville, looking out at the Spanish moss hanging off our big old tree, when the phone rang. When I stepped outside to answer, the caller (who I knew and trusted) told me they had heard that evidence existed indicating that Epstein had paid my father a sum of money way back in 2000, when I was first being trained by Epstein and Maxwell on El Brillo Way. As that was sinking in—had Dad profited from my pain?—the caller asked if I remembered my father getting a financial windfall around that time, but my mind was blank. I did not want to believe this.

After I hung up, I went to tell Robbie what I'd heard. The thought of a father knowingly accepting hush money from the middle-aged predator who was abusing his teenage daughter was horrifying. I felt like I'd gone into shock. But for my husband, this moment was the last straw. If he saw my dad on our property again, he said, he wasn't sure he could restrain himself. "I want to kill that man," he said. While I'd fantasized for years about a happy family reunion in Florida, the state was proving too small for the Roberts-Giuffre clan. I'd always told Robbie I wanted him to understand where I came from. Well, now he did, in ways we'd never anticipated. It was time to leave.

When Robbie and I put our minds to something, we get it done. I called a moving company. We rented a minivan and packed our bags. I remember the furniture was already on a truck, heading to Colorado, when I called my father and confronted him. "Dad, I know Epstein paid you off," I said. There was a brief silence, and then he started yelling at me about being an ungrateful daughter. "Here's the thing, Dad," I said. "If one of my kids, God forbid, ever accused me of something as disgusting as this, I would tell them the truth. If I hadn't done it, I'd say I hadn't done it. But I'm not hearing you say that. You're not saying a thing."

I don't know if he hung up or I did. I was seething. How many times could this one person fail me? A little more than an hour later, Robbie headed to the backyard to mow our lawn one last time. We were putting our Titusville house on the market, and he wanted it to show well. That meant I was standing inside our empty house alone, looking out at the street, when I saw Dad pull up and get out of his sports car.

I opened the front door, and I could see from the way he was swaggering toward me that he was ready to fight. But I put my hand on his chest and told him he wasn't coming in. "Dad, I need you to stop," I said. "Think for a second. Do you want your grandchildren to see you and Robbie down on the floor, trying to kill each other, with blood everywhere? Because that's what is about to happen. If you don't turn around right now, I'm calling the police."

I must have scared him, because he stopped pushing me. I could see Dad looking over my shoulder, registering the lack of furniture in the living room. "What's going on?" he asked.

"We're moving," I said. "You're never going to see us again. This is the last time."

The look on his face then—I would like to erase it from my memory, but I can't. It was like his features were collapsing inward, like he was being flattened by an invisible force.

"Can I see my grandchildren?" he stammered.

"No," I said. "No, you can't."

That's when he started sobbing. My dad has always been good at making me feel bad for him. "You're my baby girl!" he wailed. "You'll always be my only baby girl." That's Dad: even in the worst situation, he can manipulate things to seem as if they should go in his favor. "If you leave, I'm gonna have no one to look after me," he said. "Who's going to take care of me?"

"Dad," I said, and now I was crying too. "Robbie doesn't know you're here. You need to get in your car, and you need to go before he finishes cutting the grass. Because if he comes in and finds you here, I won't be able to hold him back." Dad's eyes darted around, as if he was listening for the sound of the lawnmower. Then he turned, walked to his car, and drove off. And that was the last time I ever saw my father.

A few minutes later, Robbie put the lawnmower in the garage (we were leaving it for the realtor, in case the house took a while to sell). And within an hour, our family was crowded into the minivan, and we were heading west. Our destination: Penrose, Colorado, just south of Colorado Springs. My dad had broken my heart. I was done with him. Now I would try reuniting with Mom.

TWENTY-SIX

Rocky Mountain High

There's a Kelly Clarkson song that she recorded around this time, and whenever I hear it, I think of how I felt leaving Florida. In "Piece by Piece," Clarkson describes recovering from wounds her dad inflicted in childhood by finding a sustaining love, as an adult, with a kind, protective husband. "Piece by piece, he filled the holes / that you burned in me at six years old," she sings fiercely to her father, and I think of Robbie, who restored my faith in family by building a new one with me. And, of course, I think of the man who burned me: my dad.

At thirty-one years old, I'd been fighting most of my life to feel like a worthwhile person. I'd made strides, no doubt, but sometimes all that healing seemed to disappear. At those moments, I felt like a house in a pounding hurricane whose breakaway walls float away when the storm surge gets too deep. Sure, by design, such destruction may help the house survive. But there's still damage, and until it's repaired, the house is a mess. That was me for a while after we got on the road to Colorado: an unhappy mess.

It didn't help that the minivan we were driving was full to bursting with both people and animals. In addition to Robbie, Alex, Tyler, Ellie, and me, we also were transporting several Chinese fighting fish, three ferrets, a cat, three dogs (Bear, Champ, and Odie, an utterly insane Jack Russell terrier we'd adopted in Florida), a snake named Athena, and I don't even know how many hamsters. What I do know is that our first night on the road, once we'd found a cheap motel to sleep in, we left the fish and the hamsters out in the minivan. The fish froze to death, and the hamsters got loose, never to be seen again.

Now we were heading into unknown territory, both geographically and psychically. Mom and I had been in more frequent touch, but I hadn't seen her in person for years. I knew she wanted me to flourish, and of course I wanted the same for her. When she'd married again, I hadn't attended, but I told her I was happy for her, and I meant it. Whenever I'd brought up anything about abuse I'd experienced, she would tell me she just couldn't bear to talk about the past. For months now, I'd been trying to accept that if I wanted a loving relationship with my mother, I'd just have to take her as she was.

My mom and her husband, Stan, lived in a mobile home in Penrose, a farming and ranching community in Fremont County so rural that it's categorized not as a town but as a "census-designated place and post office." With our house sitting unsold in Florida, we were in no position to buy a home. Besides, we weren't feeling like making any long-term commitments. Instead we found a three-bedroom, two-bath ranch house to rent, just two miles away from my mom. I was determined to make a go of getting to know her again.

Robbie and I found a great school for the kids, which, looking back, was perfectly timed. While I'd loved playing "teacher," the kids were missing the camaraderie of having other kids around. And I was getting too busy for homeschooling, spending more time with Brad Edwards and Brittany Henderson, whom I'd asked to help me create a nonprofit organization to help survivors of sexual trafficking and abuse surmount the shame, silence, and intimidation that victims typically experience. I wasn't sure exactly what my organization could accomplish, but in December 2014, Brad and Brittany helped me file the paperwork to formally get Victims Refuse Silence, as I then called it, registered as a 501(c)(3).

That same month, Brad and a colleague, former federal judge Paul Cassell, put the finishing touches on the motion that sought for me and another victim to join the lawsuit that Courtney Wild had filed against the US attorney's office back in 2008. As I've said, that suit alleged that the government had failed to protect the rights of Epstein's victims guaranteed by the CVRA: the right to confer, to have reasonable notice, and to be treated with fairness. In response, the government had argued that those rights did not apply to Wild because no federal charges had ever been filed against Epstein. But the judge in the case rejected that position, which cleared the way for Brad to try to get me and the other victim attached to the case.

Brad knew he had to be careful. He didn't want the judge to think he was unnecessarily expanding the lawsuit's scope. But he felt it was important to show there were different kinds of victims who'd been impacted. The other woman he was seeking to add, Jane Doe 4, was one of a dozen or so women whom Brad had identified as victims of Epstein's underage sex abuse but whose existence the government had never formally acknowledged. That was because the government had stopped investigating when it entered into the broad immunity agreement for Epstein that we found so abhorrent. In the wake of that, Brad had pushed the US attorney's office to consider these unnamed women as opportunities to go after Epstein again. As Brad wrote in his book, "Because the government, having stopped its investigation, did not know their identities at the time the non-prosecution agreement was signed . . . there could not possibly be any restriction against filing a new indictment against Epstein for those newly discovered crimes committed against these newly discovered victims. Right?" Wrong. Despite Brad's urging, no new charges had been brought. That was why he wanted Jane Doe 4 attached to his suit.

He wanted me attached, meanwhile, because unlike the case's original petitioners, who were abused only in Palm Beach, I'd traveled the world with Epstein and been lent out to several prominent men, some of whom Brad was planning to name. I would be kept anonymous, he said, and referred to as Jane Doe 3.

Brad decided we would file our motion for joinder, as it's called, the day before New Year's Eve 2014. He hoped the filing would go unnoticed, given the holiday. And perhaps it would have, but for Josh Gerstein of *Politico*. On December 31, Gerstein blogged about the filing in general, but mostly about me. "A woman allegedly kept as a sex slave by politically connected billionaire investor Jeffrey Epstein, who went to jail for having sex with underage girls, is accusing several prominent friends of the financier of having taken part in the debauchery, according to a new court filing," Gerstein wrote. "The woman—referred to in court papers as Jane Doe #3—leveled the allegations Tuesday."

Gerstein's story went on to quote this part of our filing: "Epstein . . . trafficked Jane Doe #3 for sexual purposes to many other powerful men, including numerous prominent American politicians, powerful business executives, foreign presidents . . . and other world leaders. Epstein required Jane Doe #3 to describe the events that she had with these men so that he could potentially blackmail them."

When the *Politico* story hit, it unleashed a firestorm of press, and for Maxwell, who we'd referenced by name in the complaint, that was particularly unwelcome. Maxwell had been attempting a reputational makeover by founding the TerraMar Project, a self-described environmental nonprofit organization that was vaguely focused on creating a "global ocean community" (whatever that means) based on the idea of shared ownership of the high seas. She was in the midst of fundraising. So it was no surprise when, on January 2, 2015, Maxwell issued a statement through her publicist identifying me by name and calling me a liar.

"Jane Doe 3 [sic] is Virginia Roberts," the statement began. "The original allegations are not new and have been fully responded to and shown to be untrue," it went on. "Each time the story is retold it changes with new salacious details about public figures and world leaders . . . Ms. Roberts' claims are obvious lies and should be treated as such and not publicized as news, as they are defamatory."

On January 13, 2015, Sharon Churcher—determined to capitalize on my being back in the news—wrote a misleading news story about the handwritten pages about my time with Prince Andrew that I'd handed her the day we first met in 2011. Photos of those pages—my loopy handwriting on lined paper—accompanied a story by Churcher on the gossip site Radar Online, and its headline couldn't have been more breathless or error-ridden: "Diary Entries of 'Teen Sex Slave' Detail Sordid Hook-Up with Prince Andrew—in Her Own Handwriting." Billed as a "bombshell world exclusive," the story was inaccurate in that it described the twenty-four pages I'd given her as a "secret diary" and implied I'd written them as a teenager, when I was with Epstein, not a decade later, when she asked me to. Reading those pages again, I was embarrassed by the girlish tone. But more than that, I was disgusted by Churcher. Once I'd believed she was my friend; now I saw she was nothing but a bottom-feeder. How long, I wondered, would she try to dine out on her years-old interviews with me?

It's no fun being called a liar. It sucks to be the subject of erroneous muckraking. Dr. Lightfoot, my psychologist, had taught me breathing exercises to help with my anxiety attacks, but in these weeks right after the joinder motion, it was all I could do to not hyperventilate.

But then something amazing happened. Boies had a colleague in his firm's Fort Lauderdale office named Sigrid McCawley. She'd been on maternity leave after having her fourth child, and as she was preparing to return to work, Boies mentioned my case to her. While her background was in contractual and securities litigation, McCawley had volunteered for years on behalf of abused women and foster children. When the CVRA case put me squarely in the spotlight in early 2015, Boies reached out to McCawley and asked her to meet me. I flew to New York, and the moment I met McCawley, a striking, willowy blond with an assertive demeanor, my life changed for the better.

I'd always be grateful for Brad Edwards. He'd been the first lawyer to stand up for me; he'd taught me so much, and he would continue to do so. But in Siggy, as I'd begun calling McCawley after hearing her mom use this nickname, I felt as if I'd found a sister in arms: smart, fearless, relentless. Together, David Boies, Brad, and Siggy were the legal dream team I needed to begin truly holding my abusers to account.

Not that doing so was going to be easy. Can you remember America before the #MeToo movement? As I write this, it's been less than seven years since three brave reporters and their sources sparked a conversation about sexual harassment, assault, gender, and power by revealing countless bad acts by movie producer Harvey Weinstein. Still, many have forgotten how dangerous it was then for women to confront their abusers. It's still dangerous, to be sure, but it was way worse then. Even if we wanted to, Siggy and I will never be able to forget.

When she and I joined forces in early 2015, it was more than two years before Weinstein's depravity would be unmasked, and many people were unaware of the existence of serial abusers like him. Moreover, many were skeptical then of female victims who came forward. Actually, I'm being too polite. Let me rephrase: at that time, survivors of abuse who took on those who'd victimized them were routinely discredited, treated like whores, and beaten up all over again in the press. Siggy and I remember what we call those "dark days" because we lived through them together. And for me, this headline about me—which appeared in the *New York Daily News* just weeks after she and I first met—says everything about what we were up against:

PRINCE "VIC" IN FALSE-RAPE FLAP
SEX SLAVE SHOCK
ACCUSER'S CLAIM TOSSED IN '98 CASE

Those words appeared on the *Daily News*' front page on February 23, 2015, superimposed on the photo of Prince Andrew with his arm around his "vic[tim]": me. "Virginia Roberts, who claims she had orgies with Prince Andrew as a sex slave, made rape claim against two teens when she was 14," read a caption. Readers who turned the page found an article based on a leaked, seventeen-year-old Palm Beach County Sheriff's Office report that had been written when I was fourteen. I've already described the disturbing details of what deputies were investigating back then: two teenage boys, one seventeen and the other eighteen, had sexually assaulted me in the back of a car while I was unconscious in 1998. Now I was thirty-one years old, and I had just named a few of my Epstein-related abusers in court filings. In response, someone had dug up this confidential report and fed it to the press.

Juvenile records—especially reports about minor victims—are supposed to be kept under seal. But a legal breach wasn't the worst thing about this article. The worst thing was that it (and its "false-rape" headline) misinterpreted what the leaked report said, making it look like prosecutors dropped the case because they didn't believe I was telling the truth. In fact, the reason the case wasn't prosecuted was murkier: the assault had been reported by a counselor at Growing Together; because I was enrolled there, investigators who wanted to interview me had difficulty contacting me, the report acknowledged; and both boys—while they confirmed they'd had sex with me—insisted it was consensual, so it was the classic he-said, she-said situation. Yes, the documents stated the case was not prosecuted "due to the victim's lack of credibility and no substantial likelihood of success at trial." But according to Siggy, that was boilerplate language used by law enforcement when a case was inconclusive.

Reached for comment, Siggy tried to point that out. "For the prosecutors to describe her as not credible means only that they did not think they had sufficient evidence to win. But she was raped," the *Daily News* quoted Siggy as saying. "And to be victimized all over again with the leak of sealed juvenile records is disgraceful . . . Despite the efforts of her critics, she will not be silenced."

I loved having this strong woman fighting for me, and I told Siggy so. I would soon nickname her "Superwoman." But even with Superwoman in my corner, the *Daily News'* callous rehashing of my awful childhood felt like a low blow. When that first story dropped, Siggy and I got on the phone, and she told me we probably needed to brace for more of the same. In her previous legal work, Siggy said, "No comment" had been her usual response to media inquiries. But we were dealing with something different here, she believed. Reading the article, it seemed the reporter had cherry-picked phrases from the leaked sheriff's report with the goal of painting as withering a portrait of me as possible. For example, the story quoted the report as saying my mother had told a detective in 1998 "about her daughter's past drug abuse and also how many kids in Royal Palm Beach are involved in drugs, witchcraft and animal sacrifice." I mean, talk about guilt by association! I've been accused of a lot of things, but animal sacrifice? No one loves animals more than I do.

Five days after the leaked rape report article, the *Daily News* came after me again. This piece, cowritten by the author of the earlier piece, was headlined "Jeffrey Epstein Accuser Was Not a Sex Slave, but a Money-Hungry Sex Kitten, Her Former Friends Say." The story, which described me as "a hard-partying teen who eagerly traded sex for cash," relied heavily on a Loxahatchee, Florida, resident named Philip Guderyon, who said he'd been at Growing Together at the same time I was (though I had no memory of him). Guderyon claimed I was Epstein's "head bitch" and said I never looked like I "was being held captive." What the article didn't say was that Guderyon had a rap sheet that included grand theft, trafficking in stolen property, cocaine possession, and resisting an officer. Guderyon would also later be convicted and sentenced to ten years in prison for striking a man in the head and causing his death at a bar.[*] Guderyon was not exactly a reputable source who knew me well.[†]

Again, Siggy tried to defend me. "To say that our client acquiesced in this abuse, or that the abuse was OK because she was paid for it, leaves out the fact that this is why we have laws in the United States to protect minor children who are groomed and sexually trafficked by adults," she told the *Daily News*. "Blaming a minor child who was being sexually trafficked by a wealthy and incredibly powerful individual is irresponsible and works only to silence other victims and reward the abuser."

But Siggy might as well have been screaming into the wind. She

---

[*] In February 2025, the South Carolina Supreme Court reversed the conviction and ordered a new trial, finding that the lower court failed to give the jury proper instructions regarding Guderyon's defense.
[†] We would later learn that in the days after my joinder motion that named names, Epstein and Maxwell had communicated about how to convince people to discredit me. "You can issue a reward," Epstein had written Maxwell in an email dated January 12, 2015, "to any of Virginia's friends, acquaints, family, that come forward to help prove her allegations are false."

and Brad and I were coming to the conclusion that if we wanted to battle these smear campaigns and focus attention on the truth, we needed to do more than have Siggy comment. After some media reports insinuated that I was an inadequate mother who was setting a bad example for her three children by lying, I wholeheartedly agreed. These stories proved to me that certain critics of mine would stop at nothing to hurt me and my family. I guess I shouldn't have been surprised that people affiliated with Epstein, a legendary pedophile, were quick to throw shade on my children. But that was the last straw for me. It was time to take back control of my narrative from those who sought to shame me.

I had come so far. Just thirteen years before, I'd flown to a foreign country with little idea of how I would break free from Epstein and Maxwell. Now not only had I liberated myself, but I'd also fortified my resolve, transforming from a skittish teenager who wished only to disappear into a strong woman whose name and face were becoming linked in the public sphere with the idea that victims should hold their abusers to account. But when my critics took aim at my ability to parent my children, that pushed me to a new level of ferocity.

I'd built a family with Robbie. I'd drawn a line with my father. I'd unpacked some of my worst baggage with Dr. Lightfoot, and with the help of my lawyers, I'd put names to some of my abusers' faces—faces that I still could see as clearly as when I'd first laid eyes on them. I'd also taken the first steps toward joining a growing community of women who'd survived Epstein and Maxwell's abuse and who were adamant that this twosome and others in their circle pay for what they had done. On my best days, I could picture myself standing shoulder to shoulder alongside these brave women. While I still had moments of weakness, more and more I was feeling strong. It was time to fight, and for the first time in my life, I felt ready.

Part IV

WARRIOR

"Never doubt that a small group of thoughtful, committed citizens can change the world. Indeed, it is the only thing that ever has."

—Margaret Mead

TWENTY-SEVEN

The Point of No Return

Picture a family of five, mugging for the camera in their annual Christmas portrait. Every December since their first child was born, Mom has gotten Dad to take their whole brood to the local shopping mall to wait in line for a photograph with Santa Claus. Even in years that money was tight, Mom saved up to pay for this image, insisting it was worth every penny. Now, though, her two sons and one daughter are older. No one believes in Santa anymore, and so everyone—including Dad—grumbles when asked to pose each year with a chubby, bearded man in a red suit and hat. Still, Mom won't relent. She's willing to die on this holiday hill.

"You'll thank me for this later," I say. It's important, I tell my family, to revel in life's most joyous moments. Call them silly rituals all you want, I say, but we must preserve happy memories because there will be times ahead when we will need them. Happy memories can keep a person going. I know this better than most because I once had so few of them.

THE HOUSE ROBBIE and I rented in Penrose, Colorado, sat on five acres of flat, dusty farmland. To get there, you turned off J Street and drove down a curved dirt and gravel road that led only to our front door, which was white with a large oval leaded window that afforded a glimpse into our small entryway. When we moved in, I thought the see-through door had a certain country charm. But the main reason we picked it was that my mom and her husband, Stan, lived close by.

Suddenly, I was spending more time with Mom than I had since my childhood. For more than a dozen years, she and I had lived eight thousand miles apart. Now we were neighbors. It meant the world to me that she was finally getting to spend time with her grandchildren—ages eight, seven, and four. When she visited us, she doted on them. Especially when she played with Ellie, I remembered what Mom had been like with me when I was small. My mother could be so loving. It was good to see that again.

The other day, I saw an Instagram video of one of my favorite singer-songwriters, Pink, on *The Today Show*, promoting her album *Trustfall*. Describing the difficult relationship she's had with her own mother and how they've tried to reconcile, Pink said: "Love is a lifetime of coming back to the table." Boy, does that resonate with me. By moving to Penrose, I had come back to the table where my mother had been sitting for years. She was not exactly the same woman I'd grown up with, although a part of her always would be. When I was a teen, she'd kept me at a distance. Now she wanted to be part of my life.

Mom proved to be an inexperienced babysitter—the single time she offered, it lasted just twenty minutes, until Tyler somehow got his finger stuck in the trigger of a plastic Nerf gun and she called me, begging me to come back. But I wasn't eager to leave my kids alone with her anyway. And yet I was comforted knowing that she was close by. I don't want to give the false impression that we somehow resolved all our past disputes during this period. When I told her, for example, a few of the names of the men I'd been trafficked to by Epstein, she repeated what she'd said to me before: that she didn't want to hear about any of my past abuse—it made her too upset. My mother definitely doesn't believe in talking things out. Nonetheless, a girl needs her mom, and I'd gone without mine for a long time. I was feeling more attached to her than I had in forever—a feeling that only intensified when scary things started happening, things Robbie and I couldn't explain.

Since my joinder motion had been filed in the CVRA case, we had come home more than once to find evidence that strangers had been inside our house. Robbie was vigilant about placing wooden "drop bars" in the sliding windows and doors to prevent them from being opened, and he always deadbolted all our locks. Nonetheless, it was becoming routine for us to return home to find the deadbolts unlocked. One afternoon, we came back from a trip to Walmart and discovered the front door wide open. Our malamute, Bear, who we'd left inside, was out in the street. We called the sheriff's department, and when we told the deputies who responded that nothing had been stolen, they speculated that the intruders might have entered in order to install some sort of spyware on our computers. They recommended that deputies place surveillance cameras outside to record the make and model of every vehicle that drove up our driveway. Of course, we said yes, and soon, they'd rigged an elaborate system aiming every which way.

They also suggested that we obtain a means of self-defense. And so we headed to Warrior Kit, a law-enforcement supply store about twenty miles from our house, in West Pueblo. We bought two guns (and a gun safe to keep them in): a five-shot revolver known as "The Judge" for me, and a nine-millimeter handgun for Robbie. For a few months after that, we were regulars at the shooting range in Warrior Kit's basement. Both Robbie and I wanted to feel confident that if the time came, we'd know how to defend our family.

Paparazzi followed us everywhere in and around Penrose. Once, I walked out our front door and smacked right into one of them—he asked me a question, I declined to comment, and he took my picture. Soon that photo of me, with a beige coat, a black scarf, and a knit beanie on my head, was ricocheting around the world with a caption that said I was "hiding out" in Colorado. On another occasion, when the kids were sick, paparazzi snapped images of me leading them out of a doctor's office. I wanted to scream, "Get away from my family, you pricks! Leave my bloody kids out of it!" (Even in my imagination, I swear like a true Australian.) But instead of letting loose like that, I just hustled my children to the car.

All this was more than intrusive—it was dangerous. I got run off the road once by what I presumed were tabloid journalists. I sat in the locked car on the side of the road, shielding my face and trying not to panic, until they finally left me alone. We were chased so often that Robbie became adept at turning down side streets at the last moment, pulling speedy U-turns, and driving more like we were in a war zone than a rural hamlet. This was crazy-making. I would scream at Robbie to slow down. He would scream at me that the United States was a ridiculous, lawless country. I would yell that paparazzi existed everywhere on earth. He would yell that maybe it was time to put our family's welfare ahead of my desire to seek justice. I would fume. He would slam his foot down harder on the gas pedal. At times, it felt like we were skirting the outer limits of our sanity.

IN APRIL 2015, two important things happened—both of them frustrating. On April 7, Judge Kenneth Marra, the judge presiding over the CVRA case, ruled that I could not join as Jane Doe 3 because my filing was "duplicative" of the existing lawsuit. Moreover, Marra ruled that my allegations about Prince Andrew and others should be struck from the record. "At this juncture in the proceedings, these lurid details are unnecessary," Marra wrote. While he made no ruling about the veracity of my allegations, Marra said the "factual details regarding with whom and where" I had been forced to have sex were "immaterial and impertinent." However, he noted that I might yet appear as a witness in the case. Brad and I released a statement that said my legal team absolutely respected the judge's ruling. "I'm happy to get to participate in this important case," the statement quoted me as saying. But I was disappointed.

That disappointment evaporated, though, when Brad and Siggy brought me good news. For months, they'd been putting out feelers to all the major TV networks, gauging whether they wanted to interview me. Every one had said yes. I was finally going to tell my own story to a news organization that was held in high esteem. We weighed our options and, in the end, chose ABC—I was a fan of the anchor Amy Robach, and her producer Jim Hill was a top-notch investigative reporter. When the interview date was set, Robbie and I decided he would stay in Colorado and the kids would come with me. I wanted them to understand why Mommy was always either on the phone or, too often, leaving on a plane. The four of us flew to New York City from Denver, and the next day, ABC hired two nannies to take Alex, Tyler, and Ellie to the Central Park Zoo while I got prepped in a suite at the Ritz-Carlton Hotel on Central Park South.

Sitting in that elegant room, getting wired with a microphone, I was excited. This could be a game changer, I thought. I was eager to talk about how the US government had looked the other way when it came to Epstein and Maxwell's crimes. I wanted to describe the anger and betrayal I felt and that all of Epstein and Maxwell's victims felt.

After years of seeing the media as my enemy, I wanted to believe that the media could also help our cause.

Robach and I took our seats, and the interview began. I felt immediately at ease. Robach was prepared, and her tone signaled to me that she was after the truth. "This is a story about a guy who's still walking around New York City, free as a bird, who's done all these atrocious things to me and to so many," I remember telling her, "and we've never gotten any kind of justice." Robach asked, What about the fact that Epstein had admitted that he'd procured girls for prostitution in Florida? "I don't count that as justice," I said. "I don't think labeling those minor girls 'prostitutes' and then him getting only thirteen months in jail—with him leaving the jail every day—is justice. Do you?" For probably ninety minutes, I told Robach everything I knew about how Epstein and Maxwell had organized their sex-trafficking ring. I told her the names of several men I'd been trafficked to. I wept a few times when she asked me to go into detail about particular incidents of abuse. But that was okay. I felt as if I spoke from the heart.

When the interview concluded, there was a celebratory feeling in the room. People from the network told Brad and Siggy it had gone great. A segment from the interview would air on *Good Morning America*, we were told, and then the rest would appear on one of the network's longer-format shows. I felt relieved and proud. When I reunited with my kids that night, I told them, "Your mom did a good job today."

But then the waiting began. We were strung along for weeks with no explanation for the delay. Finally, someone from the network told my legal team that because I'd told Robach about being trafficked to Prince Andrew, the network had to reach out to Buckingham Palace and an attorney for Epstein. Why that was causing such delays was

THE POINT OF NO RETURN

unclear. Robach and her producer were outraged. But for whatever reason, ABC never aired the interview.*

I'd been defeated once again by the people I was trying to speak out against. And I couldn't help but wonder, if a media giant like ABC could be shut down in its attempts to reveal the truth, was there any hope for survivors like me?

---

* Four years later, on November 5, 2019, a video of Amy Robach speaking on a "hot mic" was made public that shed a bit more light on what had happened. Robach said that "every day I get more and more pissed" that her interview with me didn't air and that "what we had was unreal." In the recording, Robach said that she was told by higher-ups, "Who's Jeffrey Epstein? No one knows who that is. This is a stupid story." She also said Epstein's lawyers and the British royal family had applied pressure to nix the interview, suggesting that the network caved because it feared losing access to Prince William and Kate Middleton in the future.

TWENTY-EIGHT

Always My Daughter

In July 2015, Robbie and I decided it was time to return to Australia. Robbie's elderly father, who already had prostate cancer, had now been diagnosed with asbestosis. Between that and the unease we'd been feeling since the first break-in, we no longer felt comfortable in Colorado. This wasn't an easy call for me. I'd had a lot invested in the idea that being in the United States would let me mend some relationships in my family. I'd made some progress, especially with my brothers, but I had also lost some ground. That feeling of loss, plus the fact that my work with Brad and Siggy was far from done, made me reluctant to leave.

But any desire I had to stay in America was outweighed by how unhappy I knew Robbie was. While he wanted to work, increasingly he didn't feel like he could while still keeping our family safe. It was hard for a proud man like Robbie not to provide for his family. But he and I both had become—I was going to say paranoid, but that's not right. Paranoia is an irrational feeling that people are out to get you.

Based on what we'd been through, it was perfectly rational for us to believe that our family was in danger.

So in July 2015, Robbie flew home to Australia. The plan was that we'd resettle 1,500 miles north of Sydney, near the city of Cairns. Robbie had a friend there who said job prospects were good, and we hoped Cairns's remote location would afford us more privacy. Robbie would get things set up for us—finding work and a place to live—while I stayed behind with the kids to pack up and resolve a few loose ends.

The truth was that Siggy and I had several things to accomplish before it made sense for me to head back Down Under. Which was fine by me, because the more I got to know Siggy, the more I respected her. Raised by a single mom who worked three jobs to support her three daughters, Siggy had been ambitious and determined practically since birth. Though we were just eleven years apart in age, I looked up to her. I soon learned that she'd faced personal challenges—she'd struggled with infertility before finding a doctor who helped her and her husband have the four kids she calls "IVF miracles." At work, meanwhile, her intellect was matched only by her compassion. Siggy told me she felt she'd been preparing her whole career for a case like mine. "Life takes you places for a reason, Virginia," she said, recalling the years she'd spent volunteering in a domestic-violence shelter. "All that positioned me perfectly to hear your story and to take on your case, the most important of my career."

As I'd done with Brad, I worked closely with Siggy to meticulously study photographs of men who were known to be Epstein associates, and we confirmed several more men I remembered being trafficked to. Some of their identities shocked me, if only because they represented such a broad swath of power and influence. I remembered each of these men's faces as if it were the day they abused me. As much as I might wish to, I could never forget them. One of these men would pass away around this time. It was unclear what, if any, legal action we might take against the rest, but identifying them—even if only to myself—had a redemptive power. These were well-known, sophisticated, wealthy men—men who enjoyed a certain cachet in their respective fields. With every name I uncovered, I appreciated more fully something I had sensed as a teenager: had any of us girls reported being trafficked when we were first abused, it was unlikely that anyone would have listened. I wondered if anyone would listen now.

Siggy, meanwhile, had been studying up on defamation, an area of the law that was evolving in the wake of the #MeToo movement, as victims who'd long been silent spoke up. In response, more and more alleged perpetrators were suing their accusers, claiming they'd been defamed. But Siggy believed she'd found a different way for me to challenge Maxwell. Specifically, when Maxwell's publicist issued a statement in January 2015 that called me a liar, Siggy believed Maxwell had defamed *me*. And she thought not only that she could prove it but that such an action would allow us to describe the abuse I'd suffered without being hamstrung by the statute of limitations (which prevented me from bringing a criminal case against Maxwell).

Siggy explained that when accused persons deny the allegations against them, that does not necessarily mean they can be successful in a defamation suit. Not if it is a mere denial. "But Maxwell was somebody who sexually abused you, and *then* called you a liar," she said. "That denial is different because it is in the context of a sexual-abuse case. Now the public can assume Maxwell has information that others don't know about." That's the key: that Maxwell called me a liar based on facts that she knew but that were undisclosed. In other words, her statement *implied* an assertion of fact. "So we are going to say that was defamatory and that you have a right to defend yourself," Siggy said. "We will sue her for defamation, and in order to establish the defamation, we will have to get into details surrounding the sexual abuse." Have I mentioned that I see Siggy as a superhero? Well, here was more proof of why.

In September 2015, Siggy filed my claim against Maxwell in Manhattan federal court. It said Maxwell had made "a deliberate effort to maliciously discredit" me and to silence my efforts to expose sex crimes committed around the world by her, Epstein, and other powerful people. It said Maxwell's denials had damaged my credibility and reiterated that "with the assistance of Maxwell, Epstein was able to sexually abuse Giuffre for years until Giuffre eventually escaped." But my favorite line in my suit explained why I was suing in the first place: "Ultimately, as a mother and one of Epstein's many victims, Giuffre believed that she should speak out about her sexual abuse experiences in hopes of helping others." I wanted the world to know that becoming a mother—particularly the mother of a daughter—had fueled my determination to act.

LATE ONE NIGHT in Colorado, after Robbie had returned to Australia, I was folding laundry when I saw headlights on our long, winding driveway. As I've said, we lived on a big lot, way off the main road. There was no reason to drive down our gravel drive unless you were visiting us. I wasn't expecting anyone, so the headlights put me on high alert. The car approached slowly, then stopped. I watched for some movement, but the driver stayed put in the front seat, idling, with the high beams trained on our see-through front door.

Later I would learn that other Epstein victims had experienced exactly this kind of intimidation: bright lights aimed at their windows at night. But while I was ignorant of that then, I still knew with certainty that my family was in peril. Moving quickly through the house, I scooped a sleeping Ellie out of her bed and gently placed her on the floor of my closet. Then I woke up Alex and Tyler and led them into the closet too. They were rubbing their eyes, confused, as I grabbed the laundry I'd been folding and threw it on top of them, trying to hide them from view. "I need you to be quiet," I whispered as my sons' faces peeked out from the pile. "I'm going to mostly close this door, so you will be safe, but don't be scared," I said, trying not to sound frightened myself. "Mom is going to take care of this."

Turning back toward the front door, I went and got The Judge out of the gun safe and loaded it. Then I grabbed ahold of Bear, our malamute, because he looked scary, even though he wouldn't hurt a fly. Slowly, Bear and I approached the front door, which was lit up like a movie set by the headlights. I had the gun in one hand, and Bear's collar in the other. I'm sure the intruders could see us through the leaded-glass window, but to make sure, I opened the door just a bit, waving the gun into the blinding high beams. Then I closed the door and stood there, gun cocked, ready. For five straight minutes, we faced off like that: the car idling, me gripping the gun, Bear panting next to me. Finally, after what seemed like forever, the driver put the car in reverse and slowly backed up, then headed off into the darkness.

That's when I realized I should have already called the sheriff. So, after sticking my head into the closet to reassure the boys, I did. Within minutes, two sheriff's deputies arrived. No, I told them, I didn't see a license plate. No, I wasn't sure of the make and model of the car, and the sheriff's department had already removed their cameras in anticipation of our move, so we couldn't check any surveillance tapes. The deputies promised to stay in their cruiser outside our house until daybreak. I thanked them, then returned the kids to their beds. Ellie had slept through the whole thing, but it took me a while to get the boys back down. "Who was in the car?" they asked—the first of so many questions whose answers I didn't know. "What did they want?" "Why didn't they say anything?" Finally, Alex and Tyler wore themselves out and fell asleep. Not me, though. I didn't close my eyes at all that night, or on many of the nights thereafter.

I knew this wasn't a good idea, especially with small kids in the house, but after that, I went to bed each night with my loaded revolver on the nightstand next to me. "How far will these people take it?" I asked Robbie when he called to check in. He couldn't stand to speculate, saying only, "I want you out of there, Jenna. I want you out of there right now." I'd arrived in the United States hoping that we could start a new life here. But now, less than two years later, I agreed with Robbie: we couldn't get back to Australia fast enough.

Mom helped me pack the irreplaceable stuff—a ceramic parrot Tyler had made in the first grade as well as other mementos and keepsakes—to take back to Australia. On one of our last days in Colorado, Mom and I were boxing up a few last items in one of the kids' rooms when I heard her say my name. I looked up from the suitcase I was trying to close and saw her holding a rectangular, needlepointed pillow. "My mom gave this to me, and now I want you to have it," Mom said, smoothing the pillow's crimson velvet piping before offering it to me. The face of the pillow had a border of tiny cross-stitched red flowers and green leaves that encircled these words, in all capital letters:

ALWAYS MY DAUGHTER
NOW TOO, MY FRIEND

"This is what I want for us," she said, and her eyes were wet. In that moment, I thought, "This is probably the closest to an apology I'm ever going to get." And I was okay with that. Sitting on the floor of our Colorado rental, I had done enough healing, and maturing, to see Mom more clearly—the woman she was, but also the overwhelmed young mother of three that she once had been. I think it's important to know where you come from. For better or worse, the people who made you will always be part of who you are. I knew that I couldn't ever rely on either of my parents and that I could never change them. They were both too broken. But I also saw that part of Mom wished she could become someone better: a person capable of being there for me.

I'D LIKE TO say Australia welcomed us with open arms in October 2015. But we had a difficult reentry. The house Robbie had rented for us in Palm Cove, about twenty-five miles north of Cairns, was fine, but he'd not had time to make it a home. We had a TV and a microwave but no furniture or bedding, and we couldn't afford to go shopping. Robbie had found a job working security at a resort, but still, after we bought a used car and paid the deposit on the rental, money was tight. Those first couple of nights, we all slept on the floor.

At the end of the year, Robbie scored a better security job at a hospital. With bankruptcy no longer imminent, we both started to breathe a little easier. For years now, my increasing activism had created a push-pull between us that at times had taken Robbie's and my marriage to the brink. While we both agreed on the principle that had driven me to become a more public figure—the assholes shouldn't be allowed to win!—the fact was that my refusal to stay silent, while honorable, had real consequences for our family. At least now, I told myself, we were back in Robbie's country, where he felt more at ease. To the extent that there were more consequences looming ahead, at least my husband would be standing strong on his own turf as he helped me to meet them.

TWENTY-NINE

I Solemnly Swear

For me, 2016 would be the Year of the Deposition. As part of my defamation case against Maxwell, my lawyers would depose her twice in 2016, and her lawyers would depose me twice, both times in Denver. Also in 2016, many people I'd known when I was in Epstein's orbit would be deposed: my mother; my father; my former boyfriends, Michael and Tony; another Epstein survivor, Johanna Sjoberg; Juan "John" Alessi, Epstein's house manager in Palm Beach; and, of course, Epstein himself. (Of all these people, Epstein alone invoked the Fifth, refusing to answer so as not to incriminate himself.)

What is it like to be deposed? No matter the subject matter, it is grueling. And as you can imagine, when the questioning revolves around years-old sexual abuse, it is especially painful. During one deposition, I would become so agitated that when we took a brief break, I went to the restroom and vomited. In that same deposition, I would also flinch as a lawyer flung photos of my children on the table in front of me—as close to a Mafia-style intimidation tactic as I'd ever seen. The lawyer claimed to be making a point about my use of

Facebook (and about how I couldn't be in fear for my life, as I'd claimed, if I posted pictures of my kids there). But I saw only malevolence. Maybe it's because the lawyer's behavior brought Epstein to mind—the memory of him tossing that photo of Skydy on his desk, telling me never to go to the police, had never left me. I interpreted this brazen display of my babies' faces as a direct threat.

Please don't hear this as a plea for sympathy. No one ever promised me that challenging my abusers would be easy. I had chosen to take these vile people on, and I'd always known that would mean an uphill fight. I was still talking to my psychologist, Judith Lightfoot, every Monday on the phone. In addition to recommending meditation and breathing exercises, she was encouraging me to speak out, saying she thought that the more vocal I became, the stronger I would feel. Still, this would be a hugely tiring year. Part of that was logistical: between depositions I gave and depositions I witnessed, I traveled from Australia to the United States and back four times in 2016. (Robbie's parents were living with us, which was the only way my absences were possible. Nonno ferried the kids to and from school and Nonna cooked and kept the house tidy while Robbie did his shifts at the hospital.) But what really wore me out were the emotions all this stirred up. In her deposition, which I did not attend, my mother was asked why I'd stopped working at Mar-a-Lago. She said she didn't know anything about it but that my father had told her that I was being educated by Maxwell, who Mom described as my "new momma." In his deposition, my father said that when he met Epstein at El Brillo Way, the pedophile "seemed just fine to me. I mean, you can't tell people by looking at them." But then Dad added that he didn't like my then boyfriend Michael: "Of course, what parent cares for your daughter's boyfriend? . . . I didn't think anybody was good enough for my daughter, but that's just me." Both my parents' testimony revealed that, as usual, they were driven by a desire to protect themselves. That wasn't news, but it was still painful for me to read.

Sjoberg's deposition transcript was easier to digest because she confirmed what I had experienced. Sjoberg described how Maxwell approached her on the main campus of Palm Beach Atlantic University, where she was a twenty-one-year-old student. Maxwell said she was looking to hire someone for twenty dollars an hour to answer phones, get drinks, and help around the house. She compared the job to that of a butler but said butlers were "too stuffy." Sjoberg accompanied Maxwell to Epstein's mansion and did as she asked. But the next time Maxwell asked her to come, Sjoberg was told she would be making a hundred dollars an hour "rubbing feet." Sjoberg, who has said her relationship with Epstein was platonic at first but that later he pressured her into having sex, also traveled to Little Saint James—she remembered her and me massaging Epstein together on the beach there. And she recalled the night in Epstein's Manhattan townhouse when Maxwell gave Prince Andrew the puppet that resembled him and then put the puppet's hand on my breast.

"Did Maxwell ever share with you whether it bothered her that Jeffrey had so many girls around?" Siggy asked Sjoberg.

"No," Sjoberg replied. "Actually, the opposite . . . She let me know that she was—she would not be able to please him as much as he needed and that is why there were other girls around."

Sjoberg also confirmed that Maxwell always said she wasn't bothered by how many girls Epstein slept with. And she described how Epstein once requested that she bring a female friend of hers—a physical trainer—to his house. When the friend of Sjoberg's arrived, Epstein asked the woman, "You see that girl over there laying by the pool? . . . I just took her virginity." Sjoberg said her friend "was mortified" by Epstein's lecherous boasting. But me? When

I read this account, all I could think was, "Yep, that's Epstein, to a tee."

I couldn't attend all these depositions—I'd been away from the kids enough as it was. But there was one deposition that I knew I needed to be there for: Tony Figueroa's. I hadn't spoken to Tony since I was in Thailand, so I wasn't sure what he'd say. He knew so much that could confirm what I'd been through. But I knew Tony was upset by my disappearance from his life fourteen years before. The deposition had been scheduled by Maxwell's lawyers. Why would they seek out Tony, my lawyers wondered, unless they thought he'd give testimony that would help their client and hurt me?

Brad had a preliminary call with Tony, who gave him an earful. Tony said I'd ditched him, embarrassed him, and left him in an apartment whose rent he couldn't afford. When Brad told Tony all we needed was for him to tell the truth, Tony replied, "I'm not doing shit until I talk to Virginia. I need some explanation about why she fucked me over."

So two days before his deposition, I dialed Tony's number. When he answered, I told him I was sorry—for the way our relationship had ended in 2002 but also for causing him to be dragged into this mess in 2016. I knew he was just trying to live his life, I said, and I understood it was no fun to rehash our difficult history. Because we'd once tried to break free together to make a life outside Epstein's orbit, when I escaped on my own, I knew Tony felt abandoned. On the phone, I acknowledged that. We'd been kids together, I said. I didn't want to cause him pain—not then, and not now.

Forty-eight hours later, Brad and I headed to a Florida law office for the deposition. Tony and I said hello in the hallway, but he was nervous and looked away. I wasn't sure how this was going to go. I needn't have worried, though. Under questioning from Maxwell's lawyer, Tony recalled that while we were living together, I traveled with

Epstein two weeks per month or so. He confirmed that I'd told him I was forced to have sex with Epstein, Maxwell, and their friends. He remembered me talking about being forced to recruit other girls and about the sex toys Epstein and Maxwell liked to use on us victims. Tony recalled that when he and I tried to leave Epstein behind, I relished the freedom. "Like, she did not want to go back there," he said. Asked what I was trying to get away from, he said: "to stop being used and abused." Tony remembered me saying I'd been forced to have sex with Prince Andrew, and he described worrying about my safety while I was in London. When asked why, he responded, "Just the way she was talking to me. Like, she just sounded scared." He recalled that when I returned from that trip, he saw the photograph of Prince Andrew with his arm around me. And he remembered that after I escaped, Maxwell called him and asked if he could find any other girls for Epstein. "She just said, 'Hi. This is Ghislaine. Jeffrey was wondering if you had anybody that could come over,'" Tony said.

But the most poignant part of the deposition, for me, was when Maxwell's attorney asked Tony if we'd seen each other since I'd told him goodbye in 2002. "Nope," he said, and his face looked truly sad. It didn't feel real, he said, that I was sitting across a table from him. "It's like talking to a ghost, or seeing one," he said. Later, Brad said he thought Tony simply needed to see me to put our unresolved breakup behind him. I hoped Brad was right.

The most important person my lawyers needed to question under oath, of course, was Maxwell herself. A first deposition was scheduled, but would it happen? Maxwell had avoided being deposed before. In 2010, for example, Brad had served Maxwell with a subpoena related to his CVRA case. Just hours before it was due to start, however, Maxwell's lawyer called to say that she was leaving the country, with no plans to return, because her mother was ill. Weeks later Maxwell was back on American soil as one of four hundred guests at

Chelsea Clinton's July 31 wedding in Rhinebeck, New York. Still, Brad's deposition never took place.

Now, six years later, Brad was looking forward to finally putting Maxwell in the hot seat at the Boies Schiller Flexner offices in Manhattan. But less than twenty-four hours before, Maxwell's lawyers challenged what's known as pro hac vice—a temporary grant of permission for Paul Cassell and Brad, who were licensed in Florida, to represent me, their client, in New York. The judge ruled that Siggy would be the one questioning Maxwell. This was an unexpected curveball. "Pro hacs," as these requests for temporary permissions are known, are rarely challenged. Siggy was counsel of record and had been working day and night on my case including helping Brad prepare for the depo. But still, she told me, "it's different when you're the one in the box."

"Don't worry, Sig, Maxwell is going to take the Fifth," Brad predicted. "I mean, we know all the crimes that she's committed—there's no way she can *not* take the Fifth." Still, just to be safe, Siggy stayed up all night preparing two things: a lengthy list of questions she didn't expect to get substantive answers to and a strategy to deal with the master manipulator she knew Maxwell to be.

The deposition began just after 9:00 a.m. on April 22, 2016. After Maxwell was sworn in, Siggy asked her to state her address and her date of birth. Then, Superwoman asked her first substantive question: "When did you first recruit a female to work for Mr. Epstein?" Maxwell acted confused. "I don't understand what you mean by female," she said. "I don't understand what you mean by recruit."

Siggy didn't blink. "Are you a female?" she asked. Maxwell said yes. Then Siggy repeated her question. It would take several back-and-forths before Maxwell finally said she'd first hired a woman who was forty or fifty years old to work for Epstein, probably in 1992. This was going to be slow going, it seemed, but that was all right because, amazingly, Maxwell wasn't taking the Fifth.

"Did you ever hire someone who was under the age of eighteen?" Siggy asked.

"Never," Maxwell said.

"Did you invite Virginia Giuffre to come to Jeffrey Epstein's home when she was under the age of eighteen?" Siggy continued.

Maxwell shot back, "Virginia Roberts held herself out as a masseuse and invited herself to come and give a massage." Siggy repeated her question, word for word, which prompted Maxwell to quibble: "Again, I did not *invite* Virginia Roberts. She came as a masseuse." And so it went, for hours. Maxwell said she didn't recall meeting me at Mar-a-Lago and denied participating in that first "massage" that she'd recruited me to give Epstein. In fact, she denied *ever* giving a massage in my presence.

Siggy forged ahead. She'd begun noticing that Maxwell got agitated every time she looked down at her notes, ignoring Maxwell. So she continued not making eye contact, getting under Maxwell's skin. "Have you heard Mr. Epstein use the phrase 'the younger the better'?" she asked. Maxwell said she had no such recollection and called me "just an awful fantasist." When Maxwell didn't want to answer something, she was dismissive. "Let's move on," she demanded at one point, haughty as ever. Siggy remained calm. "I'm in charge of the deposition," Siggy said. "I say when we move on and when we don't."

When Siggy asked, "Did you have a basket of sex toys that you kept in the Palm Beach house?" Maxwell obfuscated. "First of all, what do you mean?" she asked. In response, Siggy repeated the question. She would soon have to repeat it again. And then again. And then *again*. Maxwell kept issuing denials and asking Siggy to define even simple words (*puppet, party, school, regularly*—the list went on and on). "I never ever at any single time at any point ever at all participated in anything with Virginia and Jeffrey," Maxwell said. "I barely would remember her if not for all this rubbish." Over and over, when Siggy asked Maxwell if she was aware of some particular detail in the case, Maxwell was nonresponsive, saying instead, "I am aware that Virginia has lied repeatedly."

But there were signs that Maxwell was starting to crack. "You are trying to trap me. I will not be trapped," she admonished Siggy. Maxwell denied being able to recall flying on Epstein's plane with me and then, when given flight logs that listed her initials next to mine, protested, "How do you know the GM is me?" After Siggy asked if Maxwell had ever taken photographs of naked or seminaked girls at Epstein's homes, Maxwell snapped, "I know where you're headed with this, and it's nowhere appropriate." Siggy held her ground again: "I'm not heading anywhere. I'm just asking the questions."

After a lunch break, the tightly controlled Maxwell finally lost her temper. She had repeated that she didn't remember meeting me at Mar-a-Lago, prompting Siggy to ask, "Are you saying that it was an 'obvious lie' that you approached Virginia while she was under age at Mar-a-Lago?" Maxwell's lawyer objected, but his client went off. She was particularly worked up about me getting my age wrong in my first civil suit against Epstein, way back in 2009. As I've explained, when I'd said I was fifteen when I met her (when I was actually sixteen) it had been an honest mistake. But Maxwell described it as "a lie that was perpetrated between all of you to make the story more exciting. Can we agree on that?!" she bellowed.

"That is not my question," Siggy responded, but Maxwell kept going, and now she began to slam her fists on the table as she spoke. "Can we agree she was not the age she said, and you put that in the press? That is obviously"—slam!—"manifestly"—slam!—"absolutely"—slam!—"totally a lie."

Apparently, Maxwell was a fearsome sight; as she pounded the table, the court reporter—a usually unflappable woman whom Siggy had known for years—looked more terrified than Siggy had ever seen her. But Siggy? She was a woman of steel. "I am going to put on the record," Siggy stated, "Ms. Maxwell very inappropriately and very harshly pounded our law-firm table . . . I ask she take a deep breath and calm down." The lawyers agreed it was a good time for a break. It was 1:56 p.m.

Seventeen minutes later, the deposition resumed and went on—with Maxwell denying all wrongdoing, denying that she knew I'd gone to Thailand, denying that she gave me instructions to meet a girl there, denying, denying, denying—until Siggy ran out of time at 6:43 p.m. In the end, the deposition (including breaks) had stretched over ten hours, and Siggy had interrogated Maxwell for seven of them. Since then I've read that some lawyers who've faced off against Siggy compare her to Uma Thurman's sword-wielding assassin in Quentin Tarantino's *Kill Bill* films. ("Unexpectedly deadly" is how an adversary once described her.) To me, Siggy's performance with Maxwell only confirmed that.

David Boies would also shine a few months later, when he deposed Maxwell in a second session. All my lawyers—David, Siggy, Brad, and Paul Cassell—were working so hard for me. Brad and Siggy were both by my side during my two depositions, conducted by Maxwell's lawyers in Denver. And my lawyers were also deposing scores of others who had knowledge of Maxwell's behavior. For example, they'd taken the deposition of Rinaldo Rizzo, a former chef of an Epstein associate and his wife. Rizzo said that on one occasion, Epstein and Maxwell had brought a fifteen-year-old Swedish girl to this couple's home and then left her in the kitchen with Rizzo and his wife, who were cooking dinner. At first, the girl stayed quiet, but she was quivering and shaking and appeared to be terrified. When Rizzo asked about her connection to Epstein, though, the girl began weeping and blurted out that she had been on Epstein's island with Maxwell and another woman. The girl claimed that the three adults had pressured her to have sex, but she'd declined. "Ghislaine took my passport," Rizzo recalled the girl telling him and his wife. The girl also said Maxwell had threatened her, Rizzo said, and told her not to tell anyone about their sexual advances. As someone who'd frequently had my passport held by Maxwell, I read this deposition with a queasy feeling. I knew how scary it was to be controlled by that woman. Rizzo's account was an important corroboration of my own experience.

But if I had to point to a single example of my team's excellent work, it would have to be the response to Maxwell's motion for summary judgment that Siggy filed on January 31, 2017. Maxwell's team was claiming that I'd raised no genuine issue to be tried; they had asked the judge to rule in Maxwell's favor and make this case go away. Not so fast, wrote Siggy. First, she tore apart Maxwell's argument that she could not have abused or trafficked me when I was a minor. Summarizing Maxwell's contention that "employment records show that Ms. Giuffre was either sixteen or seventeen when Defendant recruited her from her job at Mar-a-Lago for sex with Epstein, not fifteen-years-old as Plaintiff originally thought," Siggy asserted, "Call this the 'yes-I'm-a-sex-trafficker-but-only-of-sixteen-year-old-girls' defense."

In response to Maxwell's claim that she didn't "regularly participate in Epstein's sexual exploitation on minors," Siggy wrote, "Call this the 'yes-I'm-a-sex-trafficker-but-only-on-Tuesdays-and-Thursdays' defense." In response to Maxwell's argument that I couldn't have been a sex slave because I was not confined or made Maxwell's legal property, Siggy quoted an expert on sex trafficking who explained that people didn't have to be "chained to a bed" to be considered victims of contemporary forms of slavery. Siggy then characterized Maxwell's stance, "Call this the 'yes-I'm-a-sex-trafficker-but-I-didn't-use-chains' defense." When Maxwell claimed that she did not create child pornography and that the government knew she didn't, Siggy quipped,

"Call this the 'until-you-find-the-photos-I'm-innocent' defense." And when Maxwell asserted that she did not act as a "Madame" for Epstein, Siggy responded that the gist of Maxwell's argument "seems to be that Defendant believes trafficking one girl to Epstein does not a Madame make. Call this the 'yes-I-was-Virginia's-Madame-but-no-one-else's' defense."

In conclusion, Siggy wrote that if Maxwell was involved in my abuse, as we were arguing, then her January 2015 statement accusing me of "obvious lies" was defamatory. Siggy asked the court to deny Maxwell's motion for summary judgment, and on March 22, 2017, Judge Robert W. Sweet did exactly that. Trial was set for May 15.

The next few months were a frenzy of activity. Siggy and Brad and Paul were furiously preparing for trial, wrangling countless witnesses and putting more than a thousand exhibits in order. They booked us all hotel rooms for the four weeks they thought the trial would take, as well as a large war room across the street from the courthouse. And they scheduled the final deposition they needed: a third grilling of Maxwell. Because she had refused to answer certain questions in her previous depositions, this one was going to take place in the courtroom, with the judge as referee, a week before trial.

By this point, a few settlement discussions had been held and gone nowhere. My lawyers believed we were headed to trial. Still, I flew in a few weeks beforehand for a final mediation, scheduled for May 3, which David Boies and Brad's then partner, Stan Pottinger, were handling since Brad and Siggy and Paul were so swamped with trial prep. A few days later, on the eve of Maxwell's final deposition, my team and I agreed to settle, and a few weeks after that, the case was dismissed.

I am not allowed to discuss the terms of the settlement, as they are confidential. But I can talk about why I settled. We'd prepared so diligently to expose Maxwell's lies in open court, and it would have been deeply satisfying to watch her squirm. I also would have loved to watch Epstein be called to the stand, as my lawyers had planned. Even if he'd taken the Fifth, as he'd done before, it would have done me good to see him interrogated like the criminal he was.

But remember this was a civil case, not a criminal one. There was never going to be an outcome that sent Maxwell to jail—at least not directly. In the end, if we'd taken it to trial and won, the victory was always going to be about money. For me, the settlement meant I could return to my family sooner than I'd planned, and I looked forward to using my payout to take care of them. I was not the first Epstein victim to be criticized for settling, and I would not be the last. But to those who think less of me for doing so, I'd ask you to remember the devastatingly accurate assertion I'd made in my first lawsuit, *Jane Doe 102 v. Jeffrey Epstein*—the one that said I'd permanently suffered not only loss of income but "a loss of the capacity to enjoy life." Maxwell and Epstein had stolen something precious from me. Sometimes I could rise above that loss, but other times, even still, I could not.

Financially, my family had struggled. While I would've liked to reenter the workforce, I felt as if I were unemployable. At times, I grew so desperate to explain my spotty work history during the years I was trafficked that I made up fake jobs and employers to list on my résumé. All anyone had to do was Google my name to know who I was and, as I'd said in one of my depositions, "No one wants to hire a sex slave." Meanwhile, as I've said, ongoing threats to my family's safety meant that, more and more, Robbie felt he could no longer work outside the home. Especially since I'd sued Maxwell, the paparazzi were back, circling our family like vultures, and he felt he needed to deliver the kids to and from school each day.

In the end, there was this: For months now, preparing for trial had been my primary occupation. Motherhood had taken a back seat, and that had cost me in ways that are difficult to quantify. During the first half of 2017, I'd been distracted at best (and, at worst, absent). I never missed a birthday or a holiday, but anyone who is a parent will understand that I often went without something much more important: the day-to-day mundane moments that make up a mother's life: pouring bubbles in the kids' baths, making sure homework preceded playtime, even having simple arguments ("No, Alex, you may not race around our neighborhood at night in a souped-up go-cart"). Only because I had a great husband and understanding in-laws had the wheels not fallen off the bus that was the Giuffre household. When Maxwell defamed me, she'd eroded my credibility and thus my ability to help other victims. If I could use some of her money to help me heal, to let me focus on my kids, and to fuel my attempts to do good, then I was happy to take it.

THIRTY

A Reckoning Begins

Whether talking to journalists, working with law enforcement, or filing lawsuits, so many brave women have stood up to Epstein and Maxwell. But when each of them first decided to do so, I can guarantee every single one felt terrified and alone. While I'd been in Epstein and Maxwell's world, they'd safeguarded their evil enterprise by stoking rivalries, strategically keeping girls from forging alliances. In their presence, then, we'd been kept at odds with each other, and even after I'd escaped, I still felt isolated, for a long, long time.

Now, however, as I learned of other women who had come forward, that solitary feeling was starting to lift. I knew about Courtney Wild from the CVRA case. And it turned out there were two sisters, Annie and Maria Farmer, who'd been trying for nearly two decades to expose what Epstein and Maxwell had done to them. As word spread that there were a handful of lawyers representing a growing number of Epstein's victims and getting results, more women were choosing to break their silence.

A RECKONING BEGINS

In October 2016, for example, a South African woman named Sarah Ransome called Paul Cassell. She told him that she, too, had been a victim of Epstein and Maxwell in 2006 and 2007. She said she'd been following my story in the media and had found the Facebook page of my nonprofit, Victims Refuse Silence—the one Brad had helped me found in 2014. Ransome said she wanted to assist my case in any way she could. Paul gathered my legal team in a room at Boies Schiller Flexner, and they called Sarah back in Barcelona, Spain, where she was living. She said she'd been abused by Epstein and Maxwell in various locations beginning when she was twenty-two. Specifically, she said that Epstein had raped her repeatedly while on his island and that Maxwell facilitated it, while also starving, berating, and swindling her. Like me, she had photographs of herself with them. She hadn't been a minor during this period, but what had happened to her was still wrong. In early 2017, right before a ten-year statute of limitations was about to expire, Boies Schiller Flexner filed a lawsuit on Sarah Ransome's behalf against Epstein and Maxwell. The charge: violation of the federal sex-trafficking statute, which prohibits the recruiting, enticing, transporting, or soliciting of someone for sex by means of fraud, force, or coercion. Before I settled with Maxwell, Ransome had flown to New York to serve as a witness in my defamation case.

While the mounting number of cases against Epstein and Maxwell was heartening, however, there were indications that public awareness of their crimes was either fading or had never been very high in the first place. Donald Trump was now president, and in early 2017 he nominated Alexander Acosta—the former federal prosecutor based in Miami who had approved Epstein's shameful, secretive nonprosecution agreement—to be secretary of labor. Acosta was confirmed in April 2017.

At the same time, accounts describing the mistreatment of women in America were multiplying: Fox News anchor Gretchen Carlson filed a sexual-harassment suit against her boss, Roger Ailes; Uber employee Susan Fowler went public about toxic masculinity at the ride-sharing company, causing its CEO to resign. It was as if all this bad behavior were a surging river and a dam was about to break. Then it did. On October 5, 2017, *The New York Times* ran the first of several articles by Jodi Kantor and Megan Twohey about the movie mogul Harvey Weinstein's serial harassment and assault of women, and their sources' allegations were backed up by on-the-record quotes. Five days later, *The New Yorker*'s Ronan Farrow wrote of several more women who Weinstein had victimized, and Farrow, too, was just getting started. He would soon shine light on several of Weinstein's associates who sought to silence Weinstein's victims—among them, one of my own attorneys, David Boies, who had represented Weinstein and had personally signed a contract directing a private investigative firm to attempt to uncover information that would stop the publication of a *New York Times* story about Weinstein's abuses. (Boies later said this had been a mistake. While his firm didn't select or direct the investigative firm, he said, and he characterized the arrangement as "an accommodation for a client," he took personal responsibility for the error, which he said was not "thought through.")

Back in 2006, when an activist named Tarana Burke had founded a nonprofit to serve survivors of sexual harassment and abuse, Burke had called her movement "Me Too." Now, eleven years later, the actress Alyssa Milano took to Twitter and encouraged survivors of sexual harassment and assault to post #MeToo as a status update. The response from women around the world was enormous. Two days later, the first of more than 150 gymnasts who'd been abused by USA Gymnastics doctor Larry Nassar went public. It was hard not to hope that real change was coming.

A RECKONING BEGINS

On the home front, things were good. Robbie and I used part of my Maxwell settlement to buy a four-bedroom house in a gated community just north of Cairns. After more than two years as renters, we were homeowners once again. We lived on a street named Iridescent Drive, which was fitting because at times the place, which had a lovely swimming pool in the backyard, seemed to shimmer. We had an outdoor kitchen, and during hot, muggy weather (which there is a lot of in Cairns) we pushed open our accordion doors and let the breeze cool the house.

In mid-2017, my kids were no longer babies. Alex was eleven, Tyler was ten, and Ellie was seven, and more and more I was noticing that each was special in his or her own way. Alex was beginning to write rhymes that he would eventually turn into rap music. Tyler was an artist who could draw anything. And Ellie loved to regale us with fanciful stories. While she aspired to be a firefighter more than a writer then, she was becoming a great raconteur. I admired my kids and was grateful for what they taught me every day. Which is why I got it into my head that we should make our family bigger.

In Cairns at that time, there was a campaign to streamline the process of finding homes for children in Queensland's foster-care system. I'd seen brochures about the program, called "foster to adopt," at the kids' school, and the more I thought about it, the more I wanted to be part of it. Our family was so fortunate and had so much to give. Having slept in foster homes during my time at Growing Together, I knew how bad it felt to lack a safe, permanent home. I proposed the idea of adopting to Robbie, who I suspected would be open to it, since his own father had been adopted as a child. When my husband said yes, we submitted an application, and before we knew it, we'd passed the home evaluation. Robbie and I took a required class to get educated about the challenges some foster kids might have. And right away, we were matched with a three-year-old girl. Her father was absent, we were told, and her mother was in prison and had decided to give her up for adoption. I knew with all my heart that we should give this little girl a home.

But then Siggy called. She needed me to travel to the United States again. I can't remember what the reason was—it's possible that it was for a deposition in one of my Survivor Sisters' cases—but I do remember it was urgent: I had three days to get there. As I began packing, Robbie said we needed to talk. "Jenna, you know I love kids, but you've been the one pushing us to adopt," he said. "I'm on board, but it's you who really wants to give back like this. But if you're not going to be here . . ." He hesitated, which is rare for him. Finally, he said: "It's just not fair. You need to commit to one thing or the other." I understood the choice he was laying out for me: keep on fighting to expose Epstein's cabal or step back, adopt a new daughter, and stay home with my expanding family. "It's either this or that," he said.

I knew Robbie was right, even though I didn't want him to be. The tension between my desire to be an activist and my desire to put my family first was always there for me, but in this instance, it required that I make a stark choice. I wanted to do both. Especially now that I knew of a particular child whom we could help, I yearned to do so. But at the same time, what I'd started with Siggy was nowhere near done. And seeing it through, wherever it took us, would potentially help other young women and girls. So I made my choice, and a few days later got on the plane to the States. To this day, I think about that little girl I never met and wonder how all our lives would be different if she had joined our family.

It was during this period that Julie K. Brown, an investigative journalist at the *Miami Herald*, began digging into the Epstein case. She has said that she was prompted, in part, by Alex Acosta's elevation to Trump's cabinet—and by the fact that during Acosta's confirmation hearings, Epstein's name had barely come up. The *Miami Herald*'s investigations editor gave Brown the go-ahead and assigned a videographer, Emily Michot, to work with her to capture interviews with Epstein's victims on tape. In early December 2017, they recorded their first emotional on-camera interview, with Michelle Licata, who'd been sexually assaulted by Epstein when she was just fourteen. They would later conduct similar videotaped interviews with Courtney Wild and Jena-Lisa Jones, who was fourteen when Epstein fondled her during a "massage" and paid her $200 afterward. And Brown and Michot wanted to record a conversation with me.

In early 2018, David Boies and Siggy met with Brown, who told them she was determined to get the sealed court records of my defamation case against Maxwell unsealed. In her experience, victims of sexual assault often wanted to keep the details of what happened to them private, so she was expecting pushback. But my lawyers told her she'd get no opposition from us. The more light she could shine on the darkest corners of Epstein's evil world, the better, we said. In March 2018, I sat down for a video interview with Brown. We'd meet more than once, but at the end of that first interview, I told her I was fighting not just for myself, but for every Epstein victim. "I'm not going to stop," I said, "until all these girls get justice."

When I said "all" the girls, I was quite consciously including those I was sure Epstein was continuing to abuse in the present day. Remember: he was a free man who, despite being a convicted sex offender, was still unrepentant about his taste for minor girls. We know this without a doubt because in mid-August 2018, Epstein invited a *New York Times* reporter named James Stewart to his Manhattan townhouse for a chat. The meeting was "on background," which meant

Stewart could only use whatever information he gleaned if he didn't attribute it directly to Epstein.* During their conversation (ostensibly about Elon Musk, whose business dealings Stewart was investigating), Epstein offered an off-topic aside, calling the criminalization of sex with teenage girls a cultural aberration. He supported his belief by noting that at certain times in history, it had been seen as acceptable. Epstein compared the vilification of men who had sex with minor girls to the way gay and lesbian people had been treated for decades—homosexuality, he noted, had long been considered a crime and was still punishable by death in some parts of the world. Clearly, Epstein still felt righteous about having sex with whomever he pleased, regardless of age.

In November 2018, Brown's series of articles, accompanied by Michot's videos, went live. The series was called "Perversion of Justice," and in it, Brown revealed the behind-the-scenes maneuvering that had led to Epstein's nonprosecution agreement, zeroing in on Acosta's role in it. She uncovered eighty victims of Epstein, some as young as thirteen when the abuse occurred, and revealed the campaign of terror that Epstein and his cronies had used to try to silence those victims. (Remember when that car shined its headlights on our front door in Colorado? Well, Brown found a victim in Florida who'd endured the same kind of hazing.) Finally, the series documented the experience of eight survivors in detail, with on-the-record interviews. I was among them.

The series was fantastic, in no small part because of Michot. Her videos forced readers of Brown's hard-hitting reporting to see all of us who'd survived Epstein and Maxwell's abuse as human beings. As

---

* Readers of *The New York Times* wouldn't know this, however, until three days after Epstein's death in 2019. In an article titled, "The Day Jeffrey Epstein Told Me He Had Dirt on Powerful People," Stewart explained that his promise to keep their conversations on background had expired because Epstein was deceased.

A RECKONING BEGINS

The Hollywood Reporter noted, the videos acted as "something of a force multiplier, creating a three-dimensional platform for Epstein's teenage victims to tell their harrowing stories." Brown's series drove over 9.5 million unique visits to the *Miami Herald* website, while Michot's videos were watched 850,000 times on the paper's website alone and millions more times on YouTube.

"You're just thrown into a world that you don't understand," I said in one video, describing what I and so many others had gone through with Epstein and Maxwell. "And you're screaming on the inside. And you don't know how to let it come out. And you just become this numb figure who refuses to feel and refuses to speak . . . All you do is obey. That's it."

Brown has rightly been credited with refocusing the attention of the public and of law enforcement on Epstein and Maxwell's heinous acts. We now know that not long after the *Herald* ran Brown's first story, the US attorney's office in the Southern District of New York opened an investigation into Epstein. I will always be grateful for what Brown and Michot did for the countless women who'd been victimized—first by Epstein and Maxwell, but then again by their own government.

I also have to thank Brown with helping me understand that despite the problems I'd had with members of the tabloid media, working with good journalists could do a lot of good. More and more, I began to make myself available to reporters who reached out. Maybe if I spoke more about what all of us had been through, I thought, I could help increase awareness and prevent other young girls and women being abused.

It's been said that no good deed goes unpunished, however, and apparently someone thought it was high time I be punished. At some point in this period, the FBI called me in Australia to say there had been a credible threat on my life. The agent told me that Robbie and I should contact the Australian Federal Police immediately. I called right away but kept getting transferred from one person to another. I was so scared that I was shaking. Robbie stood next to me as I waited on hold, determined to stay on the phone until someone helped us. But after explaining myself over and over, only to be transferred again, I was out of patience. That's when Robbie stepped in. "Start packing," he told me. "I've got a plan."

From the earliest days of our relationship, Robbie had been my protector—my savior, even. Now, he was going to deliver us from danger once again. He rented a large mobile home and loaded the kids, the dogs, and me into it. Within a few hours, we had hit the road, heading north. I didn't think I could maneuver that big of a vehicle, so Robbie drove for eight hours straight. We ended up in a one-horse town at the top end of Queensland, not far from Cape Melville National Park. The town had no grocery—just a convenience store where we could buy milk and bread. But it was completely off the grid, which was what we needed most. There we would stay, cooking and sleeping in our RV, swatting mosquitoes, and occasionally fishing—for three weeks.

How do you decide when a credible threat to your life is no longer dangerous? The answer is: you don't. There simply comes a time when you resume normal routines. When we returned to Cairns, we let the local police know what the FBI had told me. Robbie and I tried to make the kids feel safe, even though we weren't certain that they were. Day and night, I worried that my family would be harmed by the very people who had hurt me when I was a teenager. And in addition to fear, I felt rage. How entitled and selfish do you have to be to continue hounding and threatening the very victims you've hurt before? It drove me crazy to think these people could potentially get away with silencing me for good. When someone on Twitter speculated that the FBI might kill me "to protect the ultrarich and well connected," I felt the need to respond. If I died suddenly, I tweeted, no one should believe that it was an accident.

"I am making it publicly known that in no way, shape, or form am I suicidal," I typed hastily but resolutely (making several spelling and grammatical errors that I've corrected here). "I have made this known to my therapist and GP—If something happens to me—for the sake of my family, do not let this go away and help me to protect them. Too many evil people want to see me quieted."

THIRTY-ONE

A Taste of Justice

In July 2019 came a day I'd hoped for but had never thought I'd see. I remember Siggy calling me—it was early Sunday morning in Australia. "You're not going to believe this," she said. "Do you have a chair? Because you're going to need to sit down." On July 6, Jeffrey Epstein had been arrested on federal charges related to sex trafficking, she said. He'd been apprehended after his private jet touched down at New Jersey's Teterboro Airport. I could imagine the scene, having flown into Teterboro so many times myself with Epstein. Touching my face, I realized I was crying.

We would soon learn so much more. At almost the same moment Epstein was taken into custody, federal agents had raided his New York townhouse. Inside, they found hundreds if not thousands—an "extraordinary volume," prosecutors said—of nude photographs of young-looking women. These were the tokens this superpredator had kept to remind himself of all those he'd abused over the years. They also found a safe containing forty-eight loose diamonds, $70,000 in cash, and three passports belonging to Epstein—from the United

A TASTE OF JUSTICE

States, from Israel, and from Austria. That last one, which was expired, appeared to have a photo of Epstein but included a fake name and listed a home address in Saudi Arabia. This was a man who'd prepared a getaway plan.

On July 8, Geoffrey Berman, US attorney for the Southern District of New York, unsealed an indictment alleging that Epstein and his employees brought dozens of vulnerable girls, some as young as fourteen, to his New York mansion and his Palm Beach home between 2002 and 2005. Epstein stood accused of abusing these girls sexually, paying them money, and asking some of them to recruit other girls. Noting that this had gone on for years, Berman said that "the alleged behavior shocks the conscience." Epstein faced a maximum sentence of forty-five years in prison.

Epstein's bail hearing was a week later. I wished I could attend, if only to see Epstein in shackles. But Brad Edwards assured me that other survivors would be there to represent us all. Courtney Wild, Michelle Licata, and Annie Farmer did indeed attend, and the judge let them speak. First Farmer and then Wild stood up and briefly described how much harm Epstein had done. If nothing else, Wild said, the judge should keep him behind bars "for the safety of any other girls."*

Epstein's attorneys offered to put up hundreds of millions of dollars if only the judge would allow him to post bail and go home. But prosecutors argued that he must remain in custody because he had the means and the motive to flee. A financial disclosure form Epstein was required to fill out after his arrest had listed his net worth as $559,120,954, including six properties, stocks, equities, and $57

---

* Later it would become clear, in case anyone doubted it, that when he was arrested, Epstein had likely still been keeping company with minor girls. Two weeks before Epstein's arrest, the US Marshals Service had interviewed an air-traffic control employee who reported seeing Epstein as recently as November 2018 disembarking from his jet with girls who appeared to be as young as eleven or twelve.

million in cash. Three days later, Judge Richard M. Berman ruled: no bail for Epstein.

The next day, on July 19, Alexander Acosta—whose role in the 2008 nonprosecution agreement was now being viewed more harshly—resigned from Trump's cabinet. Four days after that, on July 23, Epstein was written up for "self-mutilation" and was put in a "suicide watch" cell. But thirty-one hours later that assessment was downgraded to something less restrictive ("psychological observation"), and later still, he was returned to a normal cell. Prison records show that on two occasions while in custody, he described himself as a coward and as someone who does not like pain.

On August 9, 2019—my thirty-sixth birthday—a judge made public the first of what would soon be several batches of previously sealed documents in my defamation case against Maxwell. This batch—roughly two thousand pages in all—included excerpts of several depositions, including my own. And these excerpts made clear that in 2016, under oath, I had named not only Prince Andrew and Jean-Luc Brunel among my abusers (as I had in my 2014 joinder motion) but also Marvin Minsky, the MIT scientist; Bill Richardson, the former governor of New Mexico; and others. My sworn testimony naming Billionaires Numbers One, Two, and Three would be made public in various document dumps, and they all denied knowledge of and participation in Epstein's trafficking scheme.

Siggy and I had a joke we often told each other: if we were frustrated that one of our cases seemed stalled, all we needed to do was send Siggy on vacation. Whenever she tried to take a break with her family, something big would happen. In August 2019, Siggy flew to Africa to take her kids on safari. I guess I shouldn't have been surprised, then, when early on a Sunday morning Siggy found a satellite phone and called me in Australia.

Just hours before, on Saturday, August 10, guards had entered

Epstein's cell inside the high-security unit of the Metropolitan Correctional Center in Manhattan to bring him breakfast. Instead, they found his lifeless body, a bedsheet tied around his neck. Epstein was dead at the age of sixty-six. The news hit me with an almost physical force. I guess I didn't believe someone who'd exerted so much power over me could ever die. "I know you're disappointed," Siggy said, and she was right. This wasn't how justice was supposed to work—with the accused avoiding a reckoning by taking himself out. Some might imagine that I'd be happy that Epstein was dead, but I wasn't. Indeed, it would take time for me to realize that I was in mourning. Not because the world had lost a monster—that was a good thing. No, like all of Epstein's victims, I was grieving the death of my ability to hold him accountable for what he had done.

As the details came out, nearly everything about Epstein's death seemed fishy. Even Attorney General William Barr would acknowledge he initially had suspicions that Epstein had been murdered. Instead, he concluded otherwise: that Epstein's death was a result of "a perfect storm of screw-ups." There was the fact that Epstein had tried to harm himself before but then been taken off suicide watch. While he'd had a cellmate at some point, on the night of his death, he did not have one. Two prison guards who sat at a desk just fifteen feet from Epstein's cell were supposed to check on him every half hour from 10:30 p.m. to 6:30 a.m. Instead, they'd napped and browsed the internet, then falsified the logs to say they'd completed their rounds. Security cameras that could have captured Epstein's self-harming behavior—or, if conspiracy theorists are to be believed, the actions of whoever murdered him—were not functioning. Other cameras that were working showed that no one had entered the area where Epstein was housed on the night he died—so that seemed to rule out the possibility of an assassin sneaking in. But then his brother hired a forensic pathologist to examine the official autopsy report. That expert concluded that the broken bones and cartilage in Epstein's neck "point[ed] to homicide."

I can make a case for either suicide or murder. This was a man who bragged about his access to power—by this point in his life, he was known to have relationships with not just pretty young girls and brainiac scientists but also the likes of Microsoft cofounder Bill Gates, James "Jes" Staley, the CEO of Barclays Bank, and Leon Black, the cofounder and CEO of the private equity firm Apollo Global Management. According to court documents, Epstein also knew Google cofounders Sergey Brin and Larry Page well enough to have introduced them and others to Staley. In addition to his self-described "biological" need for sex, Epstein needed to feel important, and collecting such high-profile acquaintances had helped him feed that hunger. Now being in jail meant having no access to either the young girls he loved to abuse or the powerful men he yearned to rub shoulders with. That certainly could have made him want to end it all. On the other hand, Epstein was the ultimate narcissist. He believed he was superior to others, and I never saw in him a scintilla of self-doubt, let alone a desire for self-annihilation. He'd always suggested to me that those videotapes he so meticulously collected in the bedrooms and bathrooms of his various houses gave him power over others. He explicitly talked about using me and what I'd been forced to do with certain men as a form of blackmail, so these men would owe him favors. Could it be that someone who feared exposure by Epstein had found a way to exterminate him? I know that the official findings, including an inspector general's report issued in June 2023, say this is impossible, but I will never be entirely convinced.

I'll tell you one thing, though: while I've read that Epstein was buried in an unmarked grave not far from his parents, in Palm Beach, Florida, I don't believe that at all. Epstein had repeatedly told me exactly what would happen when he died: his body would be placed in some sort of cryogenic chamber to be preserved until technology advanced far enough to bring him back to life. That's what he'd always bragged to me, with that satisfied smirk on his face. I know it sounds far-fetched, but I wouldn't bet against the notion that he somehow got his way on this.

Investigators would soon discover that on August 8, two days before his death, Epstein had placed his entire fortune into a trust—"The 1953 Trust," apparently named for his birth year—in the Virgin Islands. This legal maneuver would be widely interpreted as Epstein's final thumbing of his nose at those who'd survived his predation, because it made it much more difficult for his victims to get restitution. Even after death, Epstein seemed to be asserting control.

It was oddly heartening, therefore, when another photo emerged in the public realm that refocused the narrative not on Epstein's maneuvering but on his perversity. Taken by a party photographer in 2001, the image is ostensibly of Naomi Campbell—the lens zeroes in on her, in a black leather bikini and a mesh black wrap, arriving at her thirty-first birthday bash on that yacht I've told you about in Saint-Tropez. But despite her undeniable beauty, the supermodel wasn't the reason this photo ran in the *New York Post* on August 13, 2019, three days after Epstein's death. I was.

"Jeffrey Epstein's 'Sex Slave' Seen at Naomi Campbell's Birthday Party in 2001" blared the headline atop the photo (which had also appeared a day earlier in England's *Daily Mail*). And with that, a single image reminded the world just how childlike the girls in Epstein's world were required to look. I'm caught in the foreground—clearly by accident—an awkward smile on my face, my long blond hair falling down my back. I am looking away, and my pink sleeveless top reveals a slender arm and a bare shoulder. I am seventeen years old. And right next to me, partially obscured, with only her dark hair and a sliver of her cheek visible, is Maxwell.

Later, I would meet a fellow Epstein survivor who would tell me this photograph was the reason she had broken her silence and come forward with her own story. The photo said something a thousand words couldn't, she said: "Everyone knew: that was a child." By "that," she meant me.

THIRTY-TWO

Survivor Sisters Unite

For decades New York State had among the most restrictive laws in the nation when it came to punishing those who'd sexually abused children: victims had to file civil lawsuits by their twenty-third birthdays or lose their chance altogether. But that changed in early 2019, when the legislature passed the Child Victims Act, which gave victims until age fifty-five to file claims against the institutions or individuals they blamed for their suffering. And thanks to a "look-back window" written into the law, for one year, starting on August 14, victims of all ages could sue even if the statute of limitations had passed. It seemed fitting that four days after Epstein's death, that look-back window opened. And later, because of the pandemic, that window would be extended for another year, allowing victims to file claims until August 14, 2021.

This was the kind of legislative change that victims' rights advocates had long been pushing for. Increasingly, research was bolstering their arguments. For example, CHILD USA, a nonprofit focused on child-abuse prevention, conducted a study of thousands of abuse victims who had been Boy Scouts; only half of those came forward before they were fifty. More and more, the public was coming to understand that being sexually abused as a child could take decades to process. And it could take even longer than that for a victim to imagine speaking publicly about that experience and naming his or her abuser.

If you ask me, statutes of limitations should be abolished entirely for cases involving the sexual abuse of children. But this look-back window in New York State was a step in the right direction, and it was particularly a boon for Epstein's victims, so many of whom had been abused in Manhattan. Over the next two years, several of us would take advantage of the window to file claims that would otherwise have been impossible.

But first we had a hearing to attend. On August 19, 2019, the US attorney's office had filed a document to withdraw the charges against Epstein, since he was deceased. Usually this results in a dismissal of the case as soon as the judge signs it. In an unusual move, however, Judge Berman said that he was aware that Epstein's death had robbed his victims of something vital to their healing. To remedy that, Berman—who is a licensed social worker as well as a judge—scheduled a hearing for a week later. On August 27, he said, he would give any of us who wished to speak the opportunity to address the court. The government would pay for our airfare and hotels. It was short notice, but I was determined to be there, as were scores of others.

Because of the enormous media attention and expected attendance, Berman moved the hearing from his usual courtroom to a larger one. Half of the seating was reserved for survivors and their attorneys, and on the day of the hearing, that side of the room was almost full. Siggy and Brad were there, as well as several other lawyers I knew. Berman heard from the lawyers first, and then, one by one, twenty-three of us rose to say what we were there to say.

SURVIVOR SISTERS UNITE

Woman after woman—now in their twenties, thirties, and forties—told a similar tale of being hurt by Epstein, and then struggling for decades afterward as memories of that trauma threatened to derail them. But for all the pain being described, it seemed each woman who spoke took strength from the woman who'd gone before her. Courtney Wild went first, and she set the perfect tone for the proceedings. At fourteen, she had been a straight-A student, the first-chair trumpet in her school band, and the captain of the cheerleading squad. Then Epstein began abusing her, "robbing me of my innocence and my mental health," she said, and all her ambitions and achievements went up in smoke. "I feel very angry and sad that justice has never been served in this case."

Another survivor said she had lost her mother to cancer when she was eleven. Afterward, she recalled being approached by "a lady" when she was playing her violin at a mall in Texas, not far from the New Mexico border. The lady told the girl she knew a wealthy man who lived nearby who'd pay to see her play. "This was the beginning of the end of my childhood," the survivor told the court.

Chauntae Davies, who'd been recruited to be a masseuse for Epstein, recalled how at first she'd tried to reject his sexual advances, but that seemed to excite him. He ended up abusing her for years, she said. "We have all suffered, and he is still winning in death," she said.

Jennifer Araoz said that she was first abused by Epstein when she was fourteen and that he forcibly raped her at fifteen. "He stole my chance at really feeling love because I was so scared to trust anyone for so many years," she said, speaking through tears.

Annie Farmer, Anouska De Georgiou, Teala Davies, Teresa Helm, Sarah Ransome, and Marijke Chartouni—these might be names you've heard, as all of them have been quoted in media accounts speaking out about what they'd been through. But they are only a few of my Survivor Sisters (as we'd soon come to call ourselves) who spoke that day. We all shared the belief that by raising our voices, we might comfort and inspire others who weren't yet ready to reveal their own suffering. Several of us thanked the prosecutors who were there for finally assembling a case against Epstein, but I was not the only one to remind them that there were others walking free who should still be held to account. "The reckoning must not end," I told the court in my remarks. "It must continue. He did not act alone, and we, the victims, know that. We trust the government is listening and that the others will be brought to justice."

After the public hearing ended, the prosecutors invited all Epstein's victims to meet with them in a private room. It was an emotional session. Geoffrey Berman, the US attorney, had tears in his eyes as he told us how sorry he was for all we had endured. William Sweeney, the head of the FBI's New York office, thanked us for our presence. And both pleaded with us to help them in their ongoing investigations into Epstein's coconspirators. Siggy and I would soon meet with them, as I know many Survivor Sisters did.

In addition to whatever leads we provided the prosecutors, the hearing and its aftermath resulted in something else that I'd never known to hope for. Being with all those resilient women in one place gave me back a piece of myself that had gone missing. When David Boies and Siggy offered to take several Survivor Sisters to the US Open, Farmer, Helm, Ransome, Chartouni, and I were among those who gathered in Queens to watch a match. As we had dinner together later and drank champagne, I felt as if, despite our differences, I could tell these women anything. There was a palpable feeling that each of us understood and supported the others. And it was more than symbolic. Some of us were still looking for answers.

For example, Marijke Chartouni told me she thought she'd been abused by Epstein around the same time I was. She was trying to identify the woman who'd recruited her, and when she described what the woman looked like, I recognized her instantly as a woman I'd known who was in Epstein's circle for a time. I remembered her first name but not her last. Marijke is like a detective—she would soon use pattern matching and public records to find what she thought must be the woman's last name, and quickly after that she found the woman's website and social-media accounts. When we looked at the photographs the woman had posted of herself, there was no denying it was her. Because this woman witnessed Marijke's assault and participated in it, Marijke felt that finding her again—seeing that she still existed—helped defang a trauma that had gnawed at her for years.

For weeks after that hearing, I mostly felt jubilant. The way all these strangers had come together, like pieces of a huge jigsaw puzzle, to comfort one another and help fill in each other's gaps was electrifying. When united—we formed a WhatsApp group chat to keep in touch—we felt as if we had power. "Now I know I'm on the right road," I said to Robbie, "because look what is happening!"

In addition to this new form of kinship, the Survivor Sisters were dealing with a full-on media frenzy. All the women who'd spoken in the courtroom in August were being asked by various news outlets to tell their stories. For me it started right after Judge Berman's hearing, when I stood in front of the courthouse with a dozen microphones in my face and tried to keep people focused on the wrongs that still needed to be righted. "It's not how Jeffrey died, but it's how he lived," I said. "And we need to get to the bottom of everybody who was involved with that, starting with Ghislaine Maxwell . . . I will never be silenced until these people are brought to justice." Before I stepped away from the mic, a reporter asked me whether that included Prince Andrew. "He knows exactly what he's done," I said, "and I hope he comes clean about it."

Soon I did a series of interviews for NBC's *Dateline*. Several other survivors were also featured. That report would air on September 30, 2019. Interviewer Savannah Guthrie was tough, but fair, and I appreciated how she let me address some people's skepticism. When she said, for example, that during my time with Epstein I'd been "coping [by using] Xanax, taking drugs, drinking. There are going to be people who say: maybe it didn't happen the way you say it happened," I responded like this: "I say when you're abused, you know your abuser. I might not have the dates or times right, and the places might not even be right, but I know their faces, and I know what they've done to me." Next, *Glamour* magazine invited Chartouni, Helm, Ransome, another Epstein survivor, named Rachel Benavidez, and me to have a roundtable discussion about what we had been through and our hopes for the future. That feature appeared in the magazine's October 2019 issue. In rapid succession, I'd be interviewed on camera by the BBC and by the producers of *Jeffrey Epstein: Filthy Rich*, a multipart documentary about Epstein and Maxwell that would eventually air on Netflix.

But perhaps my most important interview was conducted by Tara Brown of *60 Minutes Australia*. She was preparing an extensive report in which she interviewed not only me, David Boies, and Siggy but also Courtney Wild and a lawyer named Spencer Kuvin who represented many other victims of Epstein and Maxwell. As its air date approached in early November, I told Robbie (who would also make a cameo in the report) that I wanted Alex and Tyler—then thirteen and twelve—to watch it. (I felt that at nine, Ellie was still too young.) I told Robbie chances were good that some of the boys' friends and their parents might see the report and recognize me. Even though I was known as Jenna, not Virginia, in Australia, they knew my face, and this was going to be on TV in their living rooms. Our sons might get asked about it, I told Robbie. I didn't want them to be blindsided.

But there was another, more pressing reason I wanted my sons to watch it. "I want them to know what I'm fighting for—to make sure other children don't have to endure what I did," I told Robbie. "They've known for a long time that something bad happened. I think they are old enough now to understand." Of course, I knew it would be difficult for the boys to hear the details of my abuse. But those details were the truth, and if the world was going to hear them, I wanted my sons to know them too. I also thought it might be easier for them to understand because *60 Minutes* would provide the context for my experience. They would be able to see that their mother wasn't alone—not in her victimhood, certainly, but also not in her willingness to stand up to those who'd hurt so many.

The night the report aired, the four of us gathered on the couch to watch. The boys sat silently as Brown walked her audience through Epstein and Maxwell's crimes. They saw footage of the inside of El Brillo Way and photos of me as a young girl, and they heard me and Courtney Wild talk tearfully about what we'd experienced. Importantly, they heard my answer when Brown asked me why, after I was abused the first time by Epstein and Maxwell, I went back a second time to El Brillo Way. "As an adult, I know it's right to run," I told Brown. "But as a kid who had been through what I'd been through in my life already, I guess the last thought that I had was, 'Well, this is what life's about.'" When the report was over, I could tell by the way he was clenching his jaw that Alex was angry. "Why did they let that guy get away with hurting so many people?" he demanded. It just wasn't fair, he said. Tyler had a different reaction. He'd cried a few times while watching the report, and afterward he wouldn't stop hugging me. "I'm proud of you, Mom," he said. That felt good, of course, but watching alongside my sons stirred up a lot of emotion. On the one hand, I'd never wanted them to be touched by my terrible past. Now they were old enough to know the truth, but it still made me sad. On the other hand, though, I was happy for the boys to see that I was, indeed, fighting bad guys—something I was determined to keep doing. As much as this role could sometimes disrupt our family life, I wanted them to know that sometimes even one person can make a difference. And given that possibility, you have to try.

THIRTY-THREE

Unbroken

After the *60 Minutes Australia* report, Prince Andrew couldn't help but know that I was considering filing a lawsuit against him. David Boies had made clear to Tara Brown that the Duke of York's repeated denials of my allegations had put him in our crosshairs. "Prince Andrew says he was unaware of the sex trafficking," a skeptical-looking Boies had said. "But he spent days in Epstein's New York mansion, where the sex trafficking was rampant. You could not spend time there and not know what was going on . . . At some point, he's going to have to testify. He can't hide forever." When Brown said to Boies that perhaps the prince *could* hide, given that British law enforcement had ended its investigation into the case, Boies clarified: "If he wants to stay locked up in a palace and not travel outside the United Kingdom, maybe he can escape a reckoning . . . But if he comes to the United States, he can be served with a subpoena . . . I think that's quite likely."

Now, with pressure building on a variety of fronts, Prince Andrew sat down with BBC *Newsnight*'s Emily Maitlis to try to clear his name. The interview took place on November 14, and afterward the prince reportedly thought it had gone well. But when it aired two days later, it was widely viewed as a disaster. The prince expressed no regret about his long-standing relationship with Epstein—he explained being a houseguest of Epstein, a convicted sex offender, in 2010 by saying he had only visited to tell Epstein in person that their relationship was over. While insisting that his only mistake was his "tendency to be too honorable," he failed to communicate any sympathy for Epstein's victims. Regarding my allegations about him, he denied them again, saying that on the night I said I'd first been trafficked to him, he couldn't have been with me because he had taken one of his daughters out for pizza. He said he had no recollection of ever meeting me—"None whatsoever." Most outlandishly, he said he couldn't have danced sweatily with me at the Tramp nightclub, as I'd described, because he'd temporarily developed an inability to perspire after enduring "what I would describe as an overdose of adrenaline in the Falklands War when I was shot at"—a bizarre reference to his military service nineteen years prior to our meeting.

The interview's ramifications would be sweeping.* While the royal family still denied my allegations, it also effectively banned the queen of England's third child from appearing at public events and forbade him from using the honorific "His Royal Highness." So dramatic was the fallout that two streaming services—Netflix and Amazon—would soon announce they had projects in the works to dramatize how the interview was arranged and executed, and a third company embarked on a feature-length documentary.

As devastating as this interview was for Prince Andrew, for my

---

* Indeed, documents made public in a court case in 2023 would reveal that Prince Andrew had lied in the interview when he told Maitlis he'd only seen Epstein a single time, in December 2010, after Epstein was arrested and jailed. According to court papers from a civil case brought by the US Virgin Islands against JPMorgan Chase, the prince had also had lunch with Epstein in June 2010, while Epstein was on house arrest, and the two had kept in touch via email.

legal team it was like an injection of jet fuel. Its contents would not only help us build an ironclad case against the prince but also open the door to potentially subpoenaing his ex-wife, Sarah Ferguson, and their daughters, Princesses Beatrice and Eugenie. Did he really take Beatrice out for pizza on March 10, 2001, as he claimed? If we deposed the princesses, his family members could potentially poke holes in his alibi. Would his medical records really show that he had a temporary case of anhidrosis (a lack of perspiration), which typically isn't a response to adrenaline? We weren't quite ready to sue yet, but this interview gave us a lot more to work with than we'd had before.

In early December, BBC *Panorama* released a documentary called *The Prince and the Epstein Scandal*, and I was among those interviewed. This would be my first on-camera interview with a British outlet, and while it had been recorded before Prince Andrew's sit-down with the BBC, correspondent Darragh MacIntyre used my words to contradict what the disgraced royal had told Maitlis. Once again I told the story of the three times I was trafficked to Prince Andrew. I was also asked about recent suggestions that the photo of Prince Andrew with his arm around me in 2001 was a fake. "Like, his arm was elongated or the photo was doctored?" I responded. "I mean, come on—I'm calling BS on this. Because that's what it is. He knows what happened. I know what happened. And there's only one of us telling the truth, and I know that's me."

I was glad for the opportunity to reach a British audience, and at one point in the interview, I spoke to them directly. "I implore the people in the UK to stand up beside me, to help me fight this fight, to not accept this as being OK," I said, adding, "This is not some sordid sex story. This is a story of being trafficked. This is a story of abuse." If only we could keep the pressure on, I thought, maybe the prince and others could be held to account.

In February 2020, I flew from Cairns to Los Angeles to participate in a podcast called *Broken*. In the podcast's first season, *New Yorker* writer Ariel Levy and the *Miami Herald*'s Julie K. Brown had taken listeners through the litany of Epstein's crimes. Now, journalist Tara Palmeri was hosting the second season, *Broken: Seeking Justice*. Palmeri wanted to follow several of Epstein's victims as we sought to reconcile our pasts with our present-day lives. The project was backed by two terrific guys named Adam—the Hollywood director Adam McKay and the podcaster and former NPR correspondent Adam Davidson. I was impressed by the team's firepower, and I liked that Palmeri didn't give two shakes about Epstein—only about the women he'd hurt. I would be helping to gather reporting during a ten-day, cross-country journey with Palmeri. Our goal: to track down some of the people who'd worked for Epstein during the time I knew him. I was hoping that some who'd stayed silent before his death might now be willing to talk.

The first person I wanted to talk with was also named Adam: Adam Perry Lang. He'd been Epstein's personal chef from 1999 to 2003—Lang is the one who fed me pizza on Little Saint James—and he traveled regularly on Epstein's jets. Brad and I had reached out to him in 2014, but we'd never heard back. Now he lived in Southern California—Palmeri had found a couple of home addresses—and Lang had a steak restaurant in Hollywood called APL, for his initials. First we tried to visit him at home, but Lang didn't seem to be living at the places we went to. So we made a reservation at APL. When we arrived, I told the host Lang was an old friend and that I was hoping to say hello to him. We were seated in a big booth at the back of the dining room, and we ordered dinner. But Lang wasn't in the restaurant that night. We left word explaining I was trying to reach him.

A few days later, I got a text from him: "Hi, Virginia. I know this has been a traumatic and terrible time for you. I hope your fierce advocacy brings you and the other innocent victims peace and justice. I hope you know by now that I'm planning to speak with your attorney. Best, Adam." I was thrilled—I thought Lang was finally ready to help. But when I followed up, he sent a statement that reiterated what he'd said for years: that while he was in Epstein's employ, he never witnessed any sexual activity or nudity or underage girls or depraved acts or abuse.

You may be wondering what it was that I wanted from Lang. Of course, I hoped that he might have information that could help me hold Epstein's coconspirators accountable. But also, on a purely emotional level, I just wanted to hear Lang confirm my experience. He could have said something as simple as, "I saw what happened to you because I was there," and that would have helped me heal. Would I have been thrilled if he handed over incontrovertible evidence of wrongdoing? Sure. But I wasn't really expecting that. Mostly what I wanted was validation. Clearly, though, I wasn't going to get that from Lang.

We hit another dead end when we tracked down a woman—a former model whom I knew had procured girls for Epstein—who was one of several women I'd been forced to have sex with, when she was an adult and I was a minor. This woman's connection to Epstein was well-known by this point—her name is in the flight logs of his private jets. The woman now had a different last name and lived in a gated community in the Los Angeles area, which a *Broken* producer deftly entered by following another car through the gate. We parked on the street outside her house, and I went to the door and rang the bell. A moment later, the woman stuck her head out of an upstairs window and yelled at me to get off her property. "It's Virginia Roberts," I yelled back, but she slammed the window. So I buzzed the intercom. Soon, I heard her voice.

"I don't want to talk to you," the woman said. "Jeffrey's dead, and you helped kill him."

That pissed me off. "I'm not here about what Jeffrey's done," I said. "I'm here about what you've done."

"I'm calling security," she said, and soon, we were being escorted off the property.

Having exhausted our leads on the West Coast, Palmeri, her producer, and I flew to Florida, where we knew two other former Epstein employees lived. The first one we visited was Larry Visoski, Epstein's primary pilot. As I've said, Visoski had been close to Epstein, and he had never turned over his flight logs to the authorities, so I knew an interview with him was a longshot. The pilot lived in a gated community, and when we drove up, the gate attendant got Visoski on the phone and let me talk to him. "Hello, is—is this Larry?" I stammered, and when I heard him speak, I added: "Oh, my goodness. Like a voice from the past." I told him I was outside with a reporter. "Can I just come in and have a cup of coffee with you?" I asked. When he hesitated, I suggested lunch. That's when Visoski hung up on me.

Getting doors slammed in one's face is draining, to say the least. I'd been so fired up, imagining that if I just put myself in front of these people I'd known in 2000, 2001, and 2002, I could persuade them to talk to me. But once again I'd been naive. I was beginning to feel like a trained monkey, trotting out my story, over and over and over, but getting little in return. Palmeri had questioned me at length about my history with all these people—once again, I'd had to relive the dark period when I knew them. But because none were talking to us, I felt as if I'd gotten all spun up for nothing. Each night, back in our hotel, I'd call Robbie, more and more despondent. Robbie got so worried about my spiraling mood that he called Adam Davidson, one of the podcast producers, and the next day Davidson flew to Florida to try to shore me up. "I know this whole process has put a lot of pressure on you," he told me. "I can only imagine how hard that is, and I want you to know we're all standing behind you."

I appreciated Davidson's support. But still, when Palmeri and I set out to visit the second former Epstein associate who lived in Florida—Juan Alessi, Epstein's onetime house manager—I was nearly out of steam. It was Alessi who had driven me home from El Brillo Way on the night Epstein and Maxwell first abused me, and over the next two years, I'd gotten to know him and his wife, Maria, a bit. Alessi had never talked to the media, and there was little reason to think he would talk to us. When I rang the intercom on his outer gate, I would have bet you a hundred dollars that we'd strike out again. But Alessi answered right away. "Hi, Juan," I said quickly. "It's Virginia, Virginia Roberts from, like, twenty years ago . . . I've flown all the way from Australia to try to put together the pieces of my past." I told him I just wanted to talk, face-to-face. There was a pause, then a buzzing sound. Alessi was letting us in.

Moments later Alessi opened his front door, his wife, Maria, right beside him, and we all just stared at one another for a second. As two small dogs jumped around at our feet, Alessi invited Palmeri and me to sit down. At first he didn't want to be recorded, but then he changed his mind. The conversation was disjointed. Alessi, who still spoke in slightly broken English, acknowledged that he'd been driving Maxwell around on that sweltering day when she recruited me at Mar-a-Lago; he said he remembered sweating in the car as he waited for her. He insisted he had no idea of the sexual abuse going on in the house but admitted he'd told Epstein at one point, "One of these girls is going to get you in trouble, Jeffrey." He recalled seeing Prince Andrew in Epstein's homes, though he said he'd never seen him do anything wrong. I told Alessi I remembered it was often him who paid me after a "massage." I also recalled him seeing me naked. He said he didn't remember any of that.

"I swear to God, Virginia, I never saw you naked," he said. "I saw other girls, adult. But not you."

I could tell Palmeri was getting frustrated with his denials, and I understood why. Still, I felt better than I had the entire trip. Alessi remembered me! In a sense, that was what I'd come all this way for: to be acknowledged as a person, face-to-face. As we got up to leave, Alessi apologized. "Virginia, I feel so bad what happened to you, but I feel so good that I see you so great now. So good that you make up your life, that you have a family." I felt a wave of emotion then. "This has been a beautiful reunion," I said, and I meant it. "Thanks for opening your doors and your heart to me."

Alessi reiterated that he'd never imagined he'd ever see me again. "I thought you hate me," he said.

"Why would she hate you?" Palmeri asked pointedly.

"I thought, you know, she would have blamed me for not doing something," he said. "I thought these girls would go against me. Or they would have said, 'Oh, John knew it.' But I didn't."

We said our goodbyes, and as we walked to the car, Palmeri was still aggrieved that Alessi hadn't owned up to what he'd witnessed. But I was happy. "I don't expect everybody to come forward and say exactly what they saw, because that would incriminate them," I said, but I didn't blame Alessi for protecting himself. I thought he had a good heart. "He couldn't do shit about" Epstein's behavior, I concluded. "He feels horrible about it . . . Could he have talked more? Yes. But it's the beginning of a dialogue. So I'll take that as a plus. I'm grateful that he invited me into his home and treated me like a human being."

I returned to Australia. My nonstop media tour had worn me out, and it would have probably been wise for me to slow down and rest.

But after so long being vilified by the press, I felt I had to take advantage of every opportunity to tell my story, because who knew how much longer I'd be offered the chance. So in March 2020, when an Italian TV talk show offered to fly my whole family to Rome, I said yes. Right before the COVID-19 pandemic shut down much of the world, Robbie, the kids, and I visited "The City of the Seven Hills," as the guidebooks call it, and ticked off every tourist destination. I still have a photo book I made that shows the fun we had on this special Roman holiday.

All this came at a cost, however. The price of this lovely getaway for me was that I had to excavate my worst memories, one more time, on camera. I was noticing that with every interview, my storytelling was becoming a bit less emotional; at times my voice sounded almost mechanical, or even robotic, as if I were reciting something I'd memorized. And yet still, while I increasingly appeared unaffected on the outside, on the inside, every retelling of my stories of abuse hit me hard.

Robbie was watching me, and he could see I was coming apart. "When someone comes home from fighting a war, they heal, they get therapy, they put distance between what happened to them in combat and their present-day lives," he said. "But every time you relive what happened to you, it's as if you were still on the battlefield. How are you supposed to get better if you never come home from the war?" He was right. I had told myself that in order to fight for justice, I had to keep spreading the word about what Epstein and Maxwell had done. But spreading the word meant reliving my horrors, and that ate away at me. "This is the only way I know of to keep the pressure on," I told Robbie tearfully one night. He knelt down in front of me then—I'll never forget this—and took my hands in his. "Remember when I asked you to marry me—how I told you I'd have your back until we die?" he asked. "Well, this is me having your back. You are running on fumes. Your publicity schedule is affecting your health. It's affecting your family. I understand why you have given all these interviews. I really do. But, honey, it's killing you. And it's killing me to watch." My husband saw me more clearly than I saw myself: I was burned out.

THIRTY-FOUR

From Bad to Worse

What I needed, my friend said, was some time in the great outdoors. This was a new buddy of mine—the first mom I'd met when we moved to Cairns—and she had a daughter Ellie's age. This friend—her name was Blaise—knew how much I loved animals, and she'd seen the luminescent blue butterfly on my Twitter account, which was also the logo for my foundation, Victims Refuse Silence. "Let's take both our families to Butterfly Valley," Blaise said, describing a creekside sanctuary, about two hours south of our house, where visitors slept in rustic cabins and kept their eyes peeled for Cairns birdwings, whose six-inch wingspans make them the largest butterflies in Australia. The trip sounded like a perfect chance to rest and recharge in nature, and Robbie said he and the kids would come too.

So, off we went, and initially it was heaven. Butterfly Valley lived up to its name: we must've seen thousands of Cairns birdwings in all shapes, sizes, and colors. But when I returned home, I spiked a temperature and my head hurt like hell. When I became delirious, Robbie took me to the doctor, who did some tests and concluded I must've been bitten by a mosquito, because I had meningitis. I couldn't believe it: during the trip, I'd been the only one in our group slathering myself with bug spray. I was admitted to the hospital, where things got so much worse. Not realizing how delirious I'd become, at one point I got out of bed to go to the toilet and lost my footing. When I fell to the floor, I heard a cracking sound. I'd broken my neck.

I soon recovered from the meningitis, but now doctors said I needed surgery to repair my neck, which hurt constantly. They weren't quite ready to operate, however, so we waited. To cheer me up, Robbie got me a French bulldog that I named Juno, and once I was up and walking around again, I took Juno everywhere. But in April, I was back in the hospital again with pneumonia. It was as if one mosquito bite had let loose a waterfall of health problems.

I wasn't the only one struggling, of course. In spring 2020, the world was shutting down as the coronavirus raged. But still, surreally, my face and my story seemed to be everywhere, as the interviews I'd given over the previous months began to air. Even as I nursed my neck injury, in May 2020, Netflix launched its four-part series *Jeffrey Epstein: Filthy Rich*, which told the saga of Epstein and Maxwell's reign of terror. In the final episode, a healthy-looking me reiterated that Epstein had not acted alone and repeated my belief that all his coconspirators needed to be held accountable. "The monsters are still out there abusing other people," I said. "Why they have not been named and shamed yet is beyond me."

Right after Epstein's death, Maxwell had disappeared. Unconfirmed reports placed her in California, Massachusetts, France, and Israel, but all anyone knew for sure was that she was in hiding. Even her own lawyers said they did not know her location, and they refused to accept service, on her behalf, of three lawsuits filed by Annie Farmer, Jennifer Araoz, and a third Survivor Sister identified only as Jane Doe. That meant that even as federal prosecutors assembled a case against Maxwell, she couldn't be arrested until someone actually found her. Finally, investigators used a tracker on one of her mobile phones to zero in on a remote, 156-acre property in Bradford, New Hampshire. On July 2, 2020, the FBI broke through her locked gate and announced themselves at her front door, telling her to open it. Instead she fled to another room, so they broke in. She was arrested and charged with six counts that included transportation of a minor with intent to engage in criminal sexual activity and perjury. The perjury charges were personally satisfying for me because I'd enabled it—the government was alleging Maxwell had lied under oath in her depositions we'd taken in my defamation case against her. The other charges alleged that from 1994 to 1997, Maxwell helped Epstein recruit, groom, and sexually abuse girls as young as fourteen years old. These initial charges mentioned three unidentified minor victims, though I was not among them.

Because of the pandemic, Judge Alison J. Nathan held a virtual bail hearing for Maxwell in July 2020, with all the participants appearing remotely. Two victims spoke: Annie Farmer called Maxwell "a sexual predator who groomed and abused me and countless other children and young women." And a prosecutor read aloud a statement from the other victim, referred to as Jane Doe. "Without Ghislaine," this woman said, "Jeffrey could not have done what he did." Prosecutors had made clear that Maxwell knew how to evade detection; while still in hiding, she had changed her email address and registered a new phone number under the name "G Max." She also held passports from France and Britain—and had bank accounts that totaled as much as $20 million—so she would have a relatively easy time fleeing if she wished to. Judge Nathan denied Maxwell bail.

The day after Maxwell's bail hearing, I was interviewed on *CBS This Morning* by Gayle King. I said that Maxwell could "smell the vulnerability" of the young girls she recruited, and I asserted that the way Maxwell used her femininity to give girls a false sense of safety made her worse than Epstein. While Epstein was a sick pedophile, Maxwell "was vicious. She was evil," I said. "Put it this way: Epstein was Pinocchio, and she was Geppetto. She was—"

King interjected: "Pulling the strings?"

"Yes," I answered. "She was pulling the strings."

King asked, "What would justice look like for you?"

"I would like to see Ghislaine stay in jail forever," I said. "I would like her to apologize for what she's done to me and so many others."

"Does the buck stop with Ghislaine Maxwell, in your opinion?" she asked.

"No, the buck stops when every single monster gets held accountable and our children are safe," I said. "Not just my monsters. But all the monsters. And we need everyone's help."

Two weeks later, Judge Loretta Preska, who was presiding over ongoing decisions related to my defamation suit against Maxwell, gave us a little help when she made public a second batch of documents from my case. This batch included flight logs from Epstein's private jets; police reports from the 2005 to 2008 investigation of Epstein in Florida; a set of emails, dated January 2015, between Epstein and Maxwell; and emails from me to the FBI in 2014, including one in which I expressed interest in pursuing a case against Epstein and proving, as I put it, "how much pedophilia occurred." The email was just another reminder of how much time had passed while I, and other Survivor Sisters, begged law enforcement to bring these people to justice.

In August 2020, I had what's called an anterior cervical discectomy; doctors at Sunnybank Private Hospital in Brisbane went in through the front of my throat and removed a shattered disk, then attached metal swivels in my neck to allow me to continue to have some mobility. As I healed, I posted about the ordeal on Instagram, showing my postsurgery bruises and thanking my supporters for helping me get through it. "I'm too tough for something like this to take me down—and I got a bionic spine out of it," I wrote. I was not permitted to fly afterward, so when I was released from the hospital, Robbie and I drove six hours back to Cairns.

But as my body mended, everything hurt. I was taking strong painkillers but trying not to rely on them too much. Knowing how drugs had helped me escape from reality in the past, I worried about their allure. My determination to resist that temptation, however, would soon waver. In September the *Broken* podcast that I'd helped report went live, but I didn't listen to it. I was too zoned out on oxycodone.

I GREW UP a tomboy, climbing trees, making mudpies, and splashing in ponds, so I know what happens when you turn over rocks that haven't been disturbed in a long time: when daylight hits the creepy-crawly things underneath, it makes them squirm. When the deposition in which I named the late MIT scientist Marvin Minsky among my abusers became public, for example, a colleague of Minsky's blasted out an email to a mailing list for MIT's Computer Science and Artificial Intelligence Laboratory. In the email, renowned computer scientist Richard Stallman suggested that I had been a willing participant in my encounter with Minsky. Stallman questioned whether Minsky "applied force or violence" and seemed to be arguing that if he did not, I must have opted in. "The most plausible scenario is that she presented herself to him as entirely willing," Stallman wrote of me.

Stallman was criticized by some who received this email, but still it was clear that not everyone agreed that the girls and women whom Epstein and Maxwell trafficked to others were victims who deserved compassion. "They took the money, didn't they?" was the most common refrain from people in this camp—as if someone can't be victimized while being paid two hundred dollars. While I wasn't pen pals with people who believed these things, their opinions reached me through social media and, occasionally, through email. My point: Stallman wasn't alone in his skepticism.

Just as Stallman defended Minsky, many friends and colleagues of MIT Media Lab director Joichi Ito defended him after it was revealed that he had cultivated a close (and lucrative) relationship with Epstein. Ito apologized, and for a little while, it appeared he'd keep his job. Then *The New Yorker* revealed just how extensively Ito had worked to cover up Epstein's visits to the MIT campus, as well as Epstein's direct donations and donations that Epstein had helped prompt from other people. One day after that article ran, Ito resigned.

The chips were beginning to fall for other men who'd been connected to Epstein too. A month after Ito's downfall, Brown University—who'd hired an MIT fundraising official who'd worked with Ito to cultivate Epstein—put that official on leave to make sure his behavior could be reconciled with Brown's "core values." Harvard University—which had received over $9 million in gifts from Epstein—would soon shut down its program for evolutionary dynamics after investigating the link between its director, Martin Nowak, and Epstein.

The ripples of Epstein's public shunning were soon being felt outside academia as well. Leon Black would resign as chief executive of Apollo Global Management and Jes Staley would resign as CEO of Barclays Bank—both after inquiries into the two men's relationships with Epstein. And it wouldn't be long before Melinda French Gates would tell CBS's Gayle King that while there were a number of factors that led her to divorce her husband of twenty-seven years, Bill Gates, his work with Epstein was definitely one of them. "I did not like that he had meetings with Jeffrey Epstein, no. I made that clear to him," Melinda would tell King, adding that she herself met with Epstein "exactly one time" because she "wanted to see who this man was." Her reaction: "I regretted it the second I walked in the door. He was abhorrent. He was evil personified. My heart breaks for these women."

If only everyone felt such empathy for Epstein's victims. In December 2020, *The Telegraph* ran a story about me that was headlined "Prince Andrew's Accuser Was a Prostitute Paid Off by Jeffrey Epstein, Court Papers Allege." Based on a recorded conversation between a New York publisher and the tabloid journalist Sharon Churcher, who was trying to sell a book, those court papers implied that I was making up allegations as a form of blackmail, only seeking to get paid off.

In my darkest hours, especially when the pain in my neck immobilized me, reading headlines like those cut me to the quick. The fact that I suspected this was my critics' intent—Call her a whore! That'll shut her up!—didn't make it any easier to read. Ten days before Christmas 2020, when I was really struggling, I recorded a video of myself that I shared on Twitter. "I'm not asking for a pity party," I told my followers, who numbered more than one hundred thousand. "I don't want that. I just want to know I'm on the right path and helping people. Some days, it's just—" At that point my voice cracked, and tears filled my eyes. I'd spent so long believing that it was my responsibility to demand accountability from those who'd hurt me. But to the extent that meant repeating what happened to me again and again and again, as if on a tape loop, I wasn't sure how much more of that I could take. "It's hard," I said to the camera. "I just feel quite alone."

Still, there were other, less lonely times that I sensed I was part of a movement that was forcing positive change. On January 14, 2021, L Brands shareholders filed a complaint alleging that Leslie Wexner, among others, created an "entrenched culture of misogyny, bullying and harassment" at the company. They also said Wexner, who had stepped down as CEO the previous year to return to his mansion in

New Albany, Ohio, had breached his fiduciary duty because he was aware of abuses being committed by Epstein. Among other things, Epstein was alleged to have preyed on Victoria's Secret models, and shareholders claimed this caused a devaluation of the brands under the company's umbrella. Six months later, in July, the company settled, pledging to invest $90 million to clean up its act, improving sexual harassment and antiretaliation practices and ceasing to enforce nondisclosure agreements that had silenced women victims in the past.

Not even a year later, a singer and former *American Idol* contestant named Jax released an ode to body positivity that quickly climbed the pop charts. "I know Victoria's secret," she sang, "And, girl, you wouldn't believe / She's an old man who lives in Ohio / Making money off of girls like me / Cashin' in on body issues / Sellin' skin and bones with big boobs / I know Victoria's secret / She was made up by a dude." Victoria's Secret's new female CEO soon wrote Jax a letter, thanking her for raising "important issues." One by one, some in Epstein's inner circle were being called out. If I had played even a small part in that, I thought, maybe I could keep going.

THIRTY-FIVE

Backlash

On Ellie's eleventh birthday, in January 2021, we moved our family across Australia, from Cairns on the East Coast to Perth on the West Coast. Queensland had been wonderful when the kids were younger, but now I wanted them to attend the better schools Perth could offer. I continued to be amazed by my children. Ellie, for example, was a force. Tall for her age and physically strong, she was also insatiably curious about the world and a big reader. Lately, she'd discovered a manga series called *Demon Slayer: Kimetsu no Yaiba* about a fourteen-year-old girl and her older brother who have lost their entire family to demons. When the girl becomes a demon, too, her brother becomes a demon slayer and vows to transform his sister back into human form. Ellie told me she loved the idea that demons could be rehabilitated and made good again. I was buoyed by her optimism, even as I sometimes struggled to maintain my own.

In February 2021, my health worsened. First, I developed a high fever, then a place on my thigh where I'd received a steroid injection became inflamed. My doctors speculated that maybe I was having an allergic reaction to the antibiotic I'd been taking after my neck surgery, but mostly they seemed stumped. Soon my inflamed thigh turned into a staph infection that refused to heal. Then, I got another case of pneumonia. It was as if my immune system was overloaded. I couldn't catch a break.

I was still taking a lot of pain meds, among other prescribed medicines, when I headed to France in mid-June 2021 to give a deposition against Jean-Luc Brunel. The modeling agent had been arrested in Paris the previous December and charged with sexual harassment and the rape of minor victims. No charges of human trafficking were brought initially, but the investigation was continuing, and he had not been acquitted of that charge. Part of the investigation involved taking depositions from people like me, who'd been assaulted by Brunel. So I bought a plane ticket and flew from Australia to Europe to do my duty.

As I described in the introduction to this book, first, I spent several days preparing with Siggy and my French lawyers. Then, for ten hours over a single day, I sat in the same room as Brunel as I was questioned under oath. As expected, his lawyers attempted to impale me on all the sharp words that abusers usually aim at their victims: liar, money-grubber, prostitute. While Brunel wasn't supposed to speak to me directly, of course he found a way to do so. He sat in the front row, while I sat behind him in the second row, looking at the back of his skull. At one point, when we took a break, he turned and whispered, "You're a lying bitch." Looking at me with the same eyes that had once ogled me as he forced me to have sex with him, he hissed, "I've never even met you."

I soothed myself with shopping trips and two visits to the Louvre. On my first visit, I found myself facing off with a huge garish tapestry in a room that might as well have been haunted by Epstein and Maxwell's ghosts. A panic attack nearly sunk me, but a few days later, I returned to reclaim that beautiful place for myself. On a shelf in my family room in Perth, I keep the replica I bought that day of *Winged Victory of Samothrace*, the famous headless statue of the goddess Nike that has been on display at the Louvre since 1883. Compared to the nine-foot-tall original, mine—which I found in the museum's gift shop—stands only about two feet high. But its power is immense in that every day, it serves as a reminder: winning isn't always possible, but it's worth striving for.

The highlight of my visit to France, though, was finally meeting a woman named Thysia Huisman in person. In 1991, when Huisman was eighteen and a would-be model, she'd met with Brunel in Brussels at the urging of her new agents. Brunel, then in his midforties, told her that he'd make her a star if she came to Paris immediately. She did, and at his insistence, she stayed in his apartment. But within a week, she was gone. That's because, on her fourth or fifth night there, Brunel spiked her drink and raped her.

Huisman was too ashamed at the time to bring charges against him. But years later, after seeing me on TV, she had reached out to me on Twitter, and we'd begun a dialogue. She went public with her charges in 2019, joining several models who would accuse Brunel of sexual assault and rape. Now it was two years later, and she was walking into the lobby of my Paris hotel.

We greeted each other with a warm hug, and for the next two hours, we shared what we'd been through, sitting closely together on a velvet couch. Huisman, now a TV producer, gave me a copy of book she'd written: *Close-Up: Het schokkende verhaal van een Nederlands fotomodel*, which meant: "the shocking story of a Dutch fashion model." She had published this memoir in 2020, and despite the fact that I couldn't read Dutch, getting my own copy meant the world to me. On the cover was a portrait of her stunning face when she was eighteen, right before Brunel abused her. I held her hand, and we both shed tears for what these men had taken from us.

OVER THE SUMMER, Siggy and the rest of my legal team sent a letter to Prince Andrew's lawyers as time was running out to file a lawsuit against him under a New York law extending the statute of limitations for underage sex abuse claims. They didn't receive any response. In early August, the prince's ex-wife, Sarah Ferguson, told the *Financial Times* that she and Prince Andrew were the "happiest divorced couple in the world"—a PR move seemingly intended to burnish the prince's image on the eve of my likely lawsuit.

On August 9, 2021, my thirty-eighth birthday, two key things happened. First, administrators of the Epstein Victims' Compensation Fund, which had been created after his suicide to establish a process for survivors of his abuse to bring claims against his estate, announced they were winding down the program because its work was done. In all, the fund had given almost $125 million to about 150 victims. When you add that number to the many of us who'd settled with Epstein when he was still alive, there were now probably at least 200 victims (and likely many more) who had come forward to identify themselves and been compensated by Epstein or Epstein's estate. The sheer scale of that effort was and is remarkable.

The second thing that happened on August 9 was that I sued Prince Andrew in New York State for violating the Child Victims Act. My suit came just four days before the look-back window slammed shut. In my claim, I alleged that Prince Andrew had raped and battered me when I was a minor, causing me severe and lasting damage. I asked for damages to be determined by the court.

As I turned thirty-eight, I realized that I'd spent the second half of my life recovering from the first. I was nineteen when I met Robbie and set off to make a new life with him. I'd now lived almost precisely nineteen more years, and I was still fighting for justice. I'd come a long way, but I had yet to feel anywhere near whole. I wondered if that feeling would ever come.

When the news of my lawsuit broke, I guess I shouldn't have been surprised when the British tabloid newspaper *The Sun* tracked down my father in Florida. "I support my daughter one hundred percent," Dad said, calling me "persistent" and "brave." "The royals are not above the law. That's not the way it works. They can't just do what they want. People fight back. That's what Virginia is doing. . . . If Prince Andrew puts himself in my position, if this was happening to his daughter, how would he feel? He should be ashamed." Reading these supportive words, my heart softened toward my father, but only for a moment. Above all, I knew him to be manipulative, so I suspected that this interview could be his way of trying to get back into my good graces. And, given his past behavior, I couldn't help but wonder: had Dad been paid by *The Sun*?

Initially, the prince made it difficult for my lawyers to serve him with papers, fleeing to Queen Elizabeth's Balmoral Castle in Scotland and hiding behind its well-guarded gates. This was not a surprise. Back in 2020, prosecutors in the Maxwell case had noted that Prince Andrew had "sought to falsely portray himself to the public as eager and willing to cooperate," but, in fact, he had given no interview to federal authorities and had repeatedly declined requests to talk with investigators. If the prince had "completely shut the door on voluntary cooperation" with the US DOJ, as prosecutors alleged, it would have been foolhardy to expect that he would make it easy for me.

At the end of September, however, a judge scolded Prince Andrew's lawyers for engaging in "a game of hide and seek behind palace walls," and ruled that service could be made through his US-based lawyers. The case then moved forward. Soon we caught a break: a woman named Shukri Walker went public, saying she remembered seeing me dancing with Prince Andrew at the Tramp nightclub in 2001, just as I'd always said. Walker, who had already given a written statement to the FBI, said she would happily testify against the prince if my lawsuit went to trial. Her lawyer would later tell *The Guardian* that Walker remembered the night "clearly because she never saw a royal before or since. She says Prince Andrew was happy, smiling, and dancing, and Virginia did not look happy."

I'd been in the hospital again, having laparoscopic surgery to remove cysts from my ovaries and polyps from my uterus. For weeks leading up to that operation, I'd been bleeding nonstop. Doctors wondered whether my string of health problems were somehow related to the staph infection on my thigh, which was still not fully healed. No one was quite sure of anything, it seemed, except that my body seemed to be staging a revolt.

But nothing was going to stop me from helping Ellie prepare for Halloween 2021. For months she'd been talking about going as Nezuko Kamado, the girl demon in her *Demon Slayer* manga series. At first, I'd been surprised that my daughter wanted to be a character that had crossed over to the dark side. But Ellie corrected me, saying Nezuko was actually a force for good. Even though a demon had mostly erased Nezuko's memories, Ellie explained, her love of her older brother kept her from harming him. While most demons ate human flesh to get energy, Nezuko restored herself through sleep. "Kind of like you, Mom," Ellie teased, referring to how much time I was spending in bed.

Now I threw myself into transforming my beautiful daughter into Nezuko. We got Ellie a kimono, and a pair of geta, those traditional Japanese flip-flops with the elevated wooden soles. We even found a way to re-create the bamboo muzzle, secured with a sash, that Nezuko wears to prevent herself from biting anyone. When we got it all together, my little warrior tried everything on, and she couldn't have been happier. "You know, Mama," she said, "eventually, Nezuko and her brother vanquish the evil around them and then they live a peaceful life." She was beaming at me as if she'd stumbled upon a secret code for contentment. I hugged her long and hard that day. I'd been trying to protect my daughter from the world's ugliness, but she was developing her own ways of protecting herself—and passing strength to me in the process.

THIRTY-SIX

Maxwell on Trial

"I want to tell you about a young girl named 'Jane.'" This opening line, delivered by Assistant US Attorney Lara Pomerantz, kicked off Ghislaine Maxwell's trial on November 29, 2021. Epstein's enabler and coconspirator was charged with unlawful conduct that spanned from 1994 to 2004 and involved the three minor victims listed in her original indictment and a fourth woman, aged fourteen when she was abused, who had been added later. Prosecutors were seeking to prove one count of enticement of a minor to travel to engage in illegal sex acts, one count of transportation of a minor to do the same, one count of sex trafficking of a minor, and three counts of conspiracy. Exactly one month later, a jury of twelve New Yorkers would reach a verdict. This meant that for the next four weeks, I would barely sleep, since it's twelve hours later in Perth. The proceedings were not televised, but every day court was in session, I could be found between the hours of 9:00 p.m. and 5:00 a.m. Perth time poring over live-tweets from journalists who were in the courtroom.

Months earlier, the lead prosecutors, Pomerantz and Maurene Comey, had broken the news to me that I would not be testifying because, essentially, I would be too big a distraction. For example, if I were a witness, all the men that I had previously named as my abusers would likely be called by the defense as rebuttal witnesses, the prosecutors said. They feared such theatrics would dilute jurors' focus, taking the spotlight off Maxwell. At its heart, prosecuting a case is about creating a clear narrative that jurors find easy to follow. My narrative was complicated, if only because I'd named so many names. The prosecutors acknowledged they wouldn't have been able to build as strong a case against Maxwell without the discovery gathered in my prior defamation lawsuit (as I've said, Maxwell was charged separately with two counts of perjury that stemmed from her allegedly false testimony in her depositions in my case). But they wanted to tell a straightforward story about Maxwell the groomer, the procurer, and the abuser.

I was very disappointed—I had been looking forward to doing my part to send Maxwell to prison. While Siggy tried to console me that I had done my part already, being excluded from this proceeding felt unfair to me. For one thing, I expected that many people would assume prosecutors shut me out because they didn't believe me. (Indeed, just four days before the start of Maxwell's trial, Prince Andrew's camp planted a story in *The Telegraph* that ran under this headline: "Virginia Giuffre's Absence from Ghislaine Maxwell Trial Shows She Is 'Not a Credible Witness,' Says Duke's Team.") But that couldn't be helped. More worrisome to me was the possibility that by limiting their case to just four victims—none of whom had traveled outside the United States with Epstein, as I had—the prosecution might not win. There had been much speculation that Maxwell's lawyers would attempt an "empty chair" defense, arguing that Maxwell was being blamed for the actions of a man whose death prevented him from coming to court: Epstein. I worried some jurors would be swayed by that strategy.

But now it was showtime. I tried to look at the bright side: had I been called to testify, I would've missed Christmas with my kids. Instead, I hunkered down in Perth, where I'd festooned the house with tinsel and ornaments, crossed my fingers, and prayed for justice.

"JANE," A SOAP-OPERA actress, who testified under a pseudonym, told jurors that Maxwell strolled up to her in 1994, with Epstein trailing behind her, when she was a camper at Interlochen Arts Camp in Michigan. Epstein and Maxwell were donors to the renowned summer camp and boarding school—Epstein even had a "scholarship lodge" named after him. Jane's father had died of leukemia a year before, and her family—who lived in Palm Beach—was short of money, she said. Jane thought Maxwell and Epstein were married, so when they realized she lived in Florida and asked for her mother's contact information, she gave it. Later, when she was fourteen, she agreed to meet with Epstein and Maxwell in Palm Beach. Thus began a yearslong cycle of sexual abuse in Florida, New York, and New Mexico; Jane recalled that Maxwell touched her breasts and Epstein made her touch his genitals, engage in group sex, and submit to "painful" abuse with a vibrator. Jane remembered Epstein's introducing her to Prince Andrew and confirmed that she'd been awarded $5 million by the Epstein Victims' Fund, though she'd only received $2.9 million of that. Asked about the long-term impacts of her experiences with Epstein and Maxwell, she answered with a question: "How do you navigate a healthy relationship with a broken compass? I didn't know what real love was supposed to look like."

Two of Maxwell's accusers—Dr. Annie Farmer, a licensed psychologist, and "Kate," a British model and actress who also used a pseudonym—testified only after the judge instructed jurors that their description of alleged sexual conduct could not be used to convict Maxwell of the crimes charged. That was because "Kate" was above the age of consent in the jurisdiction in which she had sexual contact with Epstein and Maxwell. (She'd been seventeen at the time.) Annie had been sixteen when she was fondled by Maxwell at Epstein's ranch in New Mexico, where a sixteen-year-old is not considered a minor. But both Annie and Kate were used by the prosecution to assert that Maxwell's exploitation of vulnerable teenagers was part of a pattern. Kate, for example, said that Maxwell groomed her for Epstein to abuse and that after she gave him sexual "massages," Maxwell said, "You're such a good girl."

The fourth minor victim was Carolyn, who used only her first name. Carolyn described herself as a middle-school dropout who'd been sexually abused by her grandfather and said that I'd introduced her to Maxwell and Epstein in Palm Beach. That testimony was a complete surprise to me. Carolyn said the first time she went to El Brillo Way, I got undressed and told her to keep on her bra and underwear. She said that after she and I spent forty-five minutes massaging Epstein, he turned over, and he and I had sex while she watched from a nearby couch. I didn't doubt her account—I've acknowledged that I'd been forced to recruit girls and said that I will always regret it. But I am ashamed to say that I didn't remember Carolyn's name. Carolyn testified that after her initial encounter with Epstein, she'd visited the Palm Beach house two or three times a week for a period of years. She said she performed sexualized massages that were arranged by Maxwell, who was always in the house when Carolyn arrived. Carolyn also told jurors that Maxwell saw her naked some thirty times in Epstein's massage room. Maxwell "felt my boobs and my hips and my buttocks and said that . . . I had a great body for Mr. Epstein and his friends," Carolyn testified.

If I had to distill defense attorney Laura Menninger's arguments into a single message, it would be this: the alleged victims had at times changed their stories, or gotten details wrong, so their memories couldn't be trusted. (I'd been similarly criticized so many times about mistakes I'd made that I'd lost count.) Menninger was particularly tough on Jane, saying in her summation, "Her lapses of memory pervade this case." Jane had recalled seeing *The Lion King* during a period it wasn't on Broadway and attending the late journalist Mike Wallace's eightieth birthday party at a point in the chronology that didn't match his age. But Maxwell's own memory expert had testified that while peripheral memories tended to erode over time, core memories about trauma tended to stick. Maurene Comey, one of the prosecutors, countered Menninger's critique by posing a question to the jury: "Ladies and gentlemen, which would stand out more in your mind: how old you were on Mike Wallace's birthday or how old you were the first time a middle-aged man molested you?"

The defense also implied that the four accusers—all who had received payouts from the Epstein Victims' Fund—were incentivized to exaggerate because they'd benefited financially from the Epstein "money train." Menninger said their stories showed the influence of "memory, manipulation, and money." But Comey noted that the checks the women had accepted in their settlements with Epstein's estate had already cleared when they took the stand. That meant that they had nothing more to gain financially from the grim experience of reliving trauma (and risking prosecution if they testified falsely). "Did that look fun?" Comey asked jurors, referring to the victims' sometimes tearful testimony. "Why would they put themselves through that, when they've already gotten millions of dollars?"

In the end, while Maxwell's lawyers had said they would call thirty-five witnesses, they called only seven, in part because the judge forbade them from letting witnesses testify anonymously. Maxwell opted not to testify on her own behalf. By contrast, while I would have loved to have testified, I was not entirely absent. I saw one report that estimated my name had been mentioned 250 times during the trial. I guess that's the next best thing to being there?

On December 20, when both sides delivered closing arguments, Comey called Maxwell a sophisticated predator who caused "deep and lasting harm to young girls" and was "crucial" to Epstein's sex-trafficking operation. She noted that three of the witnesses said Maxwell had touched their breasts. "It happened again and again," she said. Menninger, meanwhile, argued Maxwell's innocence by posing a question: "Why would a proper Oxford-educated woman do this?"

The verdict came in on the afternoon of the jury's fifth full day of deliberations. Just after 5:00 p.m. on December 29, the judge read it aloud. Maxwell was guilty of sex trafficking and four other charges; she was acquitted of one count of enticing a minor to travel across state lines to engage in an illegal sexual act.

It was just after 5:00 a.m. in Perth, and I was asleep in our bedroom, but Robbie was downstairs in the kitchen, wide awake. Like me, he'd been sleeping very little. When he saw the news, he bounded upstairs and burst into our room. "Guilty, baby!" he was screaming, and I opened my eyes to see him running around the room in circles. "She's guilty!"

Soon I got on a Zoom with Siggy, who was beaming. "Home run! All the counts but one!" she said joyfully. But then her face turned serious. "She is going to prison for a very, very long time, Virginia, and all of that has to do with you. You started this, sweetheart. You did everything to keep it going. There's no way this could have happened without your bravery and your commitment. That is heroic—

and I watched you go through it. It was a horrible, difficult job, and you did it. And you took some serious hits along the way. I'm so incredibly proud of you right now."

After a strong cup of Italian coffee made the way Robbie's parents taught me to make it, I soon took to Twitter to say the verdict had been cathartic for me. "My soul yearned for justice for years and today the jury gave me just that," I wrote. "I will remember this day always. Having lived with the horrors of Maxwell's abuse, my heart goes out to the many other girls and young women who suffered at her hands and whose lives she destroyed. I hope that today is not the end but rather another step in justice being served. Maxwell did not act alone. Others must be held accountable. I have faith that they will be."

THIRTY-SEVEN

Settling Up and Settling Down

On January 12, 2022, my case against Prince Andrew got the green light. The prince's lawyers had argued that he was protected from liability by the settlement I'd signed with Epstein way back in 2009. But Judge Lewis Kaplan rejected that. "Prince Andrew Can't Avoid His Day in Court, a Judge Rules," the *New York Times* headline said. The British press went nuts, calling the decision "a huge blow for Prince Andrew" (*The Evening Standard*) and warning of a coming "hugely expensive and reputation-shredding court case" (*Daily Mail*). Already, the case had been credited with causing "Abolish the Monarchy" to trend on Twitter. Now, the day after the judge's decision, the queen stripped the prince of his royal and military titles, prompting the *Sun* to run with this front-page headline: "Throne Out." The Platinum Jubilee of Queen Elizabeth II was coming up in June—it would be the international celebration marking the seventieth anniversary of her accession to the throne. Clearly, the British media—and the royal family itself—were already weighing how Prince Andrew's troubles might affect that day.

On January 19, Prince Andrew deleted all his Twitter, Instagram, and Facebook profiles. Three days later, *Saturday Night Live* took a swipe at him, with *Weekend Update* host Colin Jost saying, "This week, Britain's most eligible bachelor, Prince Andrew, officially deleted his Twitter account after he realized that's not the app with all the dancing teenagers." Four days later, the prince formally denied my charges, but his response was met with ridicule. My lawyers, meanwhile, were seeking to depose the prince's former assistant and to see medical records, if any existed, that could prove the prince's assertion that he'd lost the ability to sweat.

The prince was not without his supporters. On January 31, a former girlfriend of his, a socialite named Lady Victoria Hervey, took to Instagram to say that in her opinion, I was "a complete whore." Then, just in case anyone had forgotten that this story is not just about sexual abuse but also about class, she added that I was "just a ghetto opportunity whose [sic] seriously mixed up." Never one to shirk her public duty, Lady Victoria—the daughter of the sixth marquess of Bristol, half sister of the seventh marquess, and sister of the eighth marquess, whatever all of that means—would give many mean-spirited interviews about me in the coming months.

The paparazzi, meanwhile, had tracked my family down in Perth. In February, the *Daily Mail* published this important news: "Prince Andrew's accuser Virginia Giuffre is spotted vaping with foils in her hair outside salon in Australia as she prepares to take oath and be quizzed by the duke's lawyers for her sex assault lawsuit." You can imagine how unflattering the accompanying photos were. I looked like a half-crazed, metal-spiked witch (who also was trying to quit smoking). Ah, the things we women do in the name of beauty. But most women don't have to worry about such things being captured by photographers. I tried not to let it bother me.

The world didn't know it, but settlement discussions with Prince

SETTLING UP AND SETTLING DOWN

Andrew's team were suddenly moving quickly. After he'd stonewalled us for months, the scheduling of his deposition, which was to take place on March 10, seemed to motivate him. Also, the newest addition to the prince's legal team, Andrew Brettler, an American who'd worked for two Hollywood figures facing their own #MeToo allegations (the actor Armie Hammer and the director Bryan Singer), was less reluctant than some of his British counterparts to face reality. David Boies would later credit Brettler with keeping the settlement talks on track. Siggy, meanwhile, felt we couldn't have been in a better position. She was ready to try the case, and she believed strongly that if we went to trial, we'd prevail. "I'm going to ask for the moon," she told me—which we'd already agreed had to be more than mere money. After casting doubt on my credibility for so long—Prince Andrew's team had even gone so far as to try to hire internet trolls to hassle me—the Duke of York owed me a meaningful apology as well. We would never get a confession, of course. That's what settlements are designed to avoid. But we were trying for the next best thing: a general acknowledgment of what I'd been through. After my lawyers hashed out the basic details on Zoom, I then participated in two days of mediation talks. Finally, at 2:30 a.m. Florida time, the prince's lawyers agreed to the statement we'd been pushing for. Siggy called me immediately and read it to me through tears, both hers and mine.

"Prince Andrew has never intended to malign Ms. Giuffre's character," the statement read in part, "and he accepts that she has suffered both as an established victim of abuse and as a result of unfair public attacks." Yes, indeed, including attacks from the prince's own camp! "It is known that Jeffrey Epstein trafficked countless young girls over many years," the statement continued, acknowledging vastly more about Epstein's predatory behavior than the prince himself had in his fateful BBC interview. "Prince Andrew regrets his association with Epstein, and commends the bravery of Ms. Giuffre and other survivors in standing up for themselves and others. He pledges to demonstrate his regret for his association with Epstein by supporting the fight against the evils of sex trafficking, and by supporting its victims."

In that moment, I would have given anything to be in the same room with Siggy. "Thank you, Siggy, for all that you've done for me," I told her shakily over the phone. She responded by repeating her assertion that representing me had been her complete honor. "At the end of my life," Siggy would tell me later, "when I look back on the best moments, that phone call will be one of them."

On February 15, the settlement was announced. We issued a joint statement that made clear Prince Andrew would pay me money, though the amount was kept confidential (later it was reported that his mother, the queen of England, had footed the bill). The statement said he would also make a "substantial donation" in support of victims' rights to my nascent nonprofit organization. I agreed to a one-year gag order, which seemed important to the prince because it ensured that his mother's Platinum Jubilee would not be tarnished any more than it already had been.

Because of the time difference, the settlement announcement came in the middle of our night in Australia. That meant when we woke up the next day—Alex's birthday—our street was choked with paparazzi. The Giuffre family has a tradition: on their birthdays, all the kids get to go shopping to pick out their own gifts. I still wanted to do that, but Robbie wasn't sure we'd be able to get out of the driveway. For a moment, I considered going out and throwing myself at the mercy of the reporters. My plan was to say I was pleased with the settlement, then explain that it was Alex's sweet sixteen and politely ask if we could have our privacy back. But then I came to my senses. Were I to try that and then attempt to take Alex to the mall, the headlines would surely read: "Epstein Survivor Rushes Out to Start Spending Prince

Andrew's Money" or some such. Robbie and I talked about it, and in the end, we promised Alex a rain check, and we all stayed home and got a cake, beer, and flowers delivered.

Three days later, Jean-Luc Brunel was found dead in the French prison where he'd been held for more than two years. He had hanged himself. I did not give any interviews. Two months earlier, a few weeks before Maxwell was convicted, my French lawyer had gotten in touch, saying Brunel was about to be let out on bond. I'd told the lawyer that I couldn't come back to Paris at that moment, but I needed him to go to court for me and argue against Brunel's release. That effort had succeeded, but now Brunel was dead. "The suicide of Jean-Luc Brunel, who abused me and countless girls and women, ends another chapter," I tweeted. "I am disappointed that I was not able to face him in a final trial and hold him accountable for his actions, but gratified that I was able to face him in person in Paris, to keep him in prison."

That same day, a consultant I'd hired to help me get my charity organized received this email, whose subject line read simply, "Explain." The email read: "Maybe Virginia can explain how this sellout from Andrew provided justice to all the girls effected by this ... SHE SOLD EVERYONE OUT and is just as bad as Epstein, Maxwell the now dead Jean and Andrew. #nosympathy." We decided not to respond to the sender of this email, though she signed her name. But I'd like to address what she said here. Everyone is entitled to his or her opinion, of course, but to equate me with four of my abusers is wrongheaded and even cruel. As with Maxwell, I'd sued Prince Andrew in federal court, which meant a financial settlement was always going to be the prime form of punishment if we were successful. But I'd gotten more out of him than that: an acknowledgment that I and many other women had been victimized and a tacit pledge to never deny that again. Finally, my receipt of funds from the settlement has enabled me to finally make good on a long-standing goal of mine: to spend less of my energy unpacking the past and more on helping people in the present. In November 2021, I'd relaunched my nonprofit (now called Speak Out, Act, Reclaim, or SOAR) with a new website and had set about updating its mission statement and the way it would be run. Respectfully, I was attempting to help survivors of abuse—the *opposite* of what Epstein had done. I only wish it hadn't taken me so long.

ALL THROUGH THIS period, I was buoyed by the knowledge that Robbie and I had organized an amazing vacation: a hard-to-get reservation on the Ningaloo Coast, a coral reef so pristine that it has been named a UNESCO World Heritage Site. The kids were excited to swim alongside whale sharks. Me, I just wanted to get some sleep. My neck was hurting so much, and the painkillers I was taking were making me dizzy and disoriented. But just when we were getting ready to travel, Robbie and Alex came down with COVID. I called Ningaloo to cancel. Then I got COVID too. Over the next several days, my blood-oxygen level went lower and lower. When my hands and feet went numb and my left arm felt as if it had fallen asleep for good, Robbie didn't wait for an ambulance. He packed me in the car and took me straight back to the hospital.

I've told you how cunning an enemy trauma can be. It hides in the shadows, then takes control of one's psyche without warning. That's what happened as I lay in that hospital bed in Perth: all my feelings of sadness and shame overtook me. I was worn out by the near-constant pain in my neck. I was weary of defending myself against vicious, hurtful words: liar, sellout, extortionist, drug addict, whore. I was sick of the nightmares: greedy, heaving men on top of me, men whose faces I recognized and would never forget, men whose faces I didn't recognize. Alarmingly, I see now, I wasn't afraid anymore; instead, I just felt hollowed out. So when my trauma tricked my brain into telling me

SETTLING UP AND SETTLING DOWN

lies, I listened: "It would be better for everyone if you weren't here," my brain said. "You bring nothing but stress and worry into your husband and children's lives. Why should they suffer because Jeffrey and Ghislaine caused you pain? You have let your family down. They deserve better. They will be happier without you." My trauma took aim at my very existence: "Aren't you exhausted? Unconsciousness would be a relief. Robbie and the kids are safe at home, so none of them will find you. It won't hurt a bit. The pills are on the bedside table. It will be easy. You can just quietly slip away."

I believed my brain, so I reached for the painkillers that I had smuggled into the hospital and I swallowed as many as I could—later they'd estimate 240 pills—before I passed out. I'm told that I was revived with Narcan, the opioid overdose treatment. My fragile self-worth had imploded. All that remained were the shards of me.

Oh, the look on Robbie's face when they told him. He couldn't bear the thought of me disappearing, and he wanted to strangle me for trying to disappear. "What were you thinking, Jenna?" he demanded, but in my mind, I had no answer for him except: "I was thinking I needed to be dead." Indeed, just days later, after I got out of the hospital, I would try to kill myself again, with more pills. It was only because our son Alex came to check on me that I did not succeed. For a second time, I woke up in the hospital, revived once more by Narcan. After that, it would be a long time before my thoughts of self-annihilation would truly begin to subside. Only then could I promise my husband and kids that I would try with all my might to believe that I mattered.

THERE IS A huge framed picture on our wall in Perth, right at the center of our home. I placed it there, at the landing at the bottom of the stairs, so that everyone in the family can see it multiple times a day.

It's a photograph of a cove on Magnetic Island in Queensland—a place where years ago, before Ellie was born, Robbie and I had taken our young sons on our first family vacation. We had no money back then—we were living paycheck to paycheck—but after Robbie was rear-ended by that Sydney police officer, he'd gotten a settlement to cover his medical expenses, and we'd used it to take our boys, ages two and three, on this trip. I remember we caught the ferry to Nelly Bay Harbour, and we didn't come home for six whole weeks.

When I think about places where I have been truly happy, Magnetic Cove tops the list. The island was crawling with koala bears, and the fishing was ridiculously good. Mackerel, tuna, sea perch—you could catch them all, and Robbie and the boys did. For my part, I walked the palm-fringed beaches collecting bits of coral and other treasures. This trip of ours was in 2009. In 2022, as I recovered from my attempts to take my own life, it felt like an eon ago. But I still thought about that vacation almost every day. In my brain, Magnetic Island had come to symbolize a path I hadn't taken. I imagined I might have lived a beautiful life there, free from all troubles, safe from all dangers, anonymous. In this fantasy, I did what most people who endure childhood trauma do: process it privately, sometimes without telling a single person other than perhaps a trusted therapist. In other words, in this fantasy, I'd made a choice that was the polar opposite of the one I'd made in real life. This idyll would never be my reality—I knew that—but imagining it helped me.

I've said that I am a visual person—always have been. Since childhood, I have been able to remember images, faces, details others miss. If I make a notation in the margin of the book I'm reading, my brain registers the placement of that scribble so I can easily find it again. I am buoyed by bright colors. So it makes sense that in my darkest time, I turned to something visual for comfort. In the weeks after I tried to kill myself, I must have stared for hours at that oversized photo of Magnetic Island. I'd bought it for Robbie in happier times. I really, truly, wanted to be happy again.

But there was something else that helped me just as much or maybe even more. I've told you how much music has helped me throughout my life. And I've described how we Giuffres enjoy music together as a family. Well, Alex was recording music now—mixing it in his room on his computer, commissioning beats and vocal tracks from various musicians he'd connected with online. Now Alex played me one of his favorite compositions. It was called "Smile Sadness," and it started with a spare ukulele track, then segued into Alex's rapping lyrics that could have been plucked straight out of my brain: "There are demons in my mind / Circling me like a haze / It's amazing / I can't get up today / I've gotta push for it / I cannot go back / If I go back, I'll be in a fucking trap." But it was another line in the song that really made me sit up straight: "I don't know what I'd do without you."

Listening to that song, that's when I vowed to get better, once and for all. For Alex. For Tyler. For Ellie. For Robbie, of course. But most of all, for myself.

IN APRIL, JUDGE Alison J. Nathan had rejected Maxwell's request for a new trial, denying her claim that her jury could not have been fair or impartial because one juror failed to disclose his own experience of sexual abuse. Now it was late June, and the day had finally come for Maxwell to be sentenced.

Because of my health problems, my doctors said I couldn't fly to New York to deliver a victim's impact statement, as I'd long planned to do. But Siggy said she would read it for me in open court. Even before she got a chance to do so, however, a copy of my statement that had been provided to the court made headlines. "Prince Andrew's Sex Accuser Says Ghislaine Maxwell 'Opened Door to Hell' for

Abuse," blared UK's *Daily Mirror*, atop a story that quoted from my statement:

"Ghislaine, twenty-two years ago, in the summer of 2000 you spotted me at the Mar-a-Lago Hotel in Florida and you made a choice. You chose to follow me and procure me for Jeffrey Epstein. Just hours later, you and he abused me together for the first time.

"Together, you damaged me physically, mentally, sexually and emotionally. Together, you did unspeakable things that still have a corrosive impact on me to this day. I want to be clear about one thing: without question, Jeffrey Epstein was a terrible pedophile. But I never would have met Jeffrey Epstein if not for you. For me, and for so many others, you opened the door to hell. And then, Ghislaine, like a wolf in sheep's clothing, you used your femininity to betray us, and you led us all through it."

At Maxwell's sentencing hearing on June 28, 2022, Annie Farmer, Sarah Ransome, and another Survivor Sister, Elizabeth Stein, were in the courtroom to deliver their victim-impact statements in person. Siggy read mine. Judge Nathan listened to everyone, including Maxwell's lawyers and the prosecutors, then told all those assembled: "The damage done to these young girls was incalculable." Then she revealed that Maxwell, then sixty, would be sentenced to twenty years in prison, plus five years of supervised release; she was also ordered to pay a $750,000 fine. With good behavior, she could leave prison in her late seventies.

The Survivor Sisters rejoiced. Together, we'd succeeded in sending one of our most malicious abusers—the woman who'd used her gender to trick so many of us into feeling safe, even as she put us in the worst sort of danger—to prison. We hadn't gotten what I'd once told Gayle King I really hoped for: an apology. Judging by the jailhouse interviews Maxwell had begun giving, she was unrepentant. Nevertheless, she'd been held accountable. Despite all her haughty denials, despite her attempts to diminish us as money-grubbing opportunists, a judge and a jury had seen through her. For all of us, that was the best thing: we'd been believed.

UNFORTUNATELY, ANY HAPPINESS I felt about Maxwell spending most of her remaining years in prison was dampened by the fact that right around this time, I was diagnosed with fibromyalgia—a chronic, long-lasting condition that causes heightened pain and tenderness throughout the body, as well as fatigue and sleep problems. This was not exactly good news, although there was some relief in knowing I wasn't crazy: the pain was real.

In October, I bought Robbie a used powerboat. He's always loved the water, and this vessel had enough beds, couches, and benches down below that our whole family could sleep on board at the same time. Its previous owner had painted its name—*The Renaissance*—on the hull in a dark blue script. I told Robbie he could change that, but he said no, *The Renaissance* was perfect. For us, he said, a revival was long overdue. I knew what he meant: he was hoping I could renew my interest in life. I wanted that too. I was taking it one day at a time. As usual, I relied on music to lift me up. Alex was playing me more and more of his tunes, and I couldn't have been more proud of him. I also clung to Sara Bareilles's song "Brave," which I'd first heard right around the time I'd said goodbye to my father for the last time. "Sometimes a shadow wins," she sang, describing my lowest feelings perfectly. But then, she helped me rally: "Maybe there's a way out of the cage where you live / Maybe one of these days you can let the light in / Show me how big your brave is."

On November 8, 2022, I announced a settlement between me and lawyer Alan Dershowitz, the Harvard professor emeritus (and friend of Epstein's) who I'd sued for defamation in 2019. In a joint statement,

I said, "I have long believed that I was trafficked by Jeffrey Epstein to Alan Dershowitz. However, I was very young at the time, it was a very stressful and traumatic environment, and Mr. Dershowitz has from the beginning consistently denied these allegations. I now recognize I may have made a mistake in identifying Mr. Dershowitz."

When I had sued Dershowitz in 2019, I'd alleged that he had made defamatory statements about me after I accused him. He had countersued seven months later. This settlement put an end to both of those claims. No payments were made by either of us to the other. And we agreed that we would say nothing about one another, other than the agreed statements we made in a joint release. (In that release, Dershowitz said of me that he had "come to believe that at the time she accused me she believed what she said . . . She has suffered much at the hands of Jeffrey Epstein, and I commend her work combating the evil of sex trafficking.")

The next day, I got an email from Dr. Annie Farmer. Annie and her sister Maria had been fighting for justice longer than any of the Survivor Sisters, and I'd gotten to know them both over the years. Annie's words meant everything to me because she so clearly understood my emotional state. "Hi Virginia, I just wanted to send a note because I imagine everything transpiring over these last few days (and throughout this long legal fight you've been battling) has been really difficult. I just wanted to let you know that you are on my mind and I'm sending big hugs and lots of love. You have focused for years now on helping others and being a strong voice in this fight. I know your advocacy will continue, but I also hope that you can find the space you need for rest and healing and soaking up time with your family with some relief from all the pressure these cases have brought with them. Xoxo annie."

I had badly needed some peace. My family had too. Now, at long last, we would set about trying to find it again.

THIRTY-EIGHT

Nobody's Girl

As I was beginning work on this book, one of my sons invited a new friend over, and when his mother—a woman I'd never met before—dropped him off, I invited her inside. When she sat down at our kitchen island, I offered her a cold drink, which is right about the time that she recognized me. "Oh, my God," she said. "It's *you*." I smiled and nodded. This had happened to me before.

The woman was uncomfortable, I could see—her eyes were darting around, as if she was now unsure what to say. For a moment, the fact that I was a well-known survivor of sexual abuse hung awkwardly in the air between us. Then the woman kindly said, "It's okay. We don't have to talk about it. It's probably embarrassing."

I kept smiling, even though inside I felt an old twinge: Why should *I* be ashamed? I'd been a child when I was abused by adults. "No, it's not embarrassing," I replied. "And we *should* be talking about it. Because this is happening out there, and it's going to continue to happen unless we talk about it." Not wanting to sound as if I were lecturing her, I suggested we go out for a drink sometime, out of the earshot of our kids.

Sexual trafficking should not be a secret, only to be whispered about in hushed tones or not at all. It is a horrible trauma-inducing crime, and we must talk about it if we ever want it to end. That's part of why I wrote this book, and I've tried, on every page, to be transparent. I've made mistakes in my life, and I've had moments I'm not proud of. But I haven't let those human flaws keep me from telling my story. As my collaborator and I worked together to finish this book, she sent me a line by the writer Helen Rosner that rings true to me: "Memoir is the art of shining a light behind you, picking at the stitches of your life to see how it was made." That's what I've tried to do: to examine my life in the hope of destigmatizing victims' experiences. Because only by speaking out can we move ourselves and others to act.

I'm sorry to say that for all that's happened, more action is needed. Much more. Because some people still think Epstein was an anomaly, an outlier. And those people are wrong. While the sheer number of victims Epstein preyed upon may put him in a class by himself, he was no outlier. The way he viewed women and girls—as playthings to be used and discarded—is not uncommon among certain powerful men who believe they are above the law. And many of those men are still going about their daily lives, enjoying the benefits of their power.

Don't be fooled by those in Epstein's circle who say they didn't know what Epstein was doing. Anyone who spent any significant amount of time with Epstein saw him touching girls in ways you wouldn't want a creepy old man touching your daughter. They can say they didn't know he was raping children. But they were not blind. (Not to mention the fact that many prominent people were still associating with him years after his conviction.) Epstein offered many of the men in his circle sex with the females he and Maxwell trafficked—both girls and women. I know because I lived it. But even the men who didn't partake of the favors Epstein offered could see the naked photos on his walls and the naked girls on his islands or by his swimming pools.

Epstein not only didn't hide what was happening, he took a certain glee in making people watch. Because he could. And people did watch—scientists, fundraisers from the Ivy League and other heralded institutions, titans of industry. They watched and they didn't care.

Epstein is dead, but the attitude that allowed him to do what he did? It's alive and well. Yes, #MeToo has led to certain prominent men losing their jobs. Other men have gone to prison.

But just because justice has been served in a handful of high-profile cases doesn't mean we've solved the larger problem: a culture that tells girls their primary worth is to appeal to men; a culture that tells men that young girls are the ideal—the younger, as Epstein said, the better. I'm not saying those cultural trends cause most men to become child molesters. But I do believe that because of those societal forces, when a molester shows his face, many people tend to look the other way.

Even as I've chronicled my history with Epstein and Maxwell, much has happened to keep the two of them in the news. The sale of Epstein's properties, for example: his Palm Beach home was sold to a developer for $18.5 million. It has been torn down and is being redeveloped with a different address; in the future, there will be no number 358 on El Brillo Way. Epstein's Manhattan townhouse sold for $51 million. His two islands in the Caribbean sold for $60 million—roughly half what they were listed for a year earlier—to a developer who plans to build a twenty-five-room resort there. His New Mexico ranch, listed for $27.5 million in July 2021, sold to an anonymous buyer for an undisclosed sum in August 2023. And most recently, his Paris apartment sold to a Bulgarian investor for 8.2 million pounds. The money raised in these transactions has gone to Epstein's estate, which has helped fund restitution for victims.

As expected, Maxwell—who resides in an all-female, low-security facility in Tallahassee—has appealed her conviction. (In August 2024, that appeal was denied.) She also gave an interview from prison in which she repeated the lie that the photo Epstein took of Prince Andrew with his arm around me is a fake. In response, Michael Thomas, the New Zealand photographer who visited me in Australia back in 2011 and took a photo of my original photo, front and back, came forward to say definitively, "It's not fake, and it never has been." Not all men are monsters.

In the wake of my settlement with Alan Dershowitz, various media outlets have suggested that Prince Andrew might try to overturn his and my settlement agreement. *The Sun*, in London, reported, for example, that the disgraced royal was consulting with US lawyers and hoping "to force a retraction or even an apology." David Boies fired back in a wide-ranging interview with the *Daily Mail*. "If they want to get out of the settlement," he said, "all they have to do is call me and let me take Andrew's deposition and go to trial." To date, Boies has received no such call.

Prince Andrew, meanwhile, was allowed to attend King Charles III's coronation in May 2023, but with no formal role and a third-row seat. In Trafalgar Square, hundreds of antimonarchy protesters stood among a throng of royal supporters, waiting for the coronation procession to pass, and I enjoyed looking at photos of the placards they held online. Many people held signs that read "Not My King," and one protester lifted a huge hand-lettered banner that said simply "God Save Virginia Giuffre."

Various Epstein-related lawsuits have continued to make their way through the courts. In March 2023, a judge ruled that two banks who had Epstein as a customer for several years—Deutsche Bank and JPMorgan Chase—had to face lawsuits alleging that the banks profited from Epstein's sex-trafficking operation. Both banks soon reached tentative settlements, promising approximately $75 million and $290 million, respectively, to the plaintiffs—more than forty women who said the banks had facilitated Epstein's abuse of them. (I was among the plaintiffs in the JPMorgan class action.) JPMorgan also eventually settled a lawsuit filed by the US Virgin Islands, agreeing to "significant commitments" to curtail human trafficking, and a $75 million payment. That suit alleged that Jes Staley, a former top executive at the bank, "may have been involved in Epstein's sex-trafficking operation." Court papers in that case showed that Epstein shared photographs of young women with Staley, and that the two men emailed each other using what appeared to be code words based on Disney characters. "That was fun. Say hi to Snow White," Staley, then fifty-three, emailed Epstein in July 2010.

"What character would you like next?" Epstein—then fifty-seven—replied.

"Beauty and the Beast," Staley responded, to which Epstein replied: "Well one side is available."

It's not hard to imagine what Epstein meant—he had "beauties" at the ready.

THE OTHER DAY, Ellie and I were in the car, heading to her volleyball practice, when she took control of the stereo and cued up a song called "Mad at Disney," performed by Salem Ilese. "You have to listen to this, Mom," she said, pushing play. "I'm mad at Disney, Disney / They tricked me, tricked me / Had me wishin' on a shootin' star," Ellie sang at top volume over the music. She knew all the words. "My fairy grandma warned me / Cinderella's story / Only ended in a bad divorce," she sang. "The prince ain't sleeping when he / Takes his sleeping beauty / To the motel on his snow-white horse." Ellie shot me a glance. At thirteen, she knows more than she lets on. As I've said, I watched *Cinderella* on repeat when I was a child, and I internalized some of the messages it taught me about femininity and what happiness looks like for a girl. As a young mother, I went into a baby boutique before Ellie's birth and said I wanted "everything princess." But now, as the mother of teenagers, I appreciate that my daughter is more skeptical than I was about some of the pressures and stereotypes society puts on girls of all ages.

Pressure to be a "good girl" is everywhere, and the last thing I wanted to do in this book is to place more of that pressure on anyone, particularly on survivors of abuse. I've written a lot about bravery because I admire people who do what is right, even when that comes at a cost, but I want to be clear: while we need to be brave about naming our abusers, we also must protect ourselves. You may notice that while I've named some men in this book, I have not named all the men I was trafficked to. Partly that is because I still don't know some of their names. Partly, too, that is because there are certain men who I fear naming. The man who brutally raped me toward the end of my time with Epstein and Maxwell, for example—the man whom I've called the former minister in court documents—I know his name, and he knows what he did to me, even though when others have sought comment from him about my allegations, he has denied them. I fear that this man will seek to hurt me if I say his name here.

There are other men whom I was trafficked to who have threatened me in another way: by asserting that they will use litigation to bankrupt me. One of those men's names has come up repeatedly in various court filings, and in response, he has told my lawyers that if I talk about him publicly, he will employ his vast resources to keep me in court for the rest of my life. While I have named him in sworn depositions and identified him to the FBI, I fear that if I do so again here, my family will bear the emotional and financial brunt of that decision. I have the same fears about another man whom I was forced to have sex with many times—a man whom I also saw having sexual contact with Epstein himself. I would love to identify him here. But this man is very wealthy and very powerful, and I fear that he, too, might engage me in expensive, life-ruining litigation.

I do not make this decision to hold back lightly. Part of me wants to shout from the highest rooftop the names of every man who ever used me for sex. Some readers will question my reluctance to name many of my abusers. If I am, indeed, a fighter for justice, why have I not called them out? My answer is simple: Because while I have been a daughter, a prisoner, a survivor, and a warrior, my most important role is that of a mother. First and foremost, I am a parent, and I won't put my family at risk if I can help it. Maybe in the future I will be ready to talk about these men. But not now.

In the meantime, there is important work to do. We need to make it easier to punish those who victimize others. Siggy and I want to eliminate laws that limit the period in which survivors can seek justice for their abusers. As I've said, New York State has made a lot of progress, first, by opening up a look-back window for child victims of sexual assault and then, in November 2022, by passing the Adult Survivors Act: a yearlong window in which people who were sexually assaulted as adults can file civil suits against their alleged abusers, no matter how long ago the assaults occurred. After the Child Victims Act opened its window, more than ten thousand lawsuits were filed—mine among them.

Other states have made changes as well. In 2020, my childhood home of Florida passed new legislation titled "Donna's Law," named after Orlando resident Donna Hedrick, who was allegedly abused by a former high school teacher in the early 1970s. This law removed the statute of limitations for prosecuting acts of sexual battery committed against children younger than eighteen years of age. However, the law only applied to crimes committed on or after July 1, 2020. There was no look-back window.

Federally, meanwhile, numerous updates have been made to the Trafficking Victims Protection Act (TVPA) of 2000. In 2022, President Joe Biden signed the Eliminating Limits to Justice for Child Sex Abuse Victims Act, which struck from the books the statute of limitations for TVPA claims brought by minor victims of sexual abuse, human trafficking, forced labor, and child pornography. After Biden did so, more states eliminated statutes of limitations, and lawmakers in other states, such as California, proposed bills that would do the same. (Currently in California, if a person is sexually abused before the age of eighteen, they must file a civil claim before turning forty.)

Awareness is growing about the need for change. And now that my settlement from Prince Andrew has come through, I have begun the slow process of turning my fledgling foundation, SOAR, into a professionally run organization. My goal is for SOAR to combat human trafficking by supporting organizations that focus on prosecution, protection, and prevention. Eventually, I plan to make grants that make it easier for members of the public to detect trafficking when they see it and that support victims' recovery. I look forward to disseminating some of the Crown's money to do some good.

But frankly, I need a rest. While finishing this book, I've had many setbacks. I've had a second surgery on my broken neck, but it still causes me immense pain; doctors believe I may need a third. And my mental health has faltered at times, too—as it may continue to falter for the rest of my life. Lately my doctors have prescribed me a series of ketamine treatments that seem to be helping to untangle my PTSD. Still though, I'm learning to accept that sometimes I will simply not be okay. That is the price of serious trauma: it lays you low, and sometimes makes you your own worst enemy. My goal now is to prevent the emotional time bomb that lives inside me—my toxic memories and devastating visualizations of myself being hurt—from ever detonating again. But sometimes I have trouble holding to that goal. There have been silver linings to my recent struggles—my mother and I have been talking more frequently on FaceTime, for the first time, she's told me she was sorry for what my father did to me when I was a child. "I should have been there for you," she told me through tears. To finally hear—and see—her acknowledge my experience had more power than I'd ever realized it would. But nevertheless, I have found myself yearning for a lasting peace.

Recently, the second of the two televised dramas I told you were in the works about Prince Andrew's interview with the BBC's Emily Maitlis aired on Amazon Prime Video. The three-part miniseries, *A Very Royal Scandal*, which is based on a book by Maitlis, focuses mostly on the planning, execution, and aftermath of that BBC interview, and I learned a few things while watching it (though I'll admit I grimaced when the miniseries's producers chose to use actual footage of me talking, and to end the show with a close-up of my actual seventeen-year-old face). But there's a particular scene in the show's final episode that really affected me. In the wake of her sit-down with the prince, Maitlis has been heralded around the world for her brilliant interview. But now, she is sitting with her laptop in her darkened kitchen, playing back audio of *herself* being interviewed. The topic: a stalker whose relentless fixation with Maitlis upended her life before he received an eight-year prison sentence. When Maitlis's husband enters the kitchen and hears what she's listening to, he asks her why.

"Because," she tells him, "I wanted to remember how it felt to be interviewed about something that wasn't my fault. And what happened to Epstein's victims wasn't their fault. Yet they still had to be witness. They still had to, you know, parade their pain in the hope of even the slightest justice. I'm not saying that what happened to me was even, you know, remotely similar. Of course it wasn't. But just the, you know, the parading—the endless bloody talking about it, to get anyone to take it seriously. Remember that?"

Her husband nods. He does remember.

"And that's true of every woman who ever complained about any kind of harassment," Maitlis, played by the actress Ruth Wilson, continues. "Always uphill. Always against the tide. Always a battle against the unspoken. You know, the look in their eyes that says, '*Really*? Did he *really*?' . . . When I sat down with Prince Andrew, I was only ever hoping to ask the right questions. I didn't know how he'd be or what he'd say. But it was the arrogance. The entitlement. He just couldn't help himself. You know, the way that certain men, whatever their sickness, assume certain rights without ever giving it a second thought. *Their* want. *Their* need. *Their* impulse."

To which I say: exactly. For fourteen years, since 2011, I've repeatedly revealed to the world what was done to me in the hope of preventing others' suffering. Like Maitlis says: parading my pain—"the endless bloody talking about it." I don't regret it, but the constant telling and retelling has been extremely painful and exhausting. With this book, I seek to free myself from my past. From now on, anyone who wants to know about what happened can sit down with *Nobody's Girl* and start reading.

Today, I'm turning my sights to the future. I like to think about a time when all my Survivor Sisters and I might gather together again. Right before the pandemic hit, I'd rented a house for all of us in Aspen and told those of us who couldn't afford the airfare that I would buy their tickets if they wanted to come for the weekend. COVID-19 forced us to cancel that plan, but I still think about reviving it. The goal isn't to reopen old wounds—we've all done enough of that. I just want to spend a few carefree days with these women, who understand me in ways no one else can.

But mostly what I need to do is to be here, fully, for my family. In recent months, Robbie and I have moved toward a healthier way of living, together. At my request, he took my pain pills, on which I'd developed an overreliance to soothe my physical and emotional pain, and locked them away in our safe, changing the combination. Day by day, it was as if I were stepping out of a dense fog into a clearing where I could see again. For months he'd been handling all our household chores, from grocery shopping to cooking to cleaning to all the drop-offs and pickups from school. Now I've begun getting up early again. Recently, when Robbie said he wanted to get more serious about his martial-arts practice, I told him he should spend a few mornings at the gym—I could make the kids' lunches and ferry Ellie to where she needs to go. (Alex and Tyler both have their driver's licenses now.) For the first time in a long time, my husband feels as if he can rely on me. That is the highest praise I could hope for: Robbie is seeing me, once again, not merely as someone to take care of but as his partner.

And my children? Alex, who is eighteen, has graduated from high school. I've teased him that I'll never let him move out, but he is planning an independent life, probably running his own business. Tyler—now seventeen—is enrolled in the highest-level high school classes, which he is acing, and his Australian Tertiary Admission Rank scores (sort of like SATs in the United States) are off the charts, which means his dreams of attending university and becoming an architect may well come true. And my daughter? Ellie's the most badass teenage girl ever, and she teaches me something every day. She has joined Australia's Emergency Services Cadets program, which teaches young people the skills needed to respond to fires, floods, earthquakes. She's planning to be a paramedic—to save people for a living—or maybe a paleontologist. Either way, she wants to learn to fly helicopters. Despite my own tomboy roots (or perhaps because of them), I'll admit there was a time when I tried to push her toward ballet lessons or the cheerleading squad. Ellie told me, "No, I'd rather climb on someone's roof or rescue their dog." I am buoyed by the knowledge that my kids will leave any realm they enter better than they found it. What more could a mother ask?

Sometimes I fantasize that Ellie and I will eventually run a therapeutic horse farm together, doing for other people what Ruth Menor's Vinceremos once did for me and so many others. And we may just pull that off. Not long ago, Robbie and I bought a forty-acre farm just outside of Perth. Already, we've got three sheep and three hives of bees, and Robbie has constructed the Taj Mahal of chicken coops. When I'm there, I wake up to the laughing sound of kookaburras and delight in watching kangaroos and emus making themselves at home right in our front yard. Robbie's next project: building me a pond with a little island in the center. After that, we plan to convert an existing outbuilding that was once a quail hatchery into four horse stalls. I may never be able to ride again because of my neck, but still, I know being around horses will do me good.

If you've read this far, I hope my story has moved you—to seek ways to free yourself from a bad situation, say, to stand up for someone else in need, or to simply reframe how you judge victims of sexual abuse. Each one of us can make positive change. I truly believe that. I hope for a world in which predators are punished, not protected; victims are treated with compassion, not shamed; and powerful people face the same consequences as anyone else. I yearn, too, for a world in which perpetrators face more shame than their victims do and where anyone who's been trafficked can confront their abusers when they are ready, no matter how much time has passed. We don't live in this world yet—I mean, seriously: Where *are* those videotapes the FBI confiscated from Epstein's houses? And why *haven't* they led to the prosecution of any more abusers?—but I believe we could someday. Imagining it is the first step. In my mind, I hold a picture of a girl reaching out for help and easily finding it. I picture a woman, too, who—having come to terms with her childhood pain—feels that it's within her power to take action against those who hurt her. If this book moves us even an inch closer to a reality like that—if it helps just one person—I will have achieved my goal.

Where to Turn for Help

My nonprofit organization, Speak Out, Act, Reclaim (SOAR), seeks to bring light to the issue of sex trafficking and empower survivors. Our goals include strategic grant-making, partnerships, and public education. SOAR's work is informed by my own journey from victim to survivor to advocate.

If you or someone you love is being endangered by sex trafficking or domestic violence, or is considering suicide, help is available.

UK

National Domestic Abuse Helpline: Run by Refuge, call **0808 2000 247** for free at any time, day or night. The staff will offer confidential, non-judgemental information and support. https://www.nationaldahelpline.org.uk/
Women's Aid has a directory of domestic abuse support services across the UK. https://www.womensaid.org.uk/information-support/womens-aid-directory/ You can also email for support: helpline@womensaid.org.uk
UK Modern Slavery & Exploitation Helpline is part of anti-slavery charity Unseen. Call the UK modern slavery & exploitation helpline on **08000 121 700**. https://www.modernslaveryhelpline.org/
Samaritans provides emotional support round the clock for anyone experiencing feelings of distress, despair or who is in crisis. Call **116 123** (free from any phone) or email jo@samaritans.org. https://www.samaritans.org/
In an emergency, call 999.

Australia

1800RESPECT is Australia's national domestic, family and sexual violence counselling, information and support service, available 24 hours a day, 7 days a week. For support call 1800 737 732, text **0458 737 732** or visit https://1800respect.org.au/

Anti-Slavery Australia can provide access to free and confidential legal and migration advice to anyone in modern slavery. Call **02 9514 8115** or visit **www.antislavery.org.au**

Lifeline Australia provides all Australians experiencing emotional distress with access to 24-hour crisis support and suicide prevention services. Call **13 11 14** or visit **https://www.lifeline.org.au/**

The Australian Government has a regional directory of crisis support services that can be accessed at **https://www.dss.gov.au/help-and-support-ending-violence**

In an emergency, call 000.

New Zealand

Women's Refuge is the country's largest nationwide organization that supports and helps women and children experiencing family violence. Call the free 24hr crisis line on **0800 733 843** or visit https://womensrefuge.org.nz/

Samaritans Aotearoa New Zealand: If you are in NZ and experiencing loneliness, depression, despair, distress or suicidal feelings, call **0800 72 66 66** for support or visit https://www.samaritans.org.nz/

In an emergency, call 111.

South Africa

SBCWC is a leading national site for providing holistic, integrated services to survivors of violence. Call **021 633 1253** or visit https://saartjiebaartman-centre.org.za/ for support.

Tears provides access to free crisis intervention, advocacy, counselling and prevention education services for those impacted by domestic violence, sexual assault and child sexual abuse. Call **08000 83277** or visit https://tears.co.za/

South African National Human Trafficking Hotline: Call **08000 737 283 (08000 rescue)** or visit https://www.a21.org/

The South African Depression and Anxiety Group (SADAG) is a leading mental health advocate and provider of free support in South Africa. Call **0800 567 567** or visit https://www.sadag.org/

In an emergency, call 10 111.

Photo Credits

Page 1: Courtesy of Virginia Roberts Giuffre
Page 1: Courtesy of Virginia Roberts Giuffre
Page 2: Courtesy of Virginia Roberts Giuffre
Page 3: Patrick McMullan via Getty Images
Page 4: Courtesy of Virginia Roberts Giuffre
Page 5: LAFARGUE/LENHOF/Gamma-Rapho via Getty Images
Page 5: Courtesy of Virginia Roberts Giuffre
Page 6: Photo by Mathew Olsen. Courtesy of Virginia Roberts Giuffre
Page 7: Courtesy of Virginia Roberts Giuffre
Page 7: Courtesy of Virginia Roberts Giuffre
Page 8: Emily Michot, *Miami Herald*, via Getty Images
Page 8: Kevin C. Downs/Redux, FILE

Permissions Acknowledgments

Grateful acknowledgment is made to the following for permission to reprint previously published material:

Emily Perl Kingsley: for permission to reprint an excerpt from "Welcome to Holland." © 1987 by Emily Perl Kingsley. All rights reserved. Reprinted by permission of the author.

Alfred Music and Hal Leonard, LLC: for permission to reprint lyrics from "Victoria's Secret," words and music by Mark Nilan Jr., Daniel Doron Henig and Jacqueline Cole Miskanic. © 2022 Jacqueline Miskanic BMI PUB DESIGNEE (BMI). © 2022 And the Melody Is, Artist 101 Publishing Group and Jacqueline Miskanic BMI PUB DESIGNEE. All rights for And the Melody Is and Artist 101 Publishing Group administered worldwide by Songs of Kobalt Music Publishing. All Rights on behalf of Jacqueline Miskanic BMI PUB DESIGNEE administered by Warner-Tamerlane Publishing Corp. All Rights Reserved. Used by Permission of Alfred Music and Hal Leonard, LLC.

Ultra International Music Publishing, LLC and Hal Leonard, LLC: for permission to reprint lyrics from "Mad at Disney," words and music by Salem Ilese Davern, Bendik Moller, and Jason Hahs. © 2024. All rights reserved. Used by permission. Copyright © 2020 Sony Music Publishing (US) LLC, Artist 101 Publishing Group, Salem Ilese Publishing, Bendik Moller Publishing, Songs of Brill Building and Jason Hahn Publishing Designee. All Rights on behalf of Sony Music Publishing (US) LLC, Artist 101 Publishing Group and Salem Ilese Publishing administered by Sony Music (US) LLC, 424 Church Street, Suite 1200, Nashville, TN 37219. All Rights on behalf of Bendik Moller Publishing and Songs of Brill Building administered worldwide by Songs of Kobalt Music Publishing. International copyright secured. All rights reserved. Reprinted by permission of Hal Leonard, LLC and Ultra International Music Publishing, LLC.